EMMANUEL LEVINAS'S TALMUDIC TURN

Cultural Memory
in
the
Present

Hent de Vries, Editor

EMMANUEL LEVINAS'S TALMUDIC TURN
Philosophy and Jewish Thought

Ethan Kleinberg

Stanford University Press
Stanford, California

STANFORD UNIVERSITY PRESS
Stanford, California

©2021 by Ethan Kleinberg. All rights reserved.

No part of this book may be reproduced or transmitted in any form or by any means, electronic or mechanical, including photocopying and recording, or in any information storage or retrieval system without the prior written permission of Stanford University Press.

Printed in the United States of America on acid-free, archival-quality paper

Library of Congress Cataloging-in-Publication Data
Names: Kleinberg, Ethan, 1967– author.
Title: Emmanuel Levinas's Talmudic turn : philosophy and Jewish thought / Ethan Kleinberg. Other titles: Cultural memory in the present.
Description: Stanford, California : Stanford University Press, 2021. | Series: Cultural memory in the present | Includes bibliographical references and index.
Identifiers: LCCN 2021005589 (print) | LCCN 2021005590 (ebook) | ISBN 9781503629448 (cloth) | ISBN 9781503629592 (paperback) | ISBN 9781503629608 (ebook)
Subjects: LCSH: Lévinas, Emmanuel—Religion. | Talmud—Criticism, interpretation, etc.—History. | Jewish philosophy—20th century.
Classification: LCC B2430.L484 K57 2021 (print) | LCC B2430.L484 (ebook) | DDC 296.1/206—dc23
LC record available at https://lccn.loc.gov/2021005589
LC ebook record available at https://lccn.loc.gov/2021005590

Text and cover design by Kevin Barrett Kane

Typeset at Stanford University Press in 11/14.4 Adobe Garamond Pro

In memory of Hayden White

Contents

Acknowledgments xi
List of Abbreviations xiii
*Chronology of Levinas's Talmudic Lectures at
 the Colloque des intellectuels juifs de langue française* xv

Introduction: God on Our Side / God on God's Own Side   1

1 **Being-Jewish, from Vilna to Paris**   The Temptation of Temptation (*Shabbath*, 88a and 88b)   15

2 **The Alliance Israélite Universelle, Shushani, and the École Normale Israélite Universelle**   Old as the World (*Sanhedrin*, 36b–37a)   53

3 **The Talmudic Lectures at the Colloque des intellectuels juifs de langue française**   Beyond Memory (*Berakhot*, 12b–13a)   89

4 **Hebrew into Greek: Translation and Exemplarism**   Contempt for the Torah as Idolatry (*Sanhedrin*, 99a and 99b)   127

Conclusion: Constitutive Dissymmetry   165

Notes 183
Index 211

Acknowledgments

This project was made possible through the support of the Colonel Return Jonathan Meigs Fund and Wesleyan University. I had the opportunity to present many of the ideas, themes, and arguments as invited lectures at the École des Hautes Études en Sciences Sociales in Paris, the Northwestern University Critical Theory Group in Paris, the Université de Rouen, the Van Leer Jerusalem Institute, Fudan University in Shanghai, the Workshop on Critical Thinking at Missouri State University, the Tauber Institute for the Study of European Jewry at Brandeis University, the Graduate Center–CUNY, and at the fourth conference of the International Network for the Theory of History in Stockholm. I want to thank the organizers of and participants at these events for the opportunity to think more deeply about Levinas and the project of history. Other aspects of this book were worked out in articles and chapters on related subjects though they appear in an original form here. I want to thank my colleagues in the History Department and College of Letters at Wesleyan. I owe a special debt to Wesleyan's Center for the Humanities, where I started this project as a faculty fellow under the directorship of Henry Abelove and then later as director of the center myself. My conversations with Henry about Torah, Talmud, and Jewish learning still ring in my ears. Axelle Karera's precision and insight challenged me to think harder and differently about Levinas and the issue of the other. My colleagues at *History and Theory* were a constant source of support, intellectual stimulation, and also levity. Thank you Brian Fay, Philip Pomper, Julie Perkins, William Vijay Pinch, Richard Vann, Laura Stark, Matthew Specter, Shahzad Bashir, Courtney Weiss Smith, Elizabeth Boyle and David Gary Shaw. Saul Friedländer's interest in and enthusiasm for this project has been a source of motivation and inspiration. Samuel Weber likewise provided encouragement, opportunities to discuss Levinas, and so much more. I am especially grateful to Catherine Chalier who offered her time, expertise, and hospitality while I was in Paris. Noël Bonneuil welcomed me to the EHESS and helped me think through the many possibilities of Levinas's use of infinity. Sarah Hammerschlag, Martin Kavka, and Joseph Cohen were all incredibly generous with their time, resources, and expertise. I've learned so much from their work. Peter Eli Gordon, Carolyn Dean, Marnie Hughes Warrington, David Myers, Kari Weil, Stefanos Geroulanos, Zvi Ben Dor Benite, and Michael Roth all provided excellent counsel and advice. Samuel Moyn was a key interlocutor at the beginning of this project as was Nitzan Lebovic and especially Eugene Sheppard throughout the duration. A special thank you to Andrew Baird and Margaret Brose. Gary Wilder and Joan Wallach Scott, my fellow members of the Wild on Collective, helped me keep my focus on the practice as well as the theory of history. I am grateful to Judith Butler for her supportive comments on the manuscript in draft form and Michael L. Morgan for his detailed, critical, and enthusiastic comments. I owe a huge debt of gratitude to Hent de Vries, Erica Wetter, Faith Wilson Stein and the editorial staff at Stanford University Press, as well as the anonymous readers.

I also want to express my love and gratitude to my friends and family. My sister Sarah and my brother Joel somehow put up with me. My mother and father, Marvin and Irene, have been waiting on this book for quite some time so it will be a relief to finally say it has been published. My daughter Lili worked as my research assistant as I finalized the manuscript for submission. Lili and Noa surprise me every day and give me hope for a better future. Of course, none of this would have happened without the love and support of my wife Tracy. I love you so much.

Abbreviations

EMMANUEL LEVINAS

AS "Au-delà du souvenir," in *A l'Heure des Nations* (Paris: Les Éditions de Minuit, 1988)

BM "Beyond Memory," in *In the Time of Nations*, trans. Michael B. Smith (New York: Continuum Press, 2007)

CTI "Contempt for the Torah as Idolatry," in *In the Time of Nations*, trans. Michael B. Smith (New York: Continuum Press, 2007)

MPI "Mépris de la Thora comme idolâtrie," in *A l'Heure des Nations* (Paris: Les Éditions de Minuit, 1988)

OW "As Old as the World," in *Nine Talmudic Lessons*, trans. Annette Aronowicz (Bloomington: Indiana University Press, 1994)

TT "The Temptation of Temptation," in *Nine Talmudic Lessons*, trans. Annette Aronowicz (Bloomington: Indiana University Press, 1994)

TTF "La tentation de la tentation," in *Quatre Lectures Talmudiques* (Paris: Les Éditions de Minuit, 1968)

VM "Vieux comme le monde?," in *Quatre Lectures Talmudiques* (Paris: Les Éditions de Minuit, 1968)

Chronology of Levinas's Talmudic Lectures at the Colloque des intellectuels juifs de langue française

4 MAY 1957   First Colloque des intellectuels juifs de langue française. No lecture by Levinas.

22 SEPTEMBER 1959   Second Colloque des intellectuels juifs de langue française, "Entre deux mondes: Biographie spirituelle de Franz Rosenzweig," in E. Amado Lévy-Valensi and J. Halpérin, La conscience juive: Données et débats, PUF, 1963.

25 SEPTEMBER 1960   Third Colloque des intellectuels juifs de langue française, "Temps messianiques et temps historiques dans le chapitre XI du 'Traité Sanhédrin'" (Sanhedrin 99a), in La conscience juive: Données et débats, PUF, 1963.

8 OCTOBER 1961   Fourth Colloque des intellectuels juifs de langue française, "Le messianisme d'après un texte talmudique" (Sanhedrin 98b–99a), in E. Amado Lévy-Valensi and J. Halpérin, La conscience juive face à l'Histoire: Le pardon, PUF, 1965.

13–14 OCTOBER 1963   Fifth Colloque des intellectuels juifs de langue française, "Envers autrui" (Yoma 87a), in E. Amado Lévy-Valensi and J. Halpérin, La conscience juive face à l'Histoire: Le pardon, PUF, 1965.

11–12 OCTOBER 1964   Sixth Colloque des intellectuels juifs de langue française, "La tentation de la tentation" (Shabbat 88a–b), in E. Amado Lévy-Valensi and J. Halpérin, Tentations et actions de la conscience juive, PUF, 1971.

24–25 OCTOBER 1965 Seventh Colloque des intellectuels juifs de langue française, "Terre promise et terre premise" (Sota 34b–35a), in E. Amado Lévy-Valensi and J. Halpérin, Israël dans la conscience juive: Données et débats, PUF, 1971.

9–10 OCTOBER 1966 Eighth Colloque des intellectuels juifs de langue française, "Vieux comme le monde?" (Sanhedrin 36b–37a), in E. Amado Lévy-Valensi and J. Halpérin, Tentations et actions de la conscience juive, PUF, 1971.

JANUARY 1968 Ninth Colloque des intellectuels juifs de langue française, "Israel" Levinas is absent.

16, 17, 18, 19 MARCH 1969 Tenth Colloque des intellectuels juifs de langue française, "Judaïsme et revolution" (Baba Metsia 83a–b), in J. Halpérin and G. Lévitte, Jeunesse et revolution. La Conscience juive: Données et débats, PUF, 1972.

25, 26 OCTOBER 1970 Eleventh Colloque des intellectuels juifs de langue française, "Jeunesse d'Israël" (Nazir 66a–b), in J. Halpérin and G. Lévitte, Jeunesse et révolution dans la conscience juive: Données et débats, PUF, 1972.

31 OCTOBER, 1 NOVEMBER 1971 Twelfth Colloque des intellectuels juifs de langue française, "Désacralisation et désensorcellement" (Sanhedrin 67a–b), in J. Halpérin, L'autre dans la conscience juive (suivi de Le sacré et le couple), PUF, 1973.

15–16 OCTOBER 1972 Thirteenth Colloque des intellectuels juifs de langue française, "Et Dieu créa la femme" (Berakhot 61a), in J. Halpérin, L'autre dans la conscience juive (suivi de Le sacré et le couple), PUF, 1973.

NOVEMBER 1973 Fourteenth Colloque des intellectuels juifs de langue française, "Sabbath." Emmanuel Levinas is absent.

10, 11 NOVEMBER 1974 Fifteenth Colloque des intellectuels juifs de langue française, "La solitude de Kippour" (Makoth 23a–b), in J. Halpérin and G. Lévitte, Solitude d'Israël: Données et débats, PUF, 1975.

9 NOVEMBER 1975 Sixteenth Colloque des intellectuels juifs de langue française, "Les dommages causés par le feu" (Baba Kima 60a–b), in J. Halpérin and G. Lévitte, La conscience juive face à la guerre, PUF, 1976.

27, 28, 29 NOVEMBER 1976 Seventeenth Colloque des intellectuels juifs de langue française, "Modèles de la permanence" (Menahot 99b–100a), in J. Halpérin and G. Lévitte, Le modèle de l'Occident, PUF, 1977.

OCTOBER 1977 Eighteenth Colloque des intellectuels juifs de langue française, "The Muslim Community." Levinas is absent.

25, 26, 27 NOVEMBER 1978 Nineteenth Colloque des intellectuels juifs de langue française, "Les villes-refuges" (Makot 10a), in J. Halpérin and G. Levitte, Jérusalem, l'Unique et l'Universelle, PUF, 1979.

24, 25, 26 NOVEMBER 1979 Twentieth Colloque des intellectuels juifs de langue française, "Qui joue le dernier ?" (Yoma 10a), in J. Halpérin and G. Levitte, Politique et religion: Données et débats, Gallimard Idées, 1981.

1980 Twenty-First Colloque des intellectuels juifs de langue française, "Le Pacte" (Sota 37a–b), in L'au delá du verset, Les Éditions de Minuit, 1982.

28, 29, 30 NOVEMBER 1981 Twenty-Second Colloque des intellectuels juifs de langue française, "Pour une place dans la Bible" (Megillah 7a), in J. Halpérin and G. Levitte, La Bible au présent, Gallimard Idées, 1982.

24, 25 APRIL 1983 Twenty-Third Colloque des intellectuels juifs de langue française, "The Translation of Scriptures" (Megillah 9a–b), in Israel le judaïsme et l'Europe, Gallimard Idées, 1984.

28, 29, 30 JANUARY 1984 Twenty-Fourth Colloque des intellectuels juifs de langue française, "Mépris de la Thora comme idolâtrie" (Sanhedrin 99a-b), in Idoles: Données et débats, Éditions Denoël, 1985.

DECEMBER 1984 Twenty-Fifth Colloque des intellectuels juifs de langue française, "Au-delà du souvenir" (Berakhot 12b–13a), in J. Halpérin and

G. Lévitte, Mémoires et histoire: Données et débats, Éditions Denoël, 1986.

Twenty-Sixth Colloque des intellectuels juifs de langue française NO RECORD FOUND.

DECEMBER 1986 Twenty-Seventh Colloque des intellectuels juifs de langue française, "Les Nations et la présence d'Israël" (Pesachim 118b), in J. Halpérin and G. Lévitte, Les soixante-dix nations: Données et débats, Éditions Denoël, 1987.

DECEMBER 1987 Twenty-Eighth Colloque des intellectuels juifs de langue française, "Socialité et argent," in J. Halpérin and G. Lévitte, L'Argent: Données et débats, Denoël, 1989.

3, 4, 5 DECEMBER 1988 Twenty-Ninth Colloque des intellectuels juifs de langue française, "Au-dela de l'Etat dans l'Etat" (Tamid 31b-32b), in J. Halpérin and G. Lévitte, La Question de l'état: Données et débats, Denoël, 1989.

9, 10, 11 DECEMBER 1989 Thirtieth Colloque des intellectuels juifs de langue française, "Qui est soi-même?" (Chullin 88b–89a), in J. Halpérin and G. Lévitte, Le "quant-à-soi: Données et débats, Denoël, 1991.

EMMANUEL LEVINAS'S TALMUDIC TURN

INTRODUCTION

God on Our Side / God on God's Own Side

On the occasion of Emmanuel Levinas's eightieth birthday, a group of his former students and colleagues held a celebration under the auspices of the École Normale Israélite Orientale and its parent organization the Alliance Israélite Universelle. At this event the president of the AIU, Ady Steg, told an apologue, or, perhaps a myth, imagining the day when Levinas would be summoned before the Heavenly/Celestial Throne:

"Emmanuel Levinas, what have you done with your life?" Levinas would be asked.

"I consecrated myself to philosophy and that which I considered to be good and just I have written in my books."

"Very well, and what else?"

"I studied with Husserl and Heidegger."

"Heidegger? Hmm . . . and what else?"

"I also studied with Shushani."

"Marvelous! It is true that Shushani was able to penetrate the soul of the Talmud. And what else?"

"I presented many Talmudic lessons for the *Colloque des Intellectuels Juifs* based on Shushani's teachings."

"Bravo! How can one possibly understand the Torah without the light of the oral Law? But what else?"

"As a result I was also able to comment on the Torah at the École Normale Israélite Orientale of the Alliance on Shabbat mornings."
"At the school?"
"Yes, I was the director of the school for many years."
"Director of the school? You, a prestigious philosopher?"
"Yes, director of the school."

With these words, Ady Steg tells us, Cherubs and Seraphs, Ofanim and Archangels would begin to sing a glorious hymn as Emmanuel Levinas is conducted to the right of the Eternal One.[1]

Given the audience, it is no surprise that the hagiographic emphasis on Levinas as Talmudist takes pride of place above and beyond his status as a "prestigious philosopher." Indeed, it is Levinas as a disciple of the enigmatic Talmudic master Shushani who is emphasized rather than Levinas as a student of Edmund Husserl or Martin Heidegger. It is Levinas's commitment to Jewish teaching and to the transmission of these teachings, rather than his writings and work as a philosopher, that earns him his place "to the right of the Eternal One." This was, of course, a celebratory speech presented before Levinas's former students and friends, and thus one must be cautious in making too much of a playful address meant to commemorate a joyful occasion. Then again, Steg's address was later published as the "Apologue" to an edited volume titled *Emmanuel Levinas: Philosopher and Teacher*, which included an interview between Levinas and Paul Ricoeur as well as essays by David Banon, Ami Bouganim, and Catherine Chalier.[2] Thus the story holds symbolic weight commencing as it does by invoking Levinas's status as philosopher of the "good and the just" and concluding with what can only be considered as the source of this philosophy, the teaching and transmission of Talmud. This conclusion is then corroborated in the essays by the three French academics.

Other more scholarly accounts of Levinas take a similar tack. In her work *Vilna on the Seine*, Judith Friedlander credits Emmanuel Levinas with introducing the French public "to a style of learning developed by the legendary [Talmudic scholar] Gaon of Vilna [1720–1797] in the late eighteenth century and passed down for generations by rabbis trained rigorously in the scholarly tradition established by this brilliant Talmudist."[3] Contemporary Jewish intellectuals such as Alain

Finkelkraut and Richard Cohen credit Levinas with leading them away from "postmodern" philosophy and back to the Eastern European Jewish traditions that were all but eradicated in the Holocaust. Benny Lévy's explanation of his own turn to Judaism and religious learning is exemplary. "The name of one person is important, a person to whom I must confess my indebtedness, Emmanuel Levinas. Here is someone who had the very same philosophical training as Sartre, the same roots in phenomenology and humanism. He was someone who was very close to Sartre in his philosophical language, and yet profoundly different, because he had roots in Talmud."[4] Statements like this have led to the belief that Levinas himself was "trained rigorously in the scholarly tradition" of the Gaon of Vilna and thus capable of passing on these teachings. Furthermore, Levinas's self-fashioning through statements regarding his relation to the study of Talmud strengthened this belief. This belief is false. Levinas was not trained as a Talmudic scholar, at least not in his formative years in Vilna nor in a traditional heder or yeshiva, and the errant assumption that he was is the myth of Emmanuel Levinas.

Then again, why shouldn't we accept Levinas as the heir to a tradition of texts and textual interpretation whose message and mission do not rely on, or should be judged by, the evidentiary standards of the modern historical guild. Is it so crazy to view Levinas's turn to the study of Talmud and his transmission of these teachings as descended directly from the Gaon of Vilna in the chain of tradition (*sheshelet kabbalah*), worthy of earning him his place "to the right of the Eternal One." The hagiography aside, why not come to this conclusion? After all, this would be in keeping with Levinas's claim that while "no one can refuse the insights of history," nonetheless "we do not think they are sufficient for everything. . . . Our approach assumes that the different periods of history can communicate around thinkable meanings, whatever the variations in the signifying material which suggests them. . . . For we assume the permanence and continuation of Israel and the unity of its self-consciousness throughout the ages."[5] Such a conclusion rests on the belief that certain texts and meanings are transcendent and thus transmitted in ways quite different from those accepted by modern secular scholarship.

This is to ask, on what grounds are we so confident that our modern secular historical analysis is the definitive one? One reason to think so is that the accounts by Friedlander, Finkelkraut, and Cohen that seek to link Levinas to the Talmudic tradition do so by employing the conventions of modern historical scholarship. As such they should be judged according to those conventions, and, as we will see, in this regard they come up short. This is an axiomatic answer, however, that does more to indicate the underlying problem than to resolve the question. The real reason we accept the conventional scholarly analysis is because we are committed to the secular bias of modern historiography and scholarship. Brad Gregory has argued that the rejection of "confessional commitments in the study of religion in favor of social scientific or humanistic theories of religion has produced not unbiased accounts, but reductionist explanations of religious belief and practice with embedded secular biases that preclude the understanding of religious believer-practitioners."[6] Levinas himself warns us of the violence done "by the impatient, busy hand that is supposedly objective and scientific" such that the Scriptures and those who interpret them are "cut off from the breath that lives within them." Under such conditions these texts "become unctuous, false, or mediocre words, matter for doxographers, for linguists and philologists."[7] Following this line, accepting Levinas's claims at face value but also his skepticism about "religion," it is not only possible but also fruitful to imagine an alternative historical account where divine authority, revelation, and election are key components that allow for critical reflection and ethical judgment (illuminating the tensions and compatibilities between Levinas's "philosophical" and "confessional" writings).

This would be a very different sort of historical account, and here we see that Gregory's diagnosis of the hierarchy that privileges secular history is instructive but also inadequate, because he arrests the hierarchy after overturning it, thus rendering "confessional commitment" the privileged means of understanding the past. The methodological approach of these two competing worldviews, secular and confessional, remain constant even if the underlying commitments by which evidence is accepted or interpreted is different. This results in an impasse, because, as Constantin Fasolt has made clear, modern historical knowledge "is knowledge that conflicts in some important ways with claims made by the historical religions, for example, about the life of Jesus, about the origins of the Old Testament, about the authorship of Moses, and so on."[8] Secular history will not cede authority to religious believer-practitioners in pursuit of historical truth, but neither will the confessional mode accept the unqualified findings of secular scholarship. To adhere to one is seemingly to discredit the other.

The impasse can be viewed in light of Levinas's formulation "God on God's own side" and "God on our side." On Levinas's account, following the Rabbi Hayyim of Volozhin who we will discuss later, "God on God's own side" refers to the infinite and absolutely transcendent qualities of God that lie beyond our finite abilities to define, conceive, or even name God. "God on our side" references God as revealed in our finite and imperfect world and as such as limited by that which we can conceive or imagine. As Levinas puts it, "'In the Image of God,' According to Rabbi Hayyim Volozhiner": "Associated with the world, God would not exhaust [God's] religious significance, for [God] would thus represent only God from the human viewpoint—God 'on our side,' as *Nafesh ha'Hayyim* expresses it. But, God also has a meaning in the Tetragrammaton, signifying something that humans cannot define, formulate, think or even name."[9] There is a fundamental cleavage between the qualities of God and what we can know of those qualities. Following this logic, the danger is that we take the qualities we know about God "on our side" to be the essence of God or we reduce God to a mere product of our imagination. The latter is what is at work in most academic scholarship.

This then raises the question of how humans can gain access to God on God's side without reducing God to a reproduction of what we know of God from our side. The answer for Levinas lies in Revelation, both in its written form revealed to Moses as Torah and in its oral form ultimately conveyed as Talmud (we will delve into this in chapter 3). The relation is not an easy one because it requires that we "understand revelation both as a modality which paradoxically preserves transcendence from what is revealed, and consequently as something that goes beyond the capacity of an intuition, and even of a concept."[10] It is thus a relation with God on God's side that "communicates" to reach us as

God on our side. The relationship is ultimately a paradox because God enters our side, pierces it, but still preserves the status of totally other or otherwise than being. "The human, therefore, would not be just a creature to whom revelation is made, but something through which the absolute of God reveals its meaning. This human impossibility of conceiving the Infinite is also a new possibility of signifying."[11] This is a logic that eschews human understanding as the means for fully comprehending God or Revelation, be it in a religious or secular formulation, but nevertheless accepts the relation as a different mode of understanding based on a new possibility of signifying.

Scholarship on Levinas has often made sense of the tension in his work under the rubric of the universal and the particular and/or the ethical and the political. The argument in these works is that Levinas's philosophical writings and his confessional or Jewish writings each do different work, with one making universal or ethical claims and the other addressing particular or political issues. The literature on Levinas is vast and the arguments myriad with some scholars arguing for a strict separation between the works, others arguing that one side holds influence over the other, and another group arguing the two bodies are inseparable.[12] I find much of the scholarship defensible as readings of Levinas's work "on our side" but nevertheless inadequate to the task of taking up Levinas on his own terms to accept the possibility and implications of "God on God's own side."

When scholars attempt to reconcile the universal aspects of Levinas's work with the particular aspects, or attempt to massage Levinas's actual statements and actions directed at political or particular issues (the State of Israel, the Jewish people) to reconcile them with a larger or more inclusive message, they do so from "our side." In this work, I pursue the possibility that for Levinas, ethics springs from a source on the other side of our finite political or particular decisions and actions. The ethical commitment on our side is inspired, or better commanded, by Revelation, which is the conduit to God on God's own side such that these ethics should, ideally, inform our politics; it is also the case that our particular or political actions are marked by all the failings of human beings as finite and fallible creatures. We do not have the attributes of God. Levinas does not assume that this leads to total failure, but neither does he presume we are capable of total success. Instead, the relation between God on God's own side and God on our side provides a model for doing right even while it conserves the reality that we will also do wrong. Levinas does not assume too much or too little in what he calls the difficult freedom of a religion for adults. To fully understand this one must engage Levinas on the plane of his own understanding of the paradoxical relation between God on God's own side and God on our side rather than transfer his thought and writings entirely into the realm of human understanding be it under the duality of universal and particular or ethical and political.

As noted, for Levinas the study of Torah and Talmud as "living Revelation" is the means for this paradoxical relationship, and thus I propose that the most fruitful way to engage with Levinas on his own terms is through a study of how he came to his Talmudic lectures or readings presented at the Colloque des intellectuels juifs de langue française from 1960 to 1989. One way to do so would be to establish how Levinas's particular approach to the reading and interpretation of Talmud is similar to or different from other approaches. This is an attempt to situate Levinas within a specific tradition of Talmudic interpretation. Lawrence Kaplan takes such a tack in "Israel under the Mountain: Emmanuel Levinas on Freedom and Constraint in the Revelation of the Torah," where he argues that Levinas's Talmudic readings should be taken as such, readings of the Talmud. "For what this proposition means is that these essays, as Levinas himself states, are works of Talmudic commentary—philosophic commentary, if you will, commentary primarily on the Talmudic *aggadah*, but, nevertheless, works of Talmudic commentary—which consequently, and here we go beyond Levinas, ought to be read, studied, and understood within the context of that genre and tradition, that is, the genre and tradition of Talmudic commentary."[13] In what follows, Kaplan considers one of Levinas's Talmudic lectures, "The Temptation of Temptation," read in relation to "such Talmudic giants among the *rishonim* [the leading Rabbis of the eleventh to fifteenth century] as Rashi, the Tosafists, and the Ramban [Maimonides], by such great commentators on the *Aggadah* as the Maharsha and the Maharal, as well as by a host of more recent rabbinic commentators and scholars who have commented upon and elucidated, oftentimes at considerable length and with considerable insight, those very Talmudic *sugyot* which form the subject matter of Levinas's essays."[14] Kaplan's conclusion is that while he finds a "common denominator" among Levinas, the Ramban, and the Maharal, he also suggests that Levinas's Talmudic reading is one that could only have occurred "in our time . . . in our post-Holocaust age."[15] Thus while one can find similarities between Levinas and his predecessors, the conclusion appears to be that Levinas's approach is a product of his time and place.

Martin Kavka is less charitable in his view of Levinas's relation to his predecessors when it comes to the reading of Talmud. In "Is There a Warrant for Levinas's Talmudic Readings?," Kavka unravels three of Levinas's Talmudic readings to demonstrate Levinas's distance from traditional readings of Talmud, but he also points to the merits of such a dissonance. In a later piece, Kavka argues that Levinas misuses Hayyim of Volozhin's work in support of his particular claims and points to what he sees as several problematic interpretations.[16] Whereas Kaplan finds a common denominator between Levinas and his predecessors, Kavka's conclusion is that Levinas lacks such a warrant for his reading of Talmud, at least in relation to traditional sources.

The conclusions of Kaplan and Kavka should not come as a surprise given that Levinas came to the study of Talmud late and under the tutelage of an enigmatic master in the person of Shushani, whose mode of instruction is as mysterious as the person himself (as we shall see in chapter 2). While such investigations into the provenance of Levinas's mode of reading Talmud are fascinating, they may also be quixotic in regard to determining the answers that the scholars pursuing such an investigation wish to provide. To my mind though, whatever the merits of such scholarship, be they historical or philological, their approach comes at the subject entirely from "on our side." In what follows, I want to conserve the conclusions of such traditional scholarship but also take seriously the possibility that Levinas's warrant for reading Talmud is determined by the relation between God on God's side and God on our side. As we will see in chapter 3, Levinas's dynamic reading of Torah privileges the book above individual interpretations of it, and it is the book that serves as the paradoxical link between the two sides.

"We have to come back to the contradiction between 'God on our side' and 'God on his own side.' . . . In this radical contradiction, neither of the two notions could efface itself before the other."[17]

Thus we reach an aporia, but, as I argued in *Haunting History: For a Deconstructive Approach to the Past*, it is the aporia that renders visible the polysemic and chaotic conditions of the past.[18] In this work, it is the conflicting registers of the immanent and transcendent or finite and infinite as appear in the formulation "God on our side" and "God on God's own side." Thus the book is divided so as to provide an account of Levinas's Talmudic lectures that comes at this history both from "our side" and from the "other side." To do so, I deploy a deconstructive approach to the past that resists the interpretative closures that limit more traditional strategies. This is done by employing what Jacques Derrida has called a double gesture (*un double geste*) or double session (*double séance*), where two distinct modes of understanding the past remain open "according to a unity that is both systematic and in and of itself divided, a double writing, that is, a writing that is in and of itself multiple."[19]

The first gesture or session of this book employs a traditional intellectual history of Emmanuel Levinas's Talmudic lectures presented in Paris, France, between 1960 and 1990; the origins of Levinas's turn to the study of Talmud in the years following World War II; and the reception of Levinas's Talmudic lectures. The thrust of this movement is to dismiss the "myth" of Levinas as a Lithuanian-trained Talmudic scholar and explain the ways and reasons that Levinas came to study Talmud in the aftermath of the Holocaust. This exposes the particular interpretative strategies and cultural allegiances that Levinas privileges for his reading of Talmud. At this level, the first session is about issues of intellectual legitimacy, intellectual authority, and cultural or interpretative preferences. It is an approach that tackles the subject from "our side."

The second gesture or session takes Levinas's claims about Revelation and Election on their own terms allowing for a logic of divine authority insofar as God is the author of the Book, wherein "the Scriptures confer a meaning upon events rather than asking for a meaning from them."[20] This gives the reader warrant to take stock of Levinas's Talmudic lectures on the grounds upon which he presented them, the counterhistorical claim that divine and ethical meaning transcends time or particular historical context. In so doing, the second session also exposes the ways that the first adheres to the modern secular bias that discounts or dismisses fundamental aspects of Levinas's thought.[21]

The first session presents a traditional intellectual history of Levinas's Talmudic lectures that provides a contextual reading of the sources and causes for his turn to Talmud as well as a critical assessment of how his interpretative strategies are at times in conflict with his stated ethical commitment to the Other. The second session simultaneously offers a counter that allows for Levinas's transcendent claims about the past, history, and the ethical opening to the Other to stand in opposition to those of the first.[22] Each session is meant to be in dialogue and conflict with the other such that the claims made in each session on the Talmudic lectures are often in direct conflict with the historical explanations offered as intellectual history. The one is historically situated and argued from "our side," while the other approaches the issue as timeless, derived from "God on God's own side," even if the lessons to be learned can and should be applied to specific moments in time. This means that it is also the case that Levinas's Talmudic readings, presented here, should be seen as applicable to our moment today. It is for this reason that I do not include the dates, places, or context when presenting the specific Talmudic lectures in the second session.

The architecture and presentation of this book is structured to facilitate this strategy as each chapter is written in two columns.[23] The column on the left provides the intellectual history of Levinas's Talmudic lectures from our side while the column on the right takes up a single Talmudic lecture from the other side.[24] The two-column approach allows for the two historical registers to unsettle each other such that every reader is forced to consider the underlying logic or assumptions that ground each interpretative strategy. This also ties this book to *Haunting History* insofar as the two-column approach enacts the unsettling of singular historical accounts and/or the positing of a singular historical origin. As noted, one important template for this strategy is the *double séance* as presented in *Haunting History*, Derrida's *Glas*, or his essay "Tympan" in *Margins of Philosophy*, but the more immediate and relevant template is the Talmud itself, wherein multiple and often conflicting commentaries and interpretations compete on a single page. The crucial distinction is that in this work the authoritative text around which the commentary is organized, the master or Urtext, is absent, and this too coincides with the arguments of *Haunting History* that question the authority and permanence of anything like an absolute original. To my mind, the past about which we write history is just such an absent text.

The deconstructive approach does place an interpretative burden on the reader, but it does so by design so as not to overdetermine the reader's conclusions. The two competing columns of text are designed to inform, challenge, and drive the reader forward. It is also playful as it encourages readers to play with the text by choosing their path through it: intellectual history first then Talmud, Talmud first, all of one and then all of the other. The reader trained to read texts from left to right will take the intellectual history to be the first session while the reader trained to read right to left will take the Talmudic lesson to be the first session.

The book, its format, and the deconstruction at work within it attempt to provide a richer and more nuanced historical account of Levinas by defamiliarizing the familiar and unsettling the idea that any book or narrative is fixed and closed. As such, it questions the assumptions of modern scholarly norms and the consensus belief that our scholarly practices are privileged because of their modernity. "Is it not perhaps the case that ideas of a thought worthy of the name rise above their own history, royally indifferent even to the historians? There are perhaps more constants through time than one is led to believe by the differences of language, differences that in most cases come only from the varieties of metaphor. Perhaps modernity, that is, the claim of deciphering all the metaphors, is but the creation of metaphors whose wisdom can already be grasped in ancient ways of speaking."[25] By placing our modern scholarly conventions into dialogue with earlier modes of analysis and understanding and exposing them as the "metaphor of deciphering all metaphors," I also hope to make evident the strangeness of the "modern" or the present to divest it and us of our privileged status. Our modern modes of analysis and judgment are no less strange than those employed in antiquity (Torah) or the middle ages (Talmud).

Is the myth of Emmanuel Levinas his authority as an authentic master of Talmud or is it the authority of modern secular scholarship that impeaches such a claim? It is a dangerous question insofar as it threatens many modern secular assumptions, but it is the one that motivates this history of Emmanuel Levinas's Talmudic lectures.

In the first three chapters I develop the metaphor of a braid to bring together three strands of influence that lead to Levinas's Talmudic lectures at the Colloque des intellectuels juifs de langue française from 1960 to 1989. The three strands are Western philosophy, French Enlightenment Universalism, and the Lithuanian Talmudic tradition. The metaphor is imperfect, as we will see, because strictly speaking no strand is truly distinct, the influences of each blend into the other. Nevertheless, over the first three chapters I weave this braid to construct a history and counterhistory of Levinas's Talmudic lectures in Paris. In chapter 4 I shift gears, gathering the strands of the braid together to address recent important engagements and criticisms of Levinas's work by thinkers such as Andrew McGettigan, John E. Drabinski, and especially Fred Moten.

In chapter 1, I present a biography of Levinas's early life and education focusing on the influence of "Western" texts and philosophy. This journey took Levinas from Kovno (Kaunas) Lithuania, to Strasbourg, France, then Freiburg, Germany, and then Paris. This is the first strand of the braid. I couple this with Levinas's Talmudic lecture from 1964, "The Temptation of Temptation." In chapter 2 we encounter the other strands, first via an exploration of Levinas's work for the Alliance Israélite Universelle and his role as director of the École Normale Israélite Orientale then through his work with the enigmatic Talmudic master known as Shushani. The first takes up the second strand of the braid, the influence of French Enlightenment Universalism as well as the colonial aspirations of that endeavor. The second brings us to the third strand, Levinas's return to, and privileging of, the Lithuanian Talmudic tradition and the danger of particularism or essentialism that resides therein. These are coupled with Levinas's Talmudic lecture from 1966, "As Old as the World." In chapter 3 we bring the three strands together to look at Levinas's Talmudic lectures for the Colloque des intellectuels juifs de langue française and an analysis of Levinas as a reader of sacred Jewish texts. This is coupled with Levinas's Talmudic lecture from 1984, "Beyond Memory." In each of the first three chapters we encounter the ways that Levinas offers a message of universal ethics but one that is centered on the particularity of sacred Jewish texts accessed with the intellectual tools of modern Western philosophy. The fourth chapter addresses this tension by taking up recent critiques of Levinas's confessional writings, which claim "there is something presupposed in Levinas's conception of Europe that not only make . . . racist and xenophobic utterances possible, but even make them necessary."[26] I do so through an engagement with Fred Moten's *The Universal Machine* and Levinas's oft-cited claim that in his Talmudic lectures, and his confessional writings in general, his purpose was to translate "Hebrew into Greek." This is coupled with Levinas's Talmudic lecture from 1984, "Contempt for the Torah as Idolatry."

In the conclusion, I bring the two sessions together, "God on our side" and "God on God's own side," to ask the question of whether the ethical message and moral urgency of Levinas's Talmudic lectures can be extended beyond the texts and beliefs of a chosen people, religion, or even the seemingly primary unit of the self or ego? To do so I employ the term "constitutive dissymmetry" in an attempt to prise a lesson of disinterested universal ethics from the seemingly particular example of reading Torah and Talmud. Here, Levinas's commitment to the study of Talmud is not just any activity but indicative of one that results in "an other me, who answers me, tearing me away from my solitude, and for whom I am answerable."[27] The study for which Levinas advocates is indicative of a dynamism that is also a dislocation of sorts, a constitutive dissymmetry. As such, it can be an understanding of oneself completely dissociated from essentialism in regard to a people, a religion, or even the seemingly primary unit of the self or ego as well as the belief that it is our position in history as the most recent or modern that justifies our norms, codes, and actions. Our constitutive dissymmetry points us to the work we have to do, not to what we have already done. As such, it provides a compass for an ethics that is open to the Other in advance of the self.

The book ends by confronting the problem that tears at the heart of Levinas's ethical project and motivates my entire study from beginning to end. This problem has often been cast in regard to the conflict between Levinas's universal philosophical claims and his particular confessional ones or as the conflict between his ethics and politics. To my mind this misses the mark because it does not take up the way that Levinas's ethics are predicated on the relation between God on God's own side and God on our side. This is an ethics that is exemplary (or perhaps paradigmatic) and thus universal in a sense but that is intended to be applicable to particular, that is localized, cases or events. The danger or problem is the possibility that this exemplarism loses its dynamism and becomes essentialism. This happens when the exemplary status of sacred Jewish texts becomes more important than the message or living revelation contained within those texts, such that the people who adhere to those texts consider themselves elevated above others rather than beholden to them based on the teachings of responsibility that the texts ask us to continuously reconsider.

In the shadow of this tension and this understanding of ethics and responsibility, Levinas takes up the relation of Jewish identity to universal ethics. This leads us to the ways that being Jewish and being an ethical person are related for Emmanuel Levinas. In his life, in his career, and in his writings. As I see it, and as laid out in this book, the issue is that of maintaining a particular identity as a means of both self-preservation and ethical restoration, which, in so doing, also maintains the identitarian or essentialist logic that is the basis for racial exclusion. Restitution or reparation cannot be made to, or by, the appropriate parties without recognition of identity, but recognition of identity retains what is worst of such an essentialist formulation as the basis for identity based hierarchies. "Why can't we just let go?"[28] This is a problem for Levinas living in the aftermath of the Holocaust, but it is also a problem for our historical moment as we come to terms with other legacies of racial injustice. Unraveling the myth of Emmanuel Levinas is my attempt to deconstruct the ways that exemplarity and essentialism collide in even the most earnest of ethical constructs and to gauge the possibility of escaping this bind by thinking otherwise about the past.

CHAPTER 1

OUR SIDE

Being-Jewish, from Vilna to Paris

THE OTHER SIDE

The Temptation of Temptation

If one were to write the story of a twentieth-century Talmudic master, Kovno (Kaunas), Lithuania, would be the perfect place to start and 1906, the year of Levinas's birth, would be the perfect date. Kovno was known for its yeshivas and heders as well as its proximity to Vilna (Vilnius), the Jerusalem of the North, home of the Rabbi ben Solomon Zalman, the Gaon of Vilna (1720–1797), his disciple Hayyim of Volozhin (1749–1821), and the Talmudic academies Reb Hayyim Volozhiner founded. This was before the devastation of World War II and the Holocaust in which those academies were destroyed and the majority of the Jewish inhabitants murdered. The story of Emmanuel Levinas could have been that of the direct transmission of Talmudic knowledge and authority from Vilna to Paris. A chain of transmission where the contingencies of history allowed the Lithuanian Talmudic tradition to survive the destruction

From the Tractate *Shabbath*, 88a and 88b:

> And they stopped at the foot of the mountain . . . (Exodus 19:17). Rav Abdimi bar Hama bar Hasa has said: This teaches us that the Holy One, Blessed be He, inclined the mountain over them like a tilted tub and that He said: If you accept the Torah, all is well, if not here will be your grave. (TT 30, TTf 67)[1]

Levinas informs us that the literal translation of the Hebrew from Exodus of the Holocaust in the person of Emmanuel Levinas. Alas, this is not the case and thus the first strand of the braid we will encounter is not Talmud but Western or European philosophy.

In 1906, Kovno was still very much a part of czarist Russia; prevalent among the Jewish inhabitants who made up 30 percent of its eighty thousand inhabitants was a spirit of Enlightenment and an assimilation of Russian culture.[1] The Maskilic, enlightened Jewish families, spoke Russian, rejected orthodoxy, and embraced traditional Russian culture while keeping kosher and observing the rituals of traditional Jewish life. The Levinas household was just such a family, and Emmanuel Levinas's parents, Yekhiel and Dvora, did not choose to send him to a Jewish elementary school or yeshiva to study Talmud but to a Jewish Gymnasium where he studied German and finished high school with an emphasis on Russian literature. Thus the story to unfold cannot be one of direct transmission.

The tension between the desire for assimilation and fidelity to Jewish tradition and transmission can be seen in the incongruities of the Levinas family's everyday life. They lived outside of the Jewish area, spoke primarily Russian at home, owned a Russian bookstore, and wanted their children to attend Russian schools. Yet they interacted primarily in Jewish circles, kept kosher, celebrated the Jewish holidays, and learned Hebrew, albeit as a modern language.[2] Emmanuel Levinas and his brothers Boris and Aminadav had a private Hebrew tutor at home and first encountered the

19:17 should be "Israel is placed below the mountain" so that in the tractate from the Talmud, "The mountain is changed into an upside down bucket. It threatens to crush the tribes of Israel if they refuse the gift of Law." Levinas then asks whether Rav Abdimi thinks that the "choice for responsibility is made under threat and that the Torah would not have been chosen freely?" (TT 37, TTf 81). If this is so, then "the choice of the Jewish way of being, of the difficult freedom of being Jewish, would have been a choice between this way and death. Already 'eyn berera!' 'the Torah or death,' 'the truth or death,' would not be a dilemma that man gives himself. The dilemma would be imposed by force or by the logic of things. The teaching, which the Torah is, cannot come to the human being as a result of a choice. That which is received in order to make

Hebrew Bible as translation material from which to learn Russian and Hebrew, without the "famous [Talmudic] commentaries that would later appear to me as being essential. The silence of these marvelous rabbinical commentaries was also an homage to modernity."[3] The silence is all the more striking given that Levinas later came to consider "the commentaries on commentaries" as "the very structure of the Torah of Israel, reflected even in the typographical features of the Tractates overladen on all sides and all margins," and we will take up this strand of the braid in due time.[4]

Growing up in Kovno, Levinas was spared the most blatant and violent forms of anti-Semitism that were prevalent in surrounding areas, but he was made well aware of the limits placed on Jews under the czarist regime. The most glaring example in Levinas's early childhood was the *numerus clausus*, the restriction on the number of Jews allowed in the Russian high school—the cause of his parents' emphasis on academic excellence.

In 1915, the German invasion of Lithuania forced the Levinas family to move out of Kovno. Their original plan was to move to Kiev, but it was closed to Jews at this time so they moved to the Ukrainian city of Kharkov instead. For five years, from age eleven, Levinas followed the Russian school program with its emphasis on Russian culture and literature. He began to study German at school while continuing with Hebrew by means of private lessons. One year after his entrance into the Russian

freedom of choice possible cannot have been chosen unless after the fact. In the beginning was violence" (TT 37, TTf 82). Surely, the story is about the existential threat facing the Jewish people (both then and in Levinas's present) or an allegory about how the Torah came to define the Jewish people as imposed by the logic of contemporary events.

We can call this the philosophical or historical reading of the story where its meaning, as well as Levinas's use of it, can be explained through either textual or contextual analysis. In this reading, the interpretative emphasis is placed on the causal logic that both history and philosophy deploy . . . "first this, then that" or "this leads to that" . . . to determine an explanation for the event in question. When faced with the alternative of death, Israel chose the Torah, which school, the czar abdicated. He spent his first year of school under the czarist regime and the following year under the regime of the February Revolution. Levinas was drawn toward the excitement and hope of communism and Leninism, but his parents insisted adamantly that he avoid politics and keep to his studies.[5]

After the German evacuation in 1919, Lithuania declared its independence and formed a republic. In 1920, the Levinases took the "first possible opportunity" to leave Kharkov and the Soviet Ukraine to return to Kovno. But the Kovno to which the Levinas family returned was not the Kovno they had left. The Russian bookstore had been sold. Furthermore, and perhaps more troubling to the Levinas family, the Russian high school had been closed as part of the reformation of the Lithuanian national school system. Emmanuel Levinas returned to the Jewish high school; his hopes of graduating from the Russian high school and entering into the culture of Russia and Europe were dashed. Here we must consider the disappointment of the Levinases as a telling sign. Emmanuel Levinas's parents did not choose to send him to a heder or yeshiva to study Talmud. Indeed, even the return to the Jewish Gymnasium was seen as a setback.

But as one "opening to Europe" and assimilation had been closed, a new one opened. Levinas recalled that the director of the Jewish school, Dr. Moses Schwabe, was a German Jew "who had discovered Eastern European Judaism during his

of course makes sense because had they not, there would be no Israel. For Levinas, providing an explanation such as this is succumbing to what he calls the temptation of temptation, the need to make the determination and offer an answer. The philosopher or historian decides for themself what the event means, ascribes that meaning and, in doing so, wrests the event and the possibilities latent in its occurrence away from the Other. In this way, the philosophical or historical account of the event gives in to the temptation of temptation, creating a closure instead of an opening. The opening to the Other that the moment prior to determination presents is closed off by the definitive answer of the explanation or the vacillation between potential right answers. As such, the temptation of temptation derails the possibility of ethics by deactivating the relation with Revelation, which lies at the heart of the story.

captivity in Russia. He was a doctor of philosophy, and it was he who taught me German."⁶ Dr. Schwabe taught courses on German literature, and Levinas became enamored with the works of Goethe. Under the instruction of Dr. Schwabe, Levinas finished high school with an emphasis on Russian literature. Philosophy classes in the traditional sense did not exist in the Russian or Lithuanian school systems, so it was through authors such as Nikolai Gogol, Aleksandr Pushkin, Feodor Dostoyevsky, Mikhail Lermontov, Leo Tolstoy, and Ivan Turgenev that Levinas was introduced to what he later termed "metaphysical unease" (*inquiétude métaphysique*).⁷ While Levinas was certainly familiar with the Bible and the Jewish traditions, it was Russian literature that provided his first step toward the investigation and interrogation of what he later referred to as the "meaning of life" (*sens de la vie*) and not his position in the Lithuanian Jewish community.⁸ During his youth in Kovno, he did not study Talmud, nor the exegetic methods of the Gaon of Vilna or Hayyim of Volozhin. He would not come to his training in, and love of, Torah, which he later considered crucial to answering these questions, until much later in life.

Emmanuel's parents had originally planned for him to attend a Russian university, but after the revolution it became clear that this was no longer an option. Given his studies with Dr. Moses Schwabe, his knowledge of German, and the proximity of Germany, the German university

If the most important thing is "to know," then mastery and calculation rule over all. Revelation becomes the subject of philosophical or historical investigations rather than the instance when such endeavors become possible. As such, Revelation holds no power or force of its own. "We want to know before we do. But we want only a knowledge completely tested through our own evidence" (TT 34, TTf 75). The emphasis is now on the investigator, the explainer, the philosopher or historian, while Revelation, as well as all it offers, is left to the side. It is the explanations and calculations of philosophers and historians that tell us what we are to take this moment to mean. Any relation prior to the calculation is lost.

Levinas tells us this "temptation of temptation may well describe the condition of Western man" (TT 32, TTf 71). It certainly describes the condition of modern scholars who system seemed a logical choice. But Emmanuel Levinas decided to venture in 1923 to the University of Strasbourg, "the city in France closest to Lithuania," where he did not speak the language well, and which was certainly more distant than many universities in Germany. Increasing anti-Semitism in Germany, the unstable value of a diploma from a Jewish school in Lithuania, and the reticence of German universities toward admitting Eastern European Jewish immigrants may have determined the choice for him.[9]

In any event, Levinas's choice was a good one. Strasbourg was a city fluent in German and French, and Levinas was able to use his German while he improved his French. In his second year he enrolled as a student of philosophy in the school of letters. This was Levinas's first foray into the academic world of philosophy. He had no formal training in philosophy but he more than made up for this with his knowledge of Russian literature and familiarity with the Torah. His approach was not that of a student brought up studying philosophy in the French school system, nor was it that of a student of Talmud. Instead, as Levinas recollected, his interest in philosophy came from the courses he had taken on

> Pushkin, Lermontov and Dostoyevsky, above all Dostoyevsky. The Russian novel, the novels of Dostoevsky and Tolstoy appeared to me to be completely preoccupied with fundamental things. Books that were

"experience everything through [their] own self but experience it without having experienced it yet, before engaging oneself in the world. For experiencing itself is already committing oneself, choosing, living, limiting oneself. To know is to experience without experiencing, before living . . . to be simultaneously outside everything and participating in everything" (TT 34, TTf 75). What else is the fantasy of objectivity if not that of experience without experiencing? A scholar standing outside of space and time as a neutral observer nevertheless participating in the phenomenon under investigation. What is presented as the realm of neutral investigation, the public sphere or scholarly consensus, is actually a mode of understanding that raises the self to the position of arbiter and aggregator of all. This is a peculiar sort of solipsism. As strange as it may appear to secular academia, traversed by anxiety, by the essential, by religious unease; but that read like a quest for the meaning of life [*sens de la vie*]. . . . It was certainly in the sentimental love of these novels that I found my first philosophical temptations.[10]

Levinas was not interested in the theoretical idealism of neo-Kantianism, which he felt was too abstract to deal with the fundamental things of everyday life, so he turned instead to the work of Henri Bergson and the fields of sociology, psychology, and theology.[11] The work of Bergson and these other disciplines seemed much closer in their concerns to the issues that Levinas had been exploring in the work of Pushkin, Lermontov, Dostoyevsky, and Tolstoy.

His first years in the Department of Philosophy at Strasbourg were spent studying with Maurice Pradines, professor of general philosophy, and Henri Carteron, professor of ancient philosophy. But soon he had branched out to psychology under Charles Blondel and sociology under Maurice Halbwachs.

> In contact with these masters the great virtues of intelligence and intellectual probity were revealed to me, but also those of clarity and the elegance of the French university. Initiation into the great philosophers Plato and Aristotle, Descartes and the Cartesians, Kant. Not yet Hegel, in those twenties at the Faculty of Letters at Strasbourg! But it was Durkheim and Bergson who seemed to me especially alive. . . . They had

"the priority of knowledge is the temptation of temptation" where any "act, in its naivete, is made to lose its innocence. Now, it will arise only after a careful weighing of pros and cons. It will no longer be either free or generous or dangerous. *It will no longer leave the other in its otherness but will always include it in the whole, approaching it, as they say today, in a historical perspective, at the horizon of the All. From this stems the inability to recognize the other person as other person, as outside all calculation, as neighbor, as first come*" (TT 35, TTf 76–77, my emphasis). All assessment and evaluation comes after calculation and through the lens of a homogenizing totality. In the end, belief in such a realm of knowledge is no less devout than that in a divine creator and is often held by the same mechanisms.[2]

It is this strange solipsism presented as consensus

incontestably been the professors our masters.¹²

Maurice Pradines was a contemporary of Max Scheler and Ernst Cassirer. A Bergsonian, Pradines's primary concern was the privileged position of ethics and morality and specifically the relation of ethics to politics. One of the first courses Levinas took with Pradines was on just this topic, and as proof of the privileged position of ethics over politics Pradines gave the example of the Dreyfus affair.¹³ This was an essential moment in Levinas's decision to embrace French culture and society as his own, and here we touch briefly on another strand of the braid, French Enlightenment Universalism.

For Levinas, as for most Jews in Eastern Europe, the Dreyfus affair was an event of mythic proportions: "Everywhere in Eastern Europe, Jews knew about Dreyfus. Old Jewish men with beards who had never seen a letter of the Latin alphabet in their life, spoke of Zola as if he were a saint. And then, suddenly, there was a professor before me in the flesh who had chosen this [the Dreyfus affair] as his example [of the superiority of ethics over politics]. What an extraordinary world!"¹⁴ Pradines's investigation into the privileged position of rationality and ethics in relation to religion is evident in Levinas's later Talmudic lectures and his writings on Judaism. Perhaps most important was the emphasis on a rational investigation with recourse to universal claims that does not veer either into pure subjective revelation or a positivist schematic of facts. The basis

that Levinas seeks to counter by means of the Talmud, but he does not counsel blind faith in the word of God. "The text, then, will shed light on whether it is possible to escape the temptation of temptation without either reverting to childhood [blind faith] or always violently restraining it [individual mastery]. Perhaps the text suggests a way of avoiding both the alternatives of an infinitely cautious old age and of an inevitably rash childhood by establishing the relation between being and knowing in another way. It may set to work a notion which takes away the value that the temptation of temptation has acquired for us" (TT 36, TTf 80). Thus Levinas seeks to chart a course in between simple unfounded belief and the radical skepticism toward all things that cannot be empirically verified. He does so by exposing the moment before either.

This is a way of "actualizing without beginning

of this de-divinized and universal reason is ethics, but the example Pradines offered, the Dreyfus affair, was highly problematic. Levinas's decision to embrace French culture and the Republican tradition as the embodiment of the privileged position of ethics over politics neglected at first the very real aspects of that tradition that led to Dreyfus's arrest and incarceration. Indeed, it was the implications of this early choice seen through the lens of Vichy France that in part led Levinas to reshape his philosophical project and turn to Talmud. His Talmudic readings, however, are a critique and recalibration, not a rejection, of Western philosophy.

Through Pradines, Levinas was introduced to the works of Henri Bergson, a figure as inspirational to Levinas for his Jewish background as for his philosophical prowess. But while the realization that a man of Jewish origin could reach the summits of popularity in the field of philosophy was encouraging, if not seductive, to the young Jewish scholar it was the realization of how the works of Bergson could guide the future of philosophy that truly sparked the interest of the young Levinas. For Levinas, Bergson seemed to represent all that was new in philosophy, and he was swept up in the novelty of this sensation. But soon Levinas came to see Bergson's philosophy as static in the sense that it had completed the task it set out to achieve. Bergson's work had opened up new horizons and new possibilities. It was the basis without which "all the new ideas developed by philosophers during the modern with the possible" (TT 43, TTf 95) in which "the Revelation which is at stake in the following text will permit us to discover this order prior to the one in which a thought tempted by temptation is to be found" (TT 36, TTf 79). Rather than beginning with assumptions about what can be or looking for cause and effect, Levinas directs us to step back and allow for a possibility that would appear impossible in the secular modern world.

> For as Rav Hama bar Hanina has said [Song of Songs 2:3]: "Like an apple tree amidst the trees of the forest is my beloved amidst young men." Why is Israel compared to an apple tree? Answer: to teach you that just as on an apple tree fruits precede leaves, Israel committed itself to doing before hearing. (TT 45, TTf 99)

It is a seemingly impossible image: one of a tree on which the fruit arrives before the leaves.

and postmodern periods, and in particular the venerable newness of Heidegger, would not have been possible."[15] But its impact lay in breaking the grip of positivism and rationalism by emphasizing the concept of free will.

For Levinas, Bergson's philosophy escaped pure objectivity but did so by going to the other extreme and was dangerously close to pure subjectivity. Levinas did not want to replace the emphasis on the object with an emphasis on the subject that was equally removed from our everyday interactions with things in the world in which we live. Here, again, his investigation was primarily concerned with the Western philosophical tradition, and Levinas would continue his search for the "concrete meaning of the very possibility of 'working in philosophy.'"[16]

While these eminent professors were responsible for the more formal aspects of Levinas's academic training and for instilling a connection between the tradition of the French "Enlightenment" and Levinas's own understanding of Judaism, perhaps the two most important figures in Levinas's development at Strasbourg were fellow student Gabrielle Peiffer and a young instructor and pastor named Jean Hering. It was Peiffer who first introduced Levinas to the work of Edmund Husserl.[17] The following year Levinas enrolled in the course of Jean Hering, who taught in the Faculty of Protestant Theology at Strasbourg. Hering had been a member of the Göttingen

A logical correction could be to assume, as Levinas suggests, that it is no apple tree at all but instead a citron tree where the fruit stays on the tree for two or three years and thus only appears to arrive before the leaves. This explanation too, yields to the temptation of temptation. Instead, we should conceive of a "marvelous orchard where the fruit comes before the leaves" to imagine, "marvel of marvels: a history whose conclusion precedes its development." This is a logic of history where "all is there from the beginning" (TT 45, TTf 99) far afield from the conventional approach that assumes a strict logic of succession. "The fruit which negates the seed is the image *par excellence* of the negativity of history and dialectics." On Levinas's account, "the fruit is there from all eternity. History does not grow but extends. The final order awaits the leaves among which other fruit circle, one of the original phenomenological groups that gathered to study around Edmund Husserl.

At the time that Levinas enrolled in Hering's course, none of Husserl's work had been translated into French (Levinas and Peiffer's translation in 1931 would be practically the first). Hering's course and his use of the phenomenological method were inspired by his personal interest in the ontological investigation of man's relation to God. Here too, the importance of theology for philosophy was not lost on Levinas, but while the *possibility* of theology was important to him at the time, the future of *philosophy* was Levinas's primary concern.

> It was with Husserl that I discovered the concrete meaning of the very possibility of "working in philosophy" without being straight away enclosed in a system of dogmas, but at the same time without running the risk of proceeding by chaotic intuitions.[18]

Husserlian phenomenology appeared to Levinas as a methodology that escaped the closed model of science that was the basis of French neo-Kantianism while at the same time avoiding the slippery slope of spiritualism that bordered on pure subjectivity and "chaotic intuitions" toward which Bergson's work veered perilously close.

Levinas spent the academic year of 1928–29 studying with Husserl, who had just retired from the University of Freiburg but was continuing his courses until a will appear" (TT 45–46, TTf 99–100). Here, history and philosophy do not presume to be the arbiters of knowledge and explanation but serve to extend a history and a knowledge that exists prior to their undertaking. This is not to suggest that one blindly accepts that the world is 5,700 years old, but instead be open to the possibilities of a world that was created for us and the responsibility we have to take care of such a gift. "The world is here so that the ethical order has the possibility of being fulfilled" (TT 41, TTf 90).

Revelation has no need for historical development or causal explanation. There is no "this then that," so it does not fall within the purview of secular history and it is not our place to tell it what it means so we are outside the realm of traditional philosophy. "The Torah is received outside any exploratory foray, outside replacement had been chosen. For Levinas, phenomenology was the possibility of moving beyond the systematic organization of knowledge under the rubric of reason to the interrogation of the dynamic act of knowing and the mechanism at its origin. In this way it moved past the subject-object split by emphasizing consciousness at the locus of the relationship between the subject and the object.

In Husserl, Levinas found a kind and rigorous professor, and like Bergson, Husserl was of Jewish origin. But ultimately Levinas felt constricted by Husserl. "At the time conversation with him [Husserl], after some questions or replies by the student, was the monologue of the master concerned to call to mind the fundamental elements of his thought."[19] But this was Husserl's last year as a lecturer, and it was he who suggested to Levinas that he should remain in Freiburg to continue his studies with Husserl's successor, Martin Heidegger.

Levinas had already been introduced to the work of Heidegger on a trip back to Strasbourg. Levinas had gone to visit Jean Hering at his hotel, and Hering had given him a copy of *Being and Time* (first published in 1927). It was with Heidegger that Levinas finally discovered a means to explore the issues of metaphysical "unease" that had been his interest since his studies with Dr. Moses Schwabe in Kovno. Husserl's phenomenology had begun the radical interrogation that allowed for the possibility of "grasping oneself," of any gradual development.... Its urgency is not a limit imposed on freedom but attests, more than freedom, more than the isolated subject that freedom establishes, to an undeniable responsibility, beyond commitments made, for in them the absolutely separated self can put itself into question, claiming to hold the ultimate secret of subjectivity" (TT 46, TTf 100). The isolated self is a fiction of sorts derived from the temptation of temptation. The relational aspect of Revelation is lost in self-reflection and the quest for self-certainty, even as it is bound up with intersubjective agreement and the violence of forced consensus that is its guarantor. "Overcoming the temptation of temptation would then mean going within oneself further than one's self" (TT 34, TTf 75). One must give up, defer, one's finite place in the present as the portal through which all meaning and value flows.

understanding relations to things as a "consciousness of," which always implies a Self that is conscience, but Heidegger took the investigation further by shifting the focus away from the intellectual activities of the specific self and toward an investigation into Being. Through *Being and Time* and then through the lectures of Heidegger himself, Levinas was introduced to

> the comprehension of the verb "to be." Ontology would be distinguished from all the disciplines which explore *that* which is, beings, that is, the "beings," their nature, their relations—while forgetting that in speaking of these beings they have already understood the meaning of the word Being, without, however, having made it explicit. These disciplines do not worry about such an explication.[20]

Heidegger's project, however, made that explication of Being its primary goal by extending and reshaping Husserl's phenomenological project. One could certainly tease out the theological implications of Levinas's pursuit of Being. It is also possible to draw a line between the hermeneutic exegesis of Heidegger and the Lithuanian Talmudic tradition, but the line is clearly disturbing to Levinas after Heidegger's political choices of the 1930s.

For the young Levinas, the chief pursuit was philosophy, and the work of Husserl seemed less convincing because it "seemed less expected. This may sound paradoxical or childish but everything seemed

The stakes are high because as Levinas states in regard to the temptation of temptation, "we Jews all try to be Westerners" (TT 32, TTf 71), "no longer equal to the culture [we] bear, [we] immediately bequeath this culture, become deadweight, to the philologists, who with difficulty, raise it to the level of their theories. There you have Judaism, without Jews, handed over to the historians!" (TT 44, TTf 96). Levinas's target is in part the Science of Judaism (*Wissenschaft des Judentums*) with its emphasis on reason, which relegated faith to the role of antiquated superstition. Here the power of secularism came to the fore as religious traditions were challenged and cultural assimilation encouraged, the ascent of reason drained all that was spiritual, transcendent, and theological from Judaism leaving only a desiccated historical shell. It also points to the modern preoccupation unexpected in Heidegger, the wonders of his analysis of affectivity, the new access toward the investigation of everyday life, the famous ontological difference he drew between Being [*être*] and beings [*étant*]."[21] Levinas's philosophical transition from Husserlian phenomenology to Heideggerian ontological phenomenology can be best traced through two of Levinas's earliest works: his article, "Sur 'les Ideen' de M. Husserl," written for the *Revue philosophique de la France et de l'étranger* in 1929, and his doctoral dissertation published in 1930 as "The Theory of Intuition in Husserl's Phenomenology." The latter introduced the philosophy of Martin Heidegger into France through Heidegger's critique of Husserl's concept of intentionality.

What is essential to our investigation is that it was in his use of Heidegger to critique Husserl that Levinas began to articulate some of the concerns that later surfaced in his Talmudic writings, concerns that were also fostered by his Strasbourg *maîtres*. In *The Theory of Intuition*, Levinas foreshadowed what would later become his foremost concern, ethics and the place of the Other:

> There is another reason why the phenomenological reduction, as we have interpreted it so far, does not reveal concrete life and the meaning that objects have for concrete life. Concrete life is not the solipsist's life of a consciousness closed in upon itself. Concrete Being is not what exists for only one consciousness. In the very idea of

with control and mastery of all phenomenon through the lens of the human actor modeled on the individuated self. In this regard, "perhaps the text wishes to speak to us of those moments of Jewish history in which Judaism remains nearly without Jews, as did Mr. André Amar and the young student who took part in yesterday's discussion [at the colloquium]. He asked whether Judaism had become a mere abstraction so greatly does reality clash with the mythical model in the books" (TT 44, TTf 96). This is to suggest that the current understanding of Judaism has lost its connection to the moment prior to the temptation of temptation and the ability to accept Torah and Talmud as having arrived "fully formed" such that it can speak to all times. In this way, any understanding of Revelation and our relation to Torah founded on historical development or contextual analysis deactivates what concrete Being is contained the idea of an inter-subjective world. If we limit ourselves to describing the constitution of objects in an individual consciousness, in an *ego*, the *egological reduction* can only be a first step toward phenomenology. We must also discover "others" and that intersubjective world.²²

At this point in his career, Levinas saw Heidegger's displacement of the primacy of the ego as the possibility of an opening to "others." Therefore, Levinas's movement away from Husserl and toward Heidegger was derived through the realization that there was no place for "others" in Husserl's phenomenological program.²³ These themes returned in Levinas's later writing and in his Talmudic readings when they were recast in relation to his renewed emphasis on Jewish thought.

In 1930, Levinas moved to Paris and took an administrative job with the Alliance Israélite Universelle (AIU), and we will look more closely at the AIU and its École Normale Israélite Orientale (ENIO) in the following chapter. Levinas's work with the AIU was more than a job; it was a return to Jewish culture but a return to Jewish culture under the rubric of the French-conceived "rights of man." Levinas described the origin and mission of the AIU as:

> constituted in 1860 with the express concern of working for the emancipation of Israelites in countries where they did not yet have the right of citizenship. The first

is most essential. The way that Revelation, and as a result the Torah, points to something beyond ourselves.

Levinas cites the passage where "Rabbi Johanan said: Moses deserved to keep them all [his crowns], for it is said just afterward (Exodus 33:7) 'Now Moses would take the tent...'" and suggests that "the text may be speaking of those times in which Judaism is practiced or studied only by a tiny minority, perhaps by only one man, when it seems to be completely contained in treatises, immobilized in book bindings, and when living Jews have lost all influence as Jews" (TT 44, TTf 96–97). This could be explained as Levinas's own moment, and at one level it is, but Levinas then turns to the story of "A Sadducee [who] saw Raba buried in study holding his fingers beneath his foot so hard that blood spurted from it" (TT 31, TTf 69). The Sadducee is appalled at of these Israelite institutions was inspired by the French Rights of Man. There were in this inspiration no Zionist sentiments. Its mission was simply to emancipate those Israelites living in countries where they were not recognized as citizens. . . . Soon these activities became scholastic work; the founding of French schools of the highest level that would express above all the ideals of the nineteenth century . . . the elevation of universal culture and the affirmation of the glorious ideals of 1789.[24]

In this light we can view Levinas's embrace of Jewish culture via the AIU as more indebted to the influence of his professors at Strasbourg and the "glorious ideals of 1789" than to his own upbringing in Lithuania. Despite the foreign nature of his work in philosophy, or perhaps because of it, Levinas adopted an allegiance of "literary chauvinism," a faith in the tolerance and equality of France as exemplified in the rights of man. His was not the nationalism of a Maurice Barrrès or a Charles Maurras but of Émile Zola. He believed in a France based not on race and roots but on culture. In October 1930, Levinas sent a letter of request for French naturalization that was supported by a letter from the dean of Strasbourg University as well as one from Sylvain Levy who was president of the AIU.[25] Levinas's decision to become French is itself a sign of his devotion to the values he saw as embodied in that culture and the Republic. So while the post at the AIU did constitute a return to Judaism, it was in no way a turn to the study

the sight of Raba lost and distracted in study and chastises him for being in such a hurry in a state of "headlong haste" such that Raba did not listen to know whether he was able to accept. The modern scholar, seduced by the temptation of temptation, would side with the Sadducee in the story who criticizes Raba for going too far too fast. For acting before thinking, before considering and weighing the logic of the choices in the light of what appears possible. The Sadducee would deploy a developmental logic to figure out how we arrived at our current situation and what choice makes the most sense. This would be a slow and careful philology perhaps, but one that is ultimately under the scholar's control. By contrast, Raba seeks to discern the eternal meaning that Torah holds beyond his personal powers of interpretation. Levinas responds: "As if by chance, to rub in such a way that blood spurts out is of Talmud in the Lithuanian tradition. Instead, in the years leading to World War II, Levinas's position at the AIU should be seen as a job that allowed him to move between the world of "Jewish thought" and Parisian philosophy.[26] Ultimately, the mission of the AIU was as colonial as it was humanitarian, exporting both French and Jewish culture simultaneously to Northern Africa, Eastern Europe, and Asia. Here we see a conflation of the Universal ideals of the French Enlightenment project and the particular identity of Judaism.

Levinas was an avid reader of German newspapers as well as Jewish journals from Germany and Eastern Europe, so he was well aware of the rising trends of nationalism and anti-Semitism. He was also aware of the actions that his former professor, Heidegger, had taken in Germany, including his choice to join the National Socialist Party, his ascension to the rectorate at Freiburg, and the implementation on April 6, 1933, of the Baden decree, which suspended all civil servants of non-Aryan origin, regardless of religious orientation, from office, including those, such as Edmund Husserl, already in retirement.[27] Levinas had begun to distance himself from Heidegger as early as 1933, the year that Heidegger publicly joined the Nazi Party. One can see this in the 1934 article, "Reflections on the Philosophy of Hitlerism," where Levinas presented reason, liberalism, and the Judeo-Christian tradition as a counter to the racialist "philosophy of Hitlerians," and we must assume that Heidegger is to be

perhaps the way one must 'rub' the text to arrive at the life it conceals." He also concedes a point that those convinced that all interpretation is subjective would hold: "Many of you are undoubtedly thinking, with good reason, that at this moment, I am in the process of rubbing the text to make it spurt blood—I rise to the challenge!" (TT 46, TTf 102). Levinas's rejoinder, "To the degree that it rests on the trust granted the author, it can only consist in this violence done to words to tear from them the secret that time and conventions have covered over with their sedimentations, a process begun as soon as these words appear in the open air of history" (TT 47, TTf 102). Levinas looks to the text to reveal a meaning prior to that imposed on it by philologists, philosophers, or historians.

Instead, he argues that "the logical integrity of subjectivity" released included in this grouping.[28] In 1935 Levinas's critical edge and distinction from Heidegger became sharper and better defined in his essay titled "On Escape," where Levinas took issue with what he saw as the limiting and ultimately solipsistic nature of Heidegger's philosophy and advocated the need to think beyond being, beyond traditional concepts of metaphysics, and beyond ontology.[29] But in both of these essays and throughout the 1930s, Levinas's interest was primarily philosophical and his confrontation focused on the issue of the limits of ontology. While the possibility of accessing something beyond being (such as in his category of the il y a) was present in Levinas's prewar work, the resolution of this confrontation was not realized until *after* the Holocaust and the war. Up until the war, the "need for escape," Levinas tells us, "leads into the heart of philosophy."[30]

Events in France forced Levinas to accept the fact that anti-Semitism was not a phenomenon to which France was exempt, despite his hopes in the 1930s that it was a mere product of importation. By the late 1930s the circle of intellectuals around Levinas had completely destabilized. Perhaps one of the most difficult blows for Levinas was the realization that at this time of rising fascism and xenophobia, even those whom he held in the highest regard were not immune to the seductions of this vulgar trend. Heidegger's political choice in Germany is the most obvious example, but equally troublesome were the assertions made by Maurice Blanchot, Levinas's best

from the temptation of temptation leads to "the direct relation with the true, excluding the prior examination of its terms, its idea—that is, the reception of Revelation—[which] can only be the relation with a person, with another." I do not tell the Torah what it is but, instead, it tells me how to act. "The Torah is given in the Light of a face. The epiphany of the other person is *ipso facto* my responsibility towards them: seeing the other is already an obligation toward them. A direct optics—without the mediation of an idea—can only be accomplished as ethics. Integral knowledge or Revelation (the receiving of the Torah) is ethical behavior" (TT 47, TTf 103–4). The remedy to the temptation is a stepping back in which humility is required in order to accept responsibility for the world and for the Other, but again, this cannot be an act of blind faith. "In question here is a *yes* older than that of naïve friend. By 1937 Blanchot had joined the ranks of the virulently anti-Semitic press, writing numerous articles for the journals *Combat* and *L'Insurgé*.[31] But while Blanchot's work paralleled the anti-Semitism of other right-wing intellectuals such as Pierre Drieu la Rochelle, Henri de Motherlant, and Robert Brassillach, it did not display the same concerns.[32]

In response to Blanchot and Heidegger, Levinas was forced to rethink his understanding of philosophy, the relation of ontology to the subject as "I," and to the relation of that subject to an Other. More germane to our discussion, Levinas was forced to consider his position as a Jew and his own proximity to two thinkers (one his friend) tainted by anti-Semitism. It is in the context of this uncertainty and instability that Levinas wrote "De l'Évasion" in 1935 for the *Revue Philosophique*. While the majority of his work from the 1930s follows the works of Heidegger and Husserl fairly closely, using the phenomenological method to explore the ontological question of *Being*,[33] this piece intimated Levinas's growing concerns with the solipsistic nature of what he would later call the totalitarian project of ontology. In 1935, the issue was escape, and here we can detect a growing unease with the Western philosophical tradition, which he had adopted, in light of its apparent rejection of Levinas as a Jew, as the Other.

In 1939 Levinas was mobilized to serve in the Tenth Army, but by June 18, 1940, his company had been captured by the spontaneity. We think, like our text, that consciousness and seeking, taken as their own preconditions, are, like naiveté, the temptation of temptation, a torturous path leading to ruin" (TT 49, TTf 106). Philosophy and history take consciousness as their precondition, but "to say that the person begins in freedom, that freedom is the first causality and that first cause is nobody, is to close one's eyes to that secret of the ego, to that relation with the past which amounts neither to placing oneself at the beginning to accept this past consciously nor to being merely the result of the past" (TT 49, TTf 107–8). Instead, history is a different sort of relation between the actor in the present and the otherness of the past, which is not the property of the historian. "Uprightness, an original fidelity to an indissoluble alliance, a belonging with, consists in confirming this alliance and not in engaging oneself headfirst for the sake

German army and the soldiers sent to prisoner of war camps. Levinas was sent to the Frontstalags in Rennes, Laval, and Vesoul, where he was held until 1942, and then to Stalag XIB at Fallingpostel near Magdeburg, Germany, where he remained until May 1945. It was due to his capture as a soldier in the French army that Levinas was not deported to the concentration camps as a Jew.³⁴ Nevertheless, Levinas lived in the barracks designated for Jewish prisoners, and the word JUD was inscribed on his uniform while he worked on a forestry detail felling trees and chopping wood.³⁵ Despite the segregation, the derogatory remarks from the inhabitants of the local village, and the constant reminder of his subhuman status inscribed on his uniform, the war passed for Levinas without incident and, according to Levinas, without the slightest news of the atrocities committed at the camp in Bergen-Belsen.

Levinas's intellectual trajectory began to shift during his time in a German prisoner of war camp. While in captivity, Levinas developed his critique and counter to Heidegger's ontological philosophy, but now, segregated with the other Jewish soldiers in a special section of the camp and made to wear the yellow star on his uniform, this counter was established on Levinas's development of "being-Jewish" as a way to think otherwise than Heidegger.³⁶ In the seven notebooks written between 1940 and 1947, with the majority of entries written before 1945, Levinas sought to develop "Judaism" or "being-Jewish" as

of engaging oneself" (TT 49, TTf 106–7).

"To be a self" on this reading is not to be the arbiter of what one can know based solely on what one can hold in their grasp, it "is to be responsible beyond what one has oneself done. *Temimut* consists in substituting oneself for others" (TT 49, TTf 107). It is in this sense to be held hostage to the world and the Other not in the form of "servileness, for the distinction between master and slave already presupposes an established ego" (TT 49, TTf 107), but in the sense of a deposition of the sovereign ego and the substitution of an ego whose principal responsibility is for others. The status of hostage can be understood as "the impossibility of escaping from God—which in this at least is not a value among others—is the 'mystery of angels,' the 'We will do and we will hear.' It lies in the depths of the ego as ego, which is a category distinct from Heidegger's Dasein.³⁷ "To start from Dasein or to start from Judaism" reads an entry from 1942 just above a note that presents "Judaism as a category."³⁸ The notebooks are filled with fragments and reflections on the role and place of Judaism in relation to philosophy and specifically to Heidegger's philosophy that foreshadow not only his later philosophical work but also what have come to be known as his confessional writings.³⁹ In the fifth notebook from 1944 he states that "one essential element of my philosophy—and this is where it is different from the philosophy of Heidegger—is the importance of the Other. Another element is that it follows the rhythm of Judaism."⁴⁰

In the POW camp, Levinas also began to reformulate his position in relation to ontology in the form of an article titled, "Il y a," or "There Is." On his return to Paris after the war this article would become the basis for *De l'Existence à l'existant* (1947), and it would be with this work that Levinas would break with the ontological project and uncover an opening to ethics that would coincide with his discovery of Talmud. Levinas describes the *il y a*, the "there is," as

> something resembling what one hears when one puts an empty shell close to the ear, as if the emptiness were full, as if the silence were a noise. It is something one can also feel when one thinks that even if there were nothing, the fact that "there is" is undeniable. Not that there is this or that; but the

not only the possibility of death, 'the possibility of impossibility,' but already the possibility of sacrifice, birth of a meaning in the obtuseness of being, of a subordination of a 'being able to die' to a 'knowing how to sacrifice oneself" (TT 50, TTf 109). The choice offered at the foot of the mountain is not between the Torah and death, death will come regardless, but one between the domination of all or accepting the Other as Other, hearing the call of the Other before positing oneself and one's claims. Is it possible to have a history that is likewise attuned not only at the level of subject or geography but in terms of actually deposing oneself in favor of the Other?

very scene of Being is open: there is. In the absolute nothing that one can imagine before creation—there is.[41]

In the impersonal, anonymous Being of the "there is," Levinas attempted to explore the space prior to the posting of a subject. But here, too, we see evidence of the growing importance of an understanding of meaning that transcends time. The *il y a* suggests a source that lies outside of time and whose meaning is transcendent.

In the notebooks and in his immediate postwar writings, we see a double move by Levinas. As he began to break definitively with the philosophy of Heidegger and to question the viability of Western philosophy, we also see an evaluation of what it means to be a Jew under Nazi rule and then after Auschwitz. Both of these questions, one announced and one performed, eventually led Levinas to the study of Talmud, which completed the inversion of his prewar emphasis on the primacy of philosophy in the investigation of the role and place of Judaism in modern thought. Thus in an entry from 1946, Levinas defines his philosophy in terms of his Judaism: "My philosophy is a philosophy of the face to face. The relation with the other without an intermediary. This is Judaism."[42] This inversion of priority began with the substitution of "Being-Jewish" for Dasein. After the war and the Holocaust, it is this category of "Being-Jewish" that Levinas sees as the necessary precondition for the study of philosophy, and that is manifest in the "joy of having Torah" (*Simchas Torah*) that Levinas announces in a note directly below the equation of his own philosophy with Judaism.[43]

The shift in emphasis is presented, albeit in Sartrean or Heideggerian language, in Levinas's essay "Being-Jewish": "to do the will of God is in this sense the condition of facticity. The fact is only possible if, beyond its power to choose itself, which cancels out its facticity, it has been chosen, that is elected,"[44] but it appears fully formed later in his 1964 Talmudic lecture on "The Temptation of Temptation."[45] Here Levinas examined a text from tractate Shabbat (pp. 88a and 88b) about the moment in Exodus when Moses brought the Torah to the Jewish people. Rav Abdima bar Hama bar Hasa instructs us that the Lord said: "If you accept the Torah, all is well, if not here will be your grave."[46] The tract is about receiving the Torah at Mount Sinai, but the emphasis is again on a seemingly predetermined choice, this time in response to the Lord's statement. The issue gets more interesting for Levinas as he tells us that the "temptation of temptation" of which he speaks "may well describe the condition of the west." This temptation of temptation is the temptation of philosophy, the seduction of reason as a tool by which humans can master and control the world around them. This too was a theme in Levinas's prison notebooks where he opposes the "infallibility" that is the subject of "classical philosophy" to the possibility of "being fallible but not feeble, living in a world where many things escape my comprehension." To this end, for Levinas "faith = knowledge without mastery."⁴⁷

We must also be aware that this temptation of temptation is one that seduced Levinas himself in the years before World War II and led him to Martin Heidegger and one that Levinas will take up in the Talmudic lecture of that name.⁴⁸ But if knowledge, philosophical, scientific, or historical, is not the answer then what is? Here Levinas returns to the text: "The revelation which is at stake in the following text will permit us to discover this order prior to the one in which a thought tempted by temptation is found."⁴⁹ This revelation is conditioned by the threat of death, but it also is the basis for choice: "The teaching, which the Torah is, cannot come to the human being as a result of a choice. That which must be received in order to make freedom of choice possible cannot have been chosen, unless after the fact."⁵⁰ This is the election that Levinas earlier articulated as an essential condition of the ontology of "Being-Jewish" in distinction from the mechanisms of "choice" in the philosophy of Jean-Paul Sartre and Heidegger. "We must advance a bit further into certain notions that the great talent of Sartre and the genius of Heidegger have substantiated in contemporary philosophy and literature."⁵¹ For Levinas, the "transformation of supreme commitment into a supreme freedom" is indicative of the temptation of temptation insofar as philosophical cunning has supplanted the idea of origin.

For Sartre, this leads to the formulation that even "not to commit oneself would still be to commit oneself; not to choose would still be to choose." For Heidegger, it is the resolute choice in the face of one's own death that results in authentic Dasein and that can be achieved at any moment. "To cut loose the fact from its origin in this way," be it via the emphasis on contingency or *Geworfenheit* that undergirds the supreme freedom in both Sartre and Heidegger, "is precisely to dwell in the modern world, which in its science has abandoned the quest for the origin, and in its religion exalts the present."[52] To Levinas's mind, Sartre and Heidegger have made "choice" and "commitment" into empty categories by cutting through the Gordian knot rather than untying it. "The past that creation and election introduce into the economy of being cannot be confused with the fatality of a history without absolute origin."[53] By contrast it is through reflection on election and revelation that we discover the "order prior to the one in which a thought tempted by temptation is to be found."[54] But here we return to the revelation conditioned by the threat of death.

In Levinas's text from 1947, the "meaning of election, and of revelation understood as election" is not initially pronounced in relation to Moses and Sinai but in relation to the rise of Hitlerism and National Socialism. "The experience of Hitlerism was not sensed by everyone to be one of those periodic returns to barbarism which, all in all, is fundamentally in order, and about which one consoles oneself by recalling the punishment that strikes it. The recourse of Hitlerian anti-Semitism to racial myth reminded the Jew of the irremissibility of his being. Not to be able to flee one's condition."[55] This is almost immediately followed by a reference to Isaiah chapter 53, and while Levinas's portrayal of the experience of Hitlerian anti-Semitism is understated, the wider implications are clear when read in concert with a notebook entry from 1945 that contains the same biblical reference: "In persecution I rediscover the original meaning of Judaism, its initial emotion. Not just any persecution—I mean absolute persecution that chases down being to seal it in the bare fact of its existence. But it is also that, [Isaiah 53] in this despair that no one can comprehend, the presence of the divine reveals itself."[56]

In his later Talmudic reading, election is the consent to Torah that is given before the revelation of the laws of Moses and that is done so when faced with the alternative of death. God chose the Jewish people. But immediately following the war, Levinas presents the signs of this election in the suffering of the Jewish people faced "with the systematic will to extermination that rendered the Geneva Convention nothing more than a piece of paper."[57] In either case, it is this election conditioned by the possibility of death that distinguishes the ontology of being-Jewish from that of everyday or presentist existence, and here again Levinas mimics the Heideggerian structure of authentic Dasein, which can only be achieved through Dasein's confrontation with the possibility of its own death. For Heidegger, death is one's ownmost possibility, but it is also the possibility of the impossible as the confrontation with one's own finitude. "In Dasein there is undeniably a constant 'lack of totality' which finds an end with death. This 'not-yet' 'belongs' to Dasein as long as it is."[58] Dasein does not complete itself until the moment of death, when all possibilities disappear for Dasein. After death Dasein has no more possibilities; it is completed, which is to say it has finished.[59] Levinas agrees with Heidegger's presentation of Dasein as a temporal construct but does not agree with Heidegger's understanding of the finitude of being localized in the singular Dasein as defined in Being-towards-death and thus the "not yet" that signifies the lack of totality takes on a different significance for Levinas.

As a prisoner of war, faced with the pressing possibility of death at any moment, Levinas came to divine a parallel between his own condition and that of Abraham as he rode out to sacrifice his son. Levinas understood this period of delay before the terrible event to come as a time of reflection and meditation. "It is because of this [Abrahams's] journey and the time that it took that the test has meaning. It is because of the misery suffered by the Jewish prisoner that he could become aware of Judaism and the seeds of a future Jewish life that transports him who only knew torture, death and Kiddush-Hashem [a martyr's sanctification of the divine name]."[60]

Thus in captivity Levinas came to fashion an understanding of the ontology of being-Jewish as a temporal construct between an elected past and a "future Jewish life" to come. Whereas the Heideggerian structure is based on the finite temporal totality of Dasein as a whole, Levinas's presentation of "being-Jewish" eschews completion in that it is always situated in the "not yet" of an "infinite time behind us" and the promise of a messianic future to come.[61] This move also allowed Levinas to differentiate this ontology of "being-Jewish" from the ontologies proffered by Heidegger and Sartre in that the Jewish "fact" of existence "receives the structure of his personhood from election. In fact, there is a contradiction in the notion of 'ego' ['*moi*'] that defines this notion. The ego is posited as a simple part of reality and, at the same time, as endowed with the exceptional privilege of the totality. The ego is equivalent to the whole of being, of which it constitutes nevertheless only one part. This is a contradiction that is overcome in the emotion of election."[62] Thus for Levinas, "being-Jewish" is a privilege and election but only insofar as it announces the ethical imperative of understanding the ego as commencing from a position of a responsibility and not absolute freedom.

This reconciliation of the finite ego with infinite being is only possible as an alternative to the "presentist" or "everyday" understanding of existence (itself a sort of annihilation by assimilation) where the finite ego retains its dominant position. In turn the move requires that Levinas refute Heidegger's presentation of Dasein's radical finitude as demonstrated in "being-towards-death" via Levinas's own presentation of the infinite time of transcendence and the possibility of an election, which is the ontological condition of being Jewish.[63]

When Levinas returned to Paris in 1945, his first concern was for his family in France. Then, slowly he began to take stock of the events that happened in Europe. Over the next few months, stories of death camps became more and more real and more and more unbelievable. Before long, Levinas found out the fate of his own family in Kovno. In June 1941 the Germans had taken control of Lithuania; on June 24, Kovno fell into German hands, and the Jews were immediately rounded up. Pogroms were incited by the Germans, and after several days of intensive violence five thousand Jews were dead. By July 13 the Jews had been segregated, and Lithuanian groups working with German Einsatzkommandos shot five hundred Jews every day around the clock. For the following months the Jews were systematically shot in groups of one thousand. On November 1, the detention center was converted into a "proper camp," and the survivors were held until they were deported to camps in Germany.[64] Levinas's family was arrested on the doorstep of their house in Kovno, and his parents, brothers, and uncles killed by the SS. His mother-in-law was deported from France and never heard from again.[65]

After the Holocaust, Levinas's critical investigation into the viability of the Western philosophical tradition became more urgent. As we have seen in our discussion of his prison notebooks, Levinas believed that for philosophy to make sense in the wake of the Holocaust, it would have to move beyond Heidegger's emphasis on Being, but it could not return to the investigation of the individual being and that being's own personal horizon. Instead, philosophy had to work through the question of ontology to the relation of an individual being to an Other. Philosophy has to first and foremost take up the issue of ethics. But how could this undertaking be possible given the historical reality of the Holocaust? For Levinas, the answer lay in the equally important question of what it meant to be a Jew after the Holocaust. Levinas realized that the Western philosophical tradition he had so readily embraced in the years prior to the war had been implicated, if not indicted by the Holocaust.

In this light, Levinas's response to Jean-Paul Sartre's *Reflections on the Jewish Question* is particularly striking as he begins by stating, "If Judaism had only the 'Jewish Question' to resolve it would have much to do, but it would be a trifling thing."[66] A trifling thing? In 1947, a trifling thing? How can one in 1947, and Levinas in particular, consider the "Jewish Question" to be no more than a trifle? The phrase itself was a product of the mid-nineteenth century as "the crystallization of a series of questions whose modern formulation goes back to the eighteenth century: Should Jews be granted civil and political rights equal to those of Christians? Would civic education make them more like Gentiles? Can they serve as loyal soldiers? Are Jews a distinctive people, race, or nation? Is there an inherent dichotomy between Judaism and modernity?"[67] All of these questions revolve around the place of the Jews in a modernizing world. Under Nazi rule, however, this Jewish question was replaced by the "Jewish problem," to which there was ultimately only one final solution. Sartre's own reflection on the Jewish question was authored on the other side of the chasm that was the Holocaust, and his treatment of the question bears the historical weight of the event. Whatever its faults, and there are many, Sartre's text was one of the first in France to address the issues of anti-Semitism and the Jewish victims of the Holocaust.[68]

Réflexions sur la question juive was published in 1946, though the work had already caused a stir when Sartre published the first section, "The Portrait of the Anti-Semite," in the December 1945 issue of *Les Temps modernes*.[69] A second printing was issued in February 1947, and soon thereafter Sartre was invited by two French Jewish organizations to present lectures based on that work. The first was held on May 31, 1947, at the request of the French League for a Free Palestine where he lectured on "Kafka, a Jewish Writer."[70] The second lecture was held on June 3, 1947, under the auspices of the Alliance Israélite Universelle where

Sartre lectured on "The Jewish Question." Excerpts from this talk were published in the June 27 issue of *Les Cahiers de l'Alliance* with a short introduction, "Anti-Semitism and Existentialism," authored by Emmanuel Levinas.[71] Levinas followed this with a more substantial response to Sartre's writings and lecture on the "Jewish Question" published as "*Être-Juif*" in *Confluences* also in 1947.[72] Here we must remember that the lectures and discussions surrounding Sartre's *Reflections on the Jewish Question* took place at the same time as the first Heidegger affair in the pages of Sartre's journal *Les temps modernes*, which focused on the extent of Heidegger's relation to National Socialism and the impact of Heidegger's political choices on existential philosophy.[73] Though Levinas directs his analysis at Sartre's text, it is really Heidegger's thinking that is at issue.

Perhaps most striking, certainly for our purposes, is the way that in his *Reflections on the Jewish Question*, Sartre presents the inauthentic "Jew" as defined by the Other: "the Jew is the one whom other men consider a Jew."[74] When defined from without, the Jew lacks "authenticity," which Sartre defines as consisting "in having a true and lucid consciousness of the situation, in assuming the responsibilities and risks it involves, in accepting in pride or humiliation, sometimes in horror and hate."[75] When placed within the logic of *Being and Nothingness*, this quite simply means that the Jew as defined by others embodies Sartrean inauthenticity. Jonathan Judaken has argued that because

Sartre categorized the "Jew" as defined by the Other, for the Jew to achieve "authenticity" they must shed this definition thus becoming what they are not. Following this reasoning we can recognize in Sartre's philosophical presentation of the "Jew" an intractable crystallization of what he had earlier defined in *Being and Nothingness* as the human condition: "The Being of human reality is suffering because it rises as perpetually haunted by a totality which it is without being able to be it. Human reality is therefore by nature an unhappy consciousness with no possibility of surpassing its unhappy state."[76] By contrast, Peter Gordon has argued that Sartre's *Reflections on the Jewish Question* marks a break with *Being and Nothingness* because Sartre allows for the possibility of Jewish authenticity wherein the transcendence of one's transcendence is merely an abject condition to be avoided through self-assertion and the "choice" of an authentic life.[77] But whether one reads Sartre in the light of Judaken or Gordon, the text and Sartre's particular take on the "Jewish Question" must be seen in relation to his larger existential phenomenology and behind this the influence of Martin Heidegger.[78]

And yet for Levinas, Sartre's emphasis on the "Jewish Question" was no more than a trifling thing. Levinas certainly credits Sartre, if not for the success of his arguments, for the "new weapons" he deploys to attack anti-Semitism "with existentialist arguments" in order to bring the Jewish Question back from the "outmoded discourses where it is often broached [enlightenment or rationalist arguments] to the very summits where the twentieth century's true, terrible, and gripping history is taking place."[79] The "Jewish Question," as presented by Sartre or by the thinkers that preceded him, merely scratches the surface, because as Levinas wrote,

> posed in exclusively political and social terms—and this is the rule for public meetings, in the press, and even in literature—the question refers to a right to live, without seeking a reason for being. This rhetoric that invokes the right to existence for an individual or for a people reduces or returns the Jewish event to a purely natural fact. No matter how much one hopes for a cultural and moral contribution to the world from the political independence of Israel, one still does no more than expect one more kind of painting or literature. But to be Jewish is not only to seek a refuge in the world but to feel for oneself a place in the economy of being.[80]

Thus for Levinas, the issue is not equal rights, citizenship, or participation, nor is the issue that of a state or nation of one's own, although these are of course essential issues in political and social terms. In all of these cases the establishment of such rights or territories simply establishes the Jews as one people among many, which at one level they are simply another kind of "painting or literature." By phrasing the "Jewish Question" in this way the universal has prevailed over the particular, and a certain assumption about assimilation is both presumed and fulfilled. If the Jews are simply another people and their ways equivalent to all others, then in fact they have been assimilated into the "modern world." What is more, as one people among many Judaism has sought to justify its survival by "rediscovering in the [politics, culture and religion of the] Christian or liberal world the harvest of ancient sowings."[81] But, Levinas continues, "to claim a message that has already fallen into the public domain is an ambition denied by the whole impulse that for one hundred and fifty years has carried Judaism toward assimilation and in which religion, shrinking more and more, is limited to a colorless ancestor worship." What matters the provenance of Jewish thought or Judaism for that matter if its ideas are simply part and parcel of the "common patrimony of humanity"?[82] Being-Jewish must mean something other than this or there is no reason to be Jewish. No reason not to assimilate.

"But toward what kind of existence does assimilation tend?" Levinas asks: "Is it reducible to a general sociological phenomenon in which a minority dissolves into a majority that encompasses it and fascinates it with its force and the very value of its being a majority?"[83] On one level this question and this text is imbued with the fear that assimilation will lead to annihilation. A worry conditioned by the "twentieth century's true, terrible, gripping history." At another, though related, level, the question provokes an answer concerning two kinds of "being": "the ontological meaning of this existence of the non-Jewish [modern] world toward which assimilation acceded" and the ontological meaning of being Jewish.[84] For Levinas, there is an "affinity among all of the non-religious manifestations of this world, and there is an affinity between these and the Christianity that remains their religion."[85] Thus, according to Levinas, the modern world is essentially Christian at least insofar as the ontological meaning of the non-religious and Christian manifestations are compatible. Levinas describes this meaning as "everyday life" that is "essentially a present: to have to deal with the immediate, to introduce oneself into time not by moving through the entire line of the past, but all at once to ignore history."[86] For Levinas, this emphasis on the present at the expense of the past is the fundamental difference between the ontological meaning of the everyday modern world and the ontological meaning of Being-Jewish.

This presentist logic is exemplified by "Alexander's sword, which does not untie knots, which does not redo the knotting motion in reverse, but which slices," this is to say severs the relation with the past. In Christianity, one is born again in the "power of a new birth promised at each instant." In science, it is the discovery that breaks with our previous understanding of the world "that is, without reference to the origin that was implied, still, by the idea of cause." For the nation-state, it is the revolution where politics are created ex nihilo the calendar restarting at the year one. All are predicated on a logic of the now that breaks with the past in pursuit of a perpetual present. In this way the relation with being in everyday life is "action" in the present that the existential philosophy of a Sartre or Heidegger sees as the basis for freedom. By contrast, Levinas asserts that Jewish existence is not an existence centered on the present but "refers to a privileged instant of the past and the Jew's absolute position within being [that] is guaranteed him by his filiality."[87] This is the moment of election, the moment when choice itself was bestowed on the Jewish people but that was not itself chosen.

It is important to point out the ways that Levinas's presentation of the presentist existence of everyday life in contrast to the privileged instant of the past that conditions Jewish existence can be seen to mirror the structure of Martin Heidegger's analysis of Dasein in his 1927 work *Being and Time*.[88] For Heidegger, the issue is the ways that our everyday existence (what Heidegger refers to as "inauthentic being") has lost track, forgotten, or has fallen from its original or "authentic" relation with being. It is not a stretch to map Levinas's characterization of the everyday existence of the modern and presentist world onto the forgetful and inauthentic mode of being in distinction from the original and originary mode of being that characterizes both Heidegger's authentic existence and Levinas's being-Jewish. Furthermore, Levinas can be said to replicate the distinction between "authentic" and "inauthentic" Jews that he finds so problematic in the text by Sartre insofar as he equates the assimilationist tendencies of the Jewish people with the "everyday" or "inauthentic" mode of being as opposed to the seemingly forgotten model of election that characterizes the essence of being-Jewish, "authentic" being-Jewish.

The symmetry is not entirely unexpected but nevertheless surprising given Levinas's break with the philosophy of Heidegger. For Levinas, this category of "being-Jewish" creates a blind spot where he conserves aspects of the authentic/inauthentic distinction inherited from the philosophy of Heidegger. It is a retention that cannot be taken lightly because in the aftermath of the Holocaust, Levinas realized all too well the potential and actual danger of this construct. And yet it is because of the Holocaust that Levinas cannot let go of this distinction for fear that the very annihilation assigned to the Jews by the Nazi final solution will come to be fulfilled by assimilation into the "modern" world. Thus we need to be wary of the ways that this hierarchical understanding of being-Jewish is retained in aspects of his Talmudic lectures despite his stated intentions. What's more, this exemplarism is reinforced by/in the mission of the AIU and ENIO as we will see in the following chapter.

CHAPTER 2

OUR SIDE

The Alliance Israélite Universelle, Shushani, and the École Normale Israélite Universelle

THE OTHER SIDE

Old as the World

Levinas began working for the Alliance Israélite Universelle soon after moving to Paris in 1930, but the AIU to which Levinas returned after World War II, now as director of the École Normale Israélite Orientale, was an institution grappling with many of the same concerns that confronted Levinas after the war. Paramount among these were issues of Jewish existence and identity. How could Judaism recover after Auschwitz? And how does one make sense of the European heritage, upon which both the AIU and Levinas's philosophical platform were grounded, in a political and cultural world that had failed the Jewish people? The issues that motivated Levinas's response to Sartre and rejection of Heidegger led him to reconsider the mission of the AIU. He now saw his position at the ENIO as a mandate to rethink, renew, and revive Judaism after Auschwitz, and the means to do so was through the study of Talmud.

From the Tractate *Sanhedrin*, 36b–37a:

Three rows of students of the Law were seated before the judges. Each knew his place; if it became necessary to invest someone, the one appointed was from the first row; in such a case, a student from the second row moved up to the first and a student from the third row to the second. The most competent person in the assembled public was chosen and was placed in the third row. And the last to come did not sit in

Before working through Levinas's turn to Talmud and the ways that this turn came to inflect his educational mission as director of the École Normale Israélite Universelle, let us first look to the AIU itself: it's original mission, Levinas's role with it in the years prior to the war, and the ways that both were changed by World War II and the Holocaust. This is the second strand of our braid.

The Alliance Israélite Universelle was founded in 1860 in response to the Damascus blood libel affair of 1840 and the Mortara case of 1858, where the Catholic church in Italy refused to return a Jewish boy, who had been secretly baptized, to his parents. But the mission of the AIU was inspired by the ideals and principles of the French Revolution as embodied in the 1790–91 emancipation of the Jews, granting them equal rights and full citizenship.[1] Cases such as the Damascus blood libel and Mortara affair were viewed as indicative of the sorts of superstitious practices that engendered prejudice and anti-Semitism. For the founders of the AIU, the light of reason was the antidote to such backward thinking, and the granting of rights and citizenship to Jews was the proof of success. In this sense, the founders of the AIU believed the march of progress to be inevitable, anti-Semitism and persecution were "relics of the past destined to disappear as modern civilization destroyed superstition and prejudice."[2] Thus the AIU, centered in Paris, saw itself as advocating on behalf of Jews less fortunate than themselves either because these Jews lived in unenlightened

the place of the first (in the row, who had gone up to the other row) but in the place which was suitable for him.[1]

The text that Levinas offers us is about the Sanhedrin, the juridical court of the Jewish people that existed in the form of the Lesser Sanhedrin composed of twenty-three judges and the Great Sanhedrin composed of seventy-one. Each city could have a Lesser Sanhedrin, but there was only one Great Sanhedrin, which served as a Supreme Court to hear appeals from the lesser courts. Levinas tells us that he takes "the Sanhedrin to be what it is claimed to be in the text, leaving out of consideration the historical side completely. It may never have existed as it is described here. The word *Sanhedrin* is Greek. The institution may be the product of diverse influences external to Judaism. But the text is to be taken regions of the world, because they themselves remained unenlightened as Jews, or both. The founding call of 1860, "*Appel à tous les Israélites*," announced the mission of the AIU: "to work throughout the world for the emancipation and moral progress of the Jews; to help effectively all those who suffer because they are Jews; to encourage all publications designed to achieve these results."[3] Of equal weight was the belief that the "influence of the principles of 1789 are all powerful and the law that follows is a law of justice that we hope will penetrate everyone's spirit."[4] Both of these sentiments can be seen in Levinas's description of the AIU, cited in chapter 1:

> Constituted in 1860 with the express concern of working for the emancipation of Israelites in countries where they did not yet have the right of citizenship. The first of these Israelite institutions was inspired by the French Rights of Man. There were in this inspiration no Zionist sentiments. Its mission was simply to emancipate those Israelites living in countries where they were not recognized as citizens. . . . Soon these activities became scholastic work; the founding of French schools of the highest level that would express above all the ideals of the nineteenth century . . . the elevation of universal culture and the affirmation of the glorious ideals of 1789.[5]

Levinas's own allegiance to the glorious ideals of 1789 should not be underestimated, and they form a crucial strand of the braid on the way to his Talmudic lectures. As we

as a given: it is through it that for at least eighteen centuries, Jewish tradition has thought about the supreme institution of justice" (OW 72, VM 154). The history of the Sanhedrin is unimportant, even its historical existence. What is important are the lessons that have been drawn from the Sanhedrin, and so Levinas asks us to suspend disbelief and take the text as given.

Levinas begins with the Mishna where, in the text, the Sanhedrin is described as forming a semicircle "so that its members could see each other." This is a court where the individuals who compose it see each other face to face, but it is not a private retreat isolated from the cares of the world. "It is, however, a semi-, or open circle. Because the point is precisely that the judges who sit on the court remain open to the outside world when they discuss the cases submitted to their jurisdiction or when they give their verdict" have seen, in the years before World War II, Levinas's faith in the tolerance and equality of France, embodied in the emancipation of the Jews and the rights of man, and his interest in philosophy/phenomenology held more weight than the traditions of his youth or the Talmudic academies of Lithuania. In this light, one can see Levinas's trajectory from Vilna to Strasbourg to Paris as aligned with the emancipatory doctrine of the French Revolution, which called on Jews to transform themselves into modern, enlightened citizens. Levinas did just that when he became a naturalized French citizen.

After the Holocaust, Levinas's faith in these enlightenment principles and in philosophy itself was shaken. The cold realization that the principles that had guided enlightened assimilated Jews were, in fact, powerless in the face of Nazi rule is the underlying theme of two pieces, composed by Levinas after his return to Paris, written in honor and memory of his teacher and friend, the neo-Kantian philosopher Léon Brunschvicg. Brunschvicg was a member of the central committee of the AIU, and for Levinas, Brunschvicg was the embodiment of a modern French assimilated Jew. After the German occupation of Paris, Brunschvicg was forced to leave his position at the Sorbonne and flee to the south of France where he died at the age of seventy-four while in hiding. In the 1949 essay, "The Diary of Léon Brunschvicg," Levinas makes clear that his friend and mentor belonged to a different time and place, "Assimilation for Brunschvicg proceeded not (OW 72, VM 155). While the members of the Sanhedrin are in close proximity to each other and deliberate while looking at each other, they are also in contact with the outside world so that the issues and concerns of the day are part and parcel of their deliberations. Levinas is also clear that the Sanhedrin is "not a synagogue in any case but a court" (OW 72, VM 156). It is an institution concerned with jurisprudence, and in this sense it should not be confused with a house of worship even if the justice served is Jewish law. As such, Levinas equates it with the universal need to adjudicate claims and grievances that arise in everyday life. The Sanhedrin is open to the problems of the world, and in this light Levinas states: "I do not know if the world needs the Jews. But the Jew needs the world, that is certain" (OW 72–73, VM156).

Even so, there is something novel about this

from betrayal [of Judaism], but from adherence to a universal ideal to which he could lay claim outside of any particularism."⁶ Brunschvicg, like many leaders of the AIU, belonged to a generation filled with optimism in the rule of reason bolstered by the apparent victory of the Dreyfus affair. This was also a generation, Levinas cautions, who "remembered less the fact that such an injustice has been possible in a civilized age than the triumph recorded by justice."⁷ Levinas laments, in characteristic understatement, that "our generation could not derive from the experience of Hitler what Brunschvicg's generation derived from the Dreyfus Affair."⁸ In the end, Brunschvicg's confidence in European civilization and "Western culture" was unfounded. His "French training at the ENS," which "bore witness to everything that is most noble about the traditions of the school" ultimately insufficient.⁹

Nevertheless, in the person and life of Brunschvicg, Levinas saw evidence that the enlightenment principles to which Brunschvicg adhered should not be entirely forsaken. Levinas begins "The Diary of Léon Brunschvicg" by means of an apology of sorts:

> I should like to tell those who never knew him of the kind of perfect humanity Léon Brunschvicg represented. I want to show all the young people enamored of action . . . how much heart there was in this Reason that was integrally reason, and how much attention it paid to life. . . . And I

court of law: "in front of the judges sit 'students of the Law,' those who study the Torah but are not yet invested as judges. The court is indeed not a synagogue, it is a little bit of a school" (OW 73, VM 157). As with Levinas's educational program at the ENIO and then his Talmudic lessons at the Colloque, the study of Torah is inextricable from the world outside the synagogue. The lessons to be learned are not confined to houses of worship but are enacted in houses of study. "Study of the Law and jurisdiction, theory and practice, rigor and mercy—in Judaism, all the polarizations of the spirit belong to the duality of the house of study and the court" (OV 73, VM 157). Judaism here is not a revealed religion but a revealed set of laws and practices that must be learned and then enacted. Justice does not simply happen but must be achieved through the work of study, and in this way Levinas's presentation of want to remind Jewish youth who, after their recent experiences, may have had enough of Europe—it's "Western culture", its "Christian Humanism," or whatever—how much civilization was embodied in this European Jew.[10]

As we saw in "Being-Jewish," Levinas recognized the assimilationist tendencies, which characterized Brunschvicg, as a liability in post-Holocaust Europe, but he also feared that the full-blown rejection of what he calls "Western culture" would foster a return to irrational or superstitious religious practice. Levinas sought to navigate the dangerous path between European complicity with the Nazi genocide and the perils of regression to superstition and mysticism. In the person of Léon Brunschvicg, philosopher and assimilated Jew, Levinas found those aspects of the European tradition he believed should be conserved because they coincided with Levinas's understanding of Judaism. Levinas asks: "But although Brunschvicg ignores Judaism, since he does not know it, does he not discover its essential strains by affirming that at the heart of the Infinite, where the intellect dwells, there is an independent man, master of his fate, who communicates with the Eternal in the clear light of intellectual and moral action?"[11] Levinas makes the connection more clear in his second piece on Brunschvicg, "Being a Westerner," published in 1951, when he compares Brunschvicg's thought, "based on the calm truth of science," to Judaism. "Judaism," Levinas writes, "also appeals to a humanity devoid of

the Sanhedrin conforms with his understanding of Jewish learning.

What is said now concerns the Lesser Sanhedrin of twenty-three people (not the Great Sanhedrin). "We are told that on the Sanhedrin of twenty-three judges there are more than twenty-three people: three rows of students are seated before the judges" (OW 73, VM 157–58). The school extends beyond the judges on the Sanhedrin to a greater public of students. "Each knew his place: it is an order excluding contingency. One did not just sit anywhere; the classification was rigorous . . . if it became necessary to invest someone, the one appointed was from the first row; in such a case, a student from the second row moved up to the first and a student from the third row to the second" (OW 74, VM 158). There is an order and logic of ascension based on knowledge and experience. The order myths—not because the marvelous is repugnant to its narrow soul but because myth, albeit sublime, introduces into the soul that troubled element, that impure element of magic and sorcery and that drunkenness of the Sacred and of war that prolong the animal within the civilized."[12] For Levinas, Judaism could not succeed in the form of the assimilationist variant endorsed and lived by Brunschvicg (and the founders of the AIU). Nevertheless, Levinas's understanding of observant Judaism lay closer to the rationalist beliefs of Brunschvicg than to a mystical understanding of Judaism founded on irrational fervor for the sacred.

This leads us to another way in which the doctrine and practices of the AIU aligned with Levinas's intellectual priorities after the war, though, at first glance, this alignment appears counterintuitive. In the 1890s, the AIU began to focus its efforts on aiding Jewish education by creating a vast network of schools in Middle Eastern countries, the Balkans, and North Africa. The educational goal was the transformation or "regeneration" of the Jews from these lands into modern enlightened people worthy of citizenship.[13] The mission, however, held the tacit assumption that Jews from these regions were in need of education, enlightenment, and regeneration. In other words, that they were backward. The privileging of French as the language of instruction at the schools of the AIU fused the ideal of the educated, enlightened, regenerated, and thus worthy Jew to French culture and ultimately to the educational directives of Paris. Aron Rodrigue argues is not chosen at random or by lots but is instead based on Jewish education. What's more, ascension by education is not reserved for a select few but extends to the general public as well, though, here too, the movement is not random. "The most competent person in the assembled public was chosen and was placed in the third row. And the last to come did not sit in the place of the first (in the row, who had gone up to the other row) but in the place which was suitable for him" (OW 70, VM 151). This is a chain of transmission based on education and learning. "Everyone thus moved up one notch. The one from the public who acceded to the rank of student took the last place." One can see this as mirroring the logic of Levinas's Rashi seminar, his lectures at the Colloque, or for those who read his books. It is an invitation to take up the call and educate oneself so as to rise from public to student to judge.

that the imposition of a cultural hierarchy "was in part a reflection of the generally negative perception of non-Western societies so prevalent in nineteenth century Europe, a perception that European Jewry shared in full."[14] There was also the added dimension, Rodrigue continues, that Western European Jewry saw their co-religionists from Muslim lands as an embarrassment because of their unenlightened beliefs and practices. Hence, the need for indoctrination into Western European (read French) culture and modern religious practices as regeneration. This sense of embarrassment and foreboding, that Gentiles would judge the recently emancipated Western European Jews by the actions of their co-religionists, was not isolated to Jews from Muslim lands but also extended to the Jews of Eastern Europe. In this light, the Lithuanian-born Levinas seems an unlikely ally for such a doctrine given his later allegiance to the teachings of the Gaon of Vilna, Hayyim of Volozhin, and the Talmudic academies of Vilna.

But the alignment makes sense when one considers the Mitnageddic tradition to which the Gaon of Vilna and Hayyim of Volozhin belong, its emphasis on highly intellectual Talmud study, and its opposition to the claims of miracles and wonders that characterized the Hassidic movement with its emphasis on prayer.[15] Levinas shared with the founders of the AIU a distrust of, and distaste for, the miraculous, the mystical, and the enchanted. He saw these as juvenile fantasy or inebriated indulgence, and this is in part why he often referred to

In doing so, "The hierarchical order remained intact." The movement or educational track is not a free-for-all of personal interpretation based on autodidacticism. It is a course of training where one learns to understand and interpret the Law in the right way. "The text confirms it again: each went to the place which was suitable for them. A rigorous hierarchy in itself, objectively; but it was also respected and known by all, a subjectively recognized hierarchy: 'Each knew his place.' An absolute order" (OW 74, VM 159–60).

The above is from Mishna, but what follows is Gemara, which introduces new perspectives into the description of the order that governs the Sanhedrin. Levinas informs us that "the masters of Gemara can either accept the teaching because it comes from an indisputable authority (it is, in any case, always disputed but remains

Judaism as a religion for adults. In an interview for *France Culture* from 1957, Levinas provides his definition of the Jew as "a type of man who lives in a demystified, disenchanted world. . . . Enthusiasm is, after all, possession by a God. Jews wish not to be possessed, but to be responsible. Their God is the master of justice; He judges in the open light of reason and discourse."[16] For Levinas, Jewish life is one governed by the light of reason echoing the program and mission of the AIU as well as what he claimed to be most "Jewish" in the thought of Brunschvicg: "The inner life for Leon Brunschvicg is not confused with either mysticism or with religious anxiety. His inner life is composed of reason and enlightenment. . . . He knows another way to reach God, one based on the coincidence of rational activity and moral consciousness."[17] To be sure, Levinas's self-fashioning squares the circle in order to bring the Mitnageddic tradition of intellectual rigor into alignment with that of the Haskalah and Western European Enlightenment in ways that likely would appear unfathomable to either the founders of the AIU or the Volozhin Yeshiva. But it is the reconciliation of the study of Talmud in the Lithuanian tradition with the French Enlightenment principles of the AIU, as well as with Levinas's own philosophical trajectory, that forms the final, crucial, strand of the braid that enabled his Talmudic lectures.

As we have seen, Levinas's recalibration of intellectual priorities began during his time as a prisoner of war and continued indisputable), or they can seek the scriptural source from which the teacher drew his teaching" (OW 75, VM 160). The matter is not settled but opened for further discussion and debate. Here again, the question is posed: "Doesn't the Sanhedrin, as its name indicates, in all likelihood refer to foreign traditions, notably to Greek civilization?" (OW 75, VM 161). This is to ask whether there is anything particular or novel about the Sanhedrin? Is it not more likely that the Sanhedrin reflects the appropriation of other cultures or values? Is it not simply a product of Hellenization? Levinas responds by arguing that "whatever the historical causality and the antecedents of ideas and institutions might be—they always conceal their origin—what matters is the discovery of the convergence of the spiritual efforts of mankind or, and this is even more likely but does not contradict the first interpretation, what matters after his return to Paris via his exploration into the ontology of being-Jewish. But Levinas's turn to the study of Talmud is inextricably bound to the enigmatic figure known as Monsieur Chouchani. Chouchani or Shushani was almost certainly not his real name, and there has been much interpretative speculation as to its significance. Some believe it is a reference to the book of Esther, which coincides with a name on one of his passports, "Mordechai ben Shushan," thus linking Shushani to the biblical figure. Elie Wiesel, who met Shushani in the years following the war, claimed that Shushani's real name was Mordechai Rosenbaum, which provides an alternative explanation if one can make the interpretative leap of translating Rosenbaum as lily, which is shushan in Hebrew. Shalom Rosenberg by contrast claimed that Shushani's real name was Hilel Perlman, a Talmudic scholar mentioned by Rabbi Abraham Isaac Hacohen Kook in two letters from 1915.[18] The uncertainty over his name is indicative of the general uncertainty about his life, all is speculation [19] "Where did he come from? What were his joys, his fears? What did he seek to attain, to forget? Nobody knew."[20]

What we do know from the testimony of Levinas, Wiesel, and others is that Shushani was a drifter who appeared and disappeared for months at a time. Shushani told Levinas that he had been trained in the Lithuanian Talmudic tradition, but he was not from Lithuania—Levinas noted that he spoke the Yiddish of Lite with a strong

is to know *in what spirit something is borrowed*" (OW 75, VM 161). One could interpret this as a justification for Levinas's own use or borrowing of extra-Talmudic resources, such as philosophy, in his pursuit of what he calls Jewish education. To do so would miss the crucial point about how one can bring one's own tradition into the material or structure that is borrowed. In the end, historical context is important for understanding how a particular message or teaching applies to its moment, but it is not the source of the meaning because these teachings are found and not made. In actuality the Sanhedrin is, no matter how Hellenistic, the vehicle through which the Jewish idea of justice can be enacted. Likewise, Levinas's reading of Talmud, no matter how saturated with Western philosophy or Enlightenment values it might be, is the vehicle through which Judaism can be rejuvenated and revitalized in the modern foreign accent and surmised that he came from Galicia or Poland.[21] It was commonly believed that Shushani was born in Eastern Europe and that this is where he spent his childhood. There are testimonies that he lived in Morocco and Algeria during the 1920s but also an account by Wiesel that he had been in the United States during this time. Moshe Schweber, a Jerusalem-based electrician and former teacher, claimed he met Shushani at his parent's restaurant in Strasbourg in the mid-1930s.[22] This corroborates the account provided by Levinas's close friend Dr. Henri Nerson, who recounted to Levinas that he began studying with Shushani in Strasbourg at that time.[23]

Nerson was an observant Jew raised in a Jewish community in Strasbourg. There he studied Talmud with Shushani, maintaining contact with the errant Talmudic master for twenty years before Nerson met Levinas.[24] The first encounter between Levinas and Nerson was in 1937, but they became close in the years following the war as neighbors on the rue Autueil in the sixteenth arrondissement of Paris. It was at this time that Levinas suffered a crisis of conviction as a Jew. On the one hand, he took the position as director of the École Normale Israélite Orientale, and, as we will see, Levinas saw this as a commitment to revitalizing the Jewish community, after it had been brought to the brink of extermination under Nazi rule, by providing knowledgeable instructors who could guarantee the perseverance of Jewish thought. On the other hand, Levinas's

world. "Given this, in seeking a foundation for borrowing in the letter of a past which is not its own, the borrower links what he is borrowing to a tradition and formulates, beyond the similarities of the structure, the meaning he is giving to what he is borrowing" (OW 75, VM 161). Ultimately, it is Judaism that provides the meaning for the structure or text that is borrowed.

The Gemara then takes us further afield from the discussion offered in the Mishna to the extent that "even if one accepts our interpretation of the maneuver which consists in going back to a Hebrew text so as to understand the basis for an institution suspected of Hellenic origin, the nature of the text chosen for this purpose will astonish us" (OW 75, VM 162). That is, even if one accepts Levinas's assertion that the meaning of the Sanhedrin comes from the Jewish tradition and not Hellenism, the textual support for the own commitment to the practice of Judaism was in doubt, and for a period of time after returning from the war he stopped keeping kosher.[25] Levinas's friendship with Henri Nerson, arguably, brought him back to observant Judaism, restoring his sense of commitment to ritual practice. His friendship with Nerson also led Levinas to Shushani and to the reading of Talmud in the Lithuanian tradition, or at least Shushani's presentation of that tradition.

Nerson introduced Levinas to Shushani in 1946, and soon Levinas was taken by this Talmudic scholar who, according to Levinas, could cite Torah, Talmud, and Zohar by heart. As Levinas recalled: "In the years immediately following the war, around 1946, 1947 . . . M. Shushani accepted a room at my apartment and he would come there once or twice a week."[26] Levinas provided Shushani with a room and Shushani taught courses in Talmud. The courses, taught in French, were not cheap and lasted five or six hours, often going on until two in the morning. This lasted for "two or three years until one fine day he left without even saying goodbye."[27]

One can only imagine the impact that Shushani must have had on Emmanuel Levinas. For Levinas, Shushani was the embodiment of a tradition associated with his childhood, his parents, his family, and his community in Lithuania. All of which Levinas had lost. The similar experience of Elie Wiesel is perhaps instructive: "It was him [Shushani] I had been seeking since the end of the war, since the death

argument comes from an unexpected source: the erotic verse of "The Songs of Songs."

> Rav Hah bar Hanina said: we learn (what was said about the Sanhedrin) from verse 3, chapter 7 (of the Song of Songs): "Your navel is like a round goblet full of fragrant wine; your belly like a heap of wheat hedged with roses."[2] (OW 70, VM 151–52)

Levinas instructs us to "enter into the Talmud's game, which is concerned with the spirit beyond the letter, yet extricates this spirit on the basis of the letter, and is, for this reason, very wonderful." The text says more to us than it appears to say, and Levinas explains that he has mused about this text for a long time. In particular about the way the navel refers to the Sanhedrin for the Sanhedrin is in session at the navel or center of the universe. Levinas finds this a beautiful image, "the creature cut off from its source of my teachers, since their fire consumed itself among the burning coals somewhere in Silesia. He alone would be in a position to take their place and show me what road to follow, and perhaps even reveal where it leads." Like Wiesel, Levinas was searching for a "road to follow" after his return from the war, but unlike for Wiesel, Shushani represented a tradition that at some level Levinas had rejected in his desire to assimilate into European culture through the pursuit of the Western philosophical tradition and French acculturation. These traditions, so dear to Levinas, had been placed in question by the event of the Holocaust, which consumed the Lithuanian Talmudic academies "among the burning coals" somewhere in Vilna. Through Shushani, Levinas found the means to forge a link in the chain of transmission from the Paris of his present to the Lithuanian Talmudic traditions of his past. To be sure, as Levinas states, "the history of the Holocaust played a much larger role in what happened to my Judaism than my encounter with this man [Shushani]. But through this man I regained my confidence in these books."[28] Levinas's restored confidence in "these books" gave him a new means by which to reconcile the ethical concerns that guided his more general philosophical endeavors with the particular problem of what it means to be a Jew after Auschwitz. The latter problem throwing the former into turmoil. In his studies with Shushani, Levinas discovered a reformulation of Judaism wherein "Judaism is not the Bible, of nourishment but the place where justice is pronounced is in the trace of creation" (OW 77, VM 164–65).

Levinas is reminded by a friend, and in recounting the story reminds us, that there is nothing particularly Jewish about the image of the navel as the center of the universe. This friend reminds Levinas "that the image of the navel of the world is Greek and that, in Aeschylus' *The Eumenides*, Delphi is called the navel of the world," and this led Levinas to "reread *The Eumenides*. In this work . . . a witness to a world that did not know the Scriptures, I found a greatness which proved to me that everything must have been thought from time immemorial. After reading *The Eumenides* one can legitimately ask oneself if there is anything left to read" (OW 77, VM 165). In *The Eumenides*, the issue of justice is dealt with in profound ways, which leads Levinas to ask:

it is the Bible seen through the Talmud, through rabbinical wisdom, questioning, and religious life." Under this formula, the Bible represents that which is particular to Israel, whereas the Talmud constitutes the Jewish contribution to the universal. Levinas's turn to Talmud marked a "new way to approach Rabbinic wisdom" but also "to understand what it meant to be human *tout court*."²⁹ Given our limited knowledge about Shushani one can only speculate as to the specifics of his Talmudic method, as what we do know is based largely on Levinas's own writings and references to Shushani as his teacher. Wiesel remarked that Shushani "possessed the superhuman power of remaking the past for himself."³⁰ This is a power he bequeathed to Levinas who used Shushani's teachings to remake his own Lithuanian past and heritage in the service of a theology that could account for his post-Holocaust reality.

At a dinner for his eightieth birthday hosted by former students from the ENIO, Levinas reflected on his earliest years as director: "After Auschwitz, I had the impression that in taking on directorship of the École Normale Israélite Orientale I was responding to an historical calling. It was my little secret."³¹ René Cassin, president of the AIU and one of the authors of the Universal Declaration of Human Rights, named Levinas director of the ENIO in 1945, a position he held until 1979. The ENIO was established in 1867 with the mission of training the directors and teachers for the schools of the AIU. The goal was

"Is Judaism necessary to the world? Isn't Aeschylus enough? All the essential problems are broached there. The Eumenides are not expelled; vengeance-justice is not simply dismissed once and for all" (OW 77, VM 165–66). It is a vote of humans, not gods, that determines the shift from the ancient gods to the new ones and the shift from vengeance-justice to justice with forgiveness, even if the final vote that breaks the deadlocked jury is cast by Athena. Indeed, given that *The Eumenides* predates the tractate *Sanhedrin*, "There would be nothing new in [Jewish] wisdom! The text of *The Eumenides* is at least five centuries older than the Mishna with which my text opens." Of course, Levinas takes solace that "*The Eumenides* is nonetheless three centuries later than the prophets of the Bible. And that was my first consolation" (OW 78, VM 166). Even given the issue of historical precedent and priority, "an essential to bring uniform quality and content to the AIU network of school in the Balkans, North Africa, and the Middle East, so in this regard the model was akin to the École Normale Superieure in Paris educating teachers for schools throughout France. World War II led to a massive disruption under Vichy rule as the leaders of the AIU took refuge in the nonoccupied zone, and the schools of the AIU were effectively cut off from the central office in Paris. In 1943, Charles de Gaulle appointed René Cassin president of the AIU, wresting the power to do so from the Central Committee, which had been forced into hibernation.[32] Cassin accepted the presidency and formed a small committee in London before setting up headquarters at the office of the AIU in Algiers.

After the liberation of Paris, Cassin reformed the Central Committee with the goal of restoring normalcy and stability to the AIU after the heart-wrenching turmoil of World War II. "It was necessary to draw up an accounting of the damage caused by the war, to bring the Alliance out of the shadows of wartime fear and poverty, and to breathe new life into and to turn to the problems of the postwar world."[33] It was to this end that Levinas was appointed director of the ENIO, but Levinas was not only looking south to the AIU schools in North Africa and the Middle East for whom the instruction of teachers and administrators would be his charge. Levinas was also looking east at the destruction of the Jewish population in Eastern Europe

question remains. Is there nothing besides the lofty lessons of Hellenistic humanism in which is called—improperly perhaps—the message of monotheism?" (OW 78, VM 167). To answer this question, Levinas tells us, we need to look deeper.

At first glance, the answer to Levinas's question appears to be "no." "The Sanhedrin believes itself to be the navel of the world, but every nation believes it is at the center of the world! The very idea of nation arises each time that a human group thinks it dwells at the navel of the world. It is precisely because of this that it wants sovereignty and claims every responsibility" (OW 78, VM 167). The very idea that one resides at the center of the universe is the source of egoism. A selfishness that when extended manifests itself as nationalism. Our homogenous group resides at the center of the universe. As such, this belief would be a and the traditions of Jewish education that were destroyed along with them. It is in this context that one should view Levinas's reflection on the ways that taking the directorship was his calling after Auschwitz.

Cassin chose Levinas to be director and was a strong supporter of his educational work. It was Cassin who wrote in support of Levinas's nomination for Légion d'honneur and who spoke at the ceremony where he bestowed the insignes de Chevalier de la Legion d'honneur on Levinas.[34] Nevertheless, there was some tension between the educational goals of the assimilated Cassin, whose "Jewishness was defined less by the injunctions of the Torah than by the emancipatory messages of the French Revolution, of Abbe Gregoire and the Universal Declaration of Human Rights of 1789 and 1793" and the Lithuania-born Levinas now profoundly under the influence of the Talmudic master Shushani.[35] At a meeting in 1952, Cassin stated that the ENIO "did not maintain the level of instruction it should attain," and that "the students felt isolated," entreating Levinas to rectify the situation.[36]

The job itself was also something of a culture clash for the Ashkenazi Levinas who was charged with the formation of students who were Sephardim. To be sure, Levinas had worked with Jews from Morocco when he began his post with the AIU in the years prior to the war, but he found the postwar students to be decidedly different from the prewar ones. To begin with, there was now a fervor for Jewish practices, the students problem and not any sort of solution. "But in returning to our text, and in examining it a little more carefully—and with a bit less mistrust—we may perhaps have occasion to discover in the Sanhedrin an aspect slightly different from the one which emerges when one reflects upon the other navels of the world" (OW 78, VM 167). Again, Levinas asks us to suspend our mistrust of this text and in so doing to put aside the biases of our modern understanding and methods as the most advanced and informed ones. This is to ask the reader to accept that the modern lens is no more privileged, and no less strange, than those that came before it.

What does the text say?

> "Your navel," that is the Sanhedrin. Then, "a goblet." The Hebrew word used for goblet by the Song of Songs is *aggan*. The Talmudist will read into [*va solliciter*]

who came in knew the Psalms by heart and were highly skilled at reading the *sefer torah* (a copy of the Pentateuch handwritten on parchment scrolls) with proper vowels and cantillation.[37] There is a confluence between the postwar students' fervor and Levinas's own restored confidence in the books of Judaism as well as his renewed sense of the importance of Jewish teaching, but the practices of the students were different from his, be it the prolonging of the songs and prayers or emphasis on the letter of the text rather than the interpretative possibilities that the text opened. Emile Amzalag, who attended the ENIO from 1946 to 1948, recalled that his image of Levinas during the daily prayers was "of him with a Bible or Talmud in hand. While we were busy with our ritual recitations, he was immersed in study. One might wonder whether the love of learning was not more urgent for him than religious practice."[38] The diagnosis is apt because for Levinas, Jewish learning *was* indeed more urgent and important than religious practice. In several essays from the early 1950s written for the AIU, he made this clear.

In "Reflections on Jewish Education," written for the *Cahiers de l'Alliance Israélite Universelle* in 1951, Levinas argues that Jewish education is essential if the Jewish people are to continue to exist. He is clear that by Jewish education he does not mean "religious instruction," which is, "in the sense understood by Catholics and Protestants, insufficient as a formula for Jewish education."[39] To Levinas's mind, this is precisely what has happened in Western

this word. They will read *meggin* in *aggan*. *Meggin* means "protects." . . . The role of Judaism, of which the Sanhedrin is the center, is a universal role, a deaconry in the service of the totality of being. (OW 78, VM 167–68)

The interpretation is willful and violent, like rubbing one's foot until it spurts blood. It leads us to a different possible understanding of the Sanhedrin as unfettered from any particular time or place. It is not the property of any one people but instead a universal deaconry in "the service of the totality of being," in the service of all being. Levinas admits that "one can certainly legitimately doubt—according to Western principles of exegesis—that the analogy between the body of the beloved and the Sanhedrin is perfect or convincing" (OW 79, VM 169). As we have seen, he also cautions us against such a dismissal. Instead, he extols us to look

Europe where "the notions that a Jewish child picks up on Sundays and Thursdays are limited—without Hebrew—to schemes whose meaning is watered down or dispersed in the face of these Christian forms of Europe to which Western humanism itself for so long has been linked."[40] Instead, Levinas advocated for the study of Hebrew as the cornerstone of Jewish education, contending that "if we detach [Jews] from the deep and real life that animates these square letters [Hebrew] with its precise rhythms, we reduce them to the poverty of a theoretical catechism."[41] Here again, we must be careful not to presume that Levinas is advocating for a turn to a more strict or orthodox form of religion and Judaism. In "Education and Prayer," Levinas writes that:

> The old fashioned Judaism is dying off, or is already dead. This is why we must return to Jewish wisdom; this is why in our recitation of this wisdom we must reawaken the reason that has gone to sleep; *this is why the Judaism of reason must take place over the Judaism of prayer: the Jew of the Talmud must take precedence over the Jew of the Psalms.*[42]

On the one hand, Levinas points to the poverty of Jewish religious instruction in Western Europe because of the ways it mimics its Christian counterparts but, on the other hand, Levinas rejects a Judaism that "imposes itself in the name of piety, which is not a reason. Traditionalism or pietism are orthodoxies, not doctrines."[43] Levinas found each of these intellectually lazy and deeper still to further explore the possibilities offered by an understanding of the Sanhedrin, which does not see it as exemplifying any particular nation or the decree of any particular god. It is the instantiation of the ethical responsibility of individual humans who have been given divine guidance but who, as humans, are prone to weakness, temptation, and failure.

This leads us back to the *Song of Songs* and the navel or belly hedged with roses. Levinas tells us that there is very little that separates humans from temptation and transgression: it is a hedge of roses. Indeed, as such, the barrier itself poses temptation. And yet, "even if the separation is only a hedge of roses, they will make no breach in it." This is because "to be a judge in Israel, one must be an exceptional man: even if only a hedge of roses separates judges from sin, they will make no breach in it" OW 79, ultimately unfulfilling. One because it follows the template of Western European religious instruction. The other because it relies entirely on what has come before with no reflection on what should be done now.

Instead, Levinas believed that "in order for the permanent values of Judaism, contained in the great texts of the Bible, the Talmud and their commentators, to be able to nurture our souls, they must once again be able to nurture our brains."⁴⁴ Here, we see the ways that the different strands of our braid come together in the service of Levinas's intellectual Jewish educational program, which privileges the Judaism of reason over the Judaism of prayer but does not succumb to the temptations of secularism or assimilation despite its commitment to rationalism and humanism. To this end, Levinas tells us "we must enlarge the science of Judaism and, fundamentally, raise it only to the level of a science" but cautions that "to raise Judaism to the level of a science does not involve submitting its sources to philology. For 150 years we have done nothing else."⁴⁵ Jewish education must be serious, rigorous, and led by reason, but it cannot subordinate itself to secular thought. This is what Levinas believed to be the case in the Haskalah when "the nineteenth century wore itself out with the philology of Judaism. Fifty centuries were catalogued—an immense Jewish epigraphy, a collusion of epigraphs—for which historical accounts were important and which had to be placed at the crossroads of different influences. What a graveyard!"⁴⁶

VM 170). Here again, one might take Levinas to be advocating an exclusionary elitism that is the sole property of the judges of Israel. Instead Levinas continues citing Rav Kahana:

> The Torah has testified for us through a hedge of roses; for even if the separation is only a hedge of roses, they will make no breach in it. (OW 81, VM 173)

Here, something new is added: "What was said before of the judge is now said of the entire Jewish people" (OW 81, VM 173). This shift in register is the key to Levinas's understanding of the Sanhedrin because the call to responsibility is now extended beyond the select members of the court. Indeed, Rav Kahana is "no longer speaking of the court. He is speaking of the Jewish people: the excellence demanded of the members of the Sanhedrin is extended to the Jewish people in its entirety. . . . All belong—or

The problem with such an approach was not the scientific rigor with which the scholars approached their object of study but the ways that the scholar took him or herself to be "more intelligent than their object" of study, the great texts of the Bible, the Talmud and their commentators. In "The State of Israel and the Religion of Israel," also published in 1951, Levinas writes that "henceforth we must return to what was strongest in rabbinical exegesis. This exegesis made the text speak while critical philology speaks of the text."[47] Levinas concludes "Reflections on Jewish Education" asserting "pure philology, which is not enough for the understanding of Goethe, is not enough for the intellection of Rabbi Akkiba or Rabbi Tarphon" but also that "pure piety is no longer enough" because "pure feelings which pass for ideas have no future." For Levinas, to turn Judaism into a science is instead to "turn these texts back into teaching texts," to return to the rigorous study of Talmud in order to see the "unfinished dialogue they open up with a world that has once more been put into question."[48]

Levinas's work with Shushani led him to the conclusion that the rigorous study of Talmud in the Lithuanian tradition was the key to Jewish survival and the survival of Judaism in the post-Holocaust world. But as we have seen, Levinas's understanding of Judaism remained fundamentally compatible with those values of humanism, reason, and philosophy that he held dear and that he longed to conserve. Thus must belong—to the elite. . . . But Judaism does not affirm any national or racial pride by this: it teaches what, in its opinion, *is possible for humanity*. And, it is through this teaching, perhaps, that the world needs Judaism" (OW 81, VM 174, my emphasis). Here we see the move from the responsibility commanded of a select few to the responsibility of and for all. In this way, Judaism is a humanism intended for all and founded on what is possible for humanity, to raise oneself up so that all belong to the elite. The elitism is a call to each and every one of us to learn and perform *mitzvot*. As such, it requires institutions of learning such as the school created by Levinas at the ENIO or the Talmudic lectures presented at the Colloque. In each case, it is not the institutions that create or actualize morality and responsibility any more than nations do so. As seen in the discussion of the Hellenistic origins of

Levinas's Talmudic lectures and his educational agenda required him to assert this compatibility without subordinating the primacy or authority of the sacred Jewish texts to the critical scholarly skills he believed necessary to interpret them. In "For a Jewish Humanism," published in the *Cahiers de l'Alliance Israélite Universelle* in 1956, Levinas writes:

> We should like to show that, without prejudicing the religious orders, the teaching of Hebrew and the Jewish school that ought to see such teaching as its principal vocation in no way betray the ideals of the secular school, and the study of Hebrew itself lends support to what today can give meaning to Judaism. It lends support to the Jewish humanism which cannot remain indifferent to the modern world in which it seeks a whole humanity.[49]

Here, on Levinas's reading, Jewish education and the teaching of Hebrew should not be the property of religious orders but in line with the ideals of secular schools. What's more, such an education, which "today can give meaning to Judaism," is one aligned with humanism but, in some way, predates humanism itself. For Levinas, "the Bible clarified and accentuated by the commentaries from the great age that precedes and follows the destruction of the Second Temple, when an ancient and uninterrupted tradition finally blossoms, is a book that leads us *not* towards the mystery of God, but towards the human tasks of man." Thus "monotheism is a humanism. Only simpletons made it into a the Sanhedrin, the institutions, while important and in some cases essential, are not the source of the ideal to be enacted, and this message extends to individuals as well. "What matters for the human being is to realize, not to invent, the ideal" (OW 82, VM 175). This is to say, the ideal need not be new. Humanism need not be a Jewish invention but, nevertheless, the tradition borrowed can be infused with the ethical ideal of Judaism and realized as such beyond the confines of the Sanhedrin and even beyond the Jewish people. The elitism is not exclusionary.

Resh Lakish said, "It can be answered on the basis of the following text (*Song of Songs* 4:3), 'Your brow (*rakkathek*) is like a pomegranate.' Even those established as good for nothings among you are full of mitzvot (of fulfilled commandments) as a pomegranate is full of seeds" (OW 83, VM 177). Resh Lakish provides an theological arithmetic. The books in which this humanism is inscribed await their humanists."⁵⁰ This statement deserves attention as it serves a number of purposes. First, Levinas asserts a continuous chain of tradition that is both ancient and uninterrupted, one presumes, to the present day. Second, and crucially, Levinas reveals that this ancient tradition is the origin of what later takes on the name "humanism," and it is only the reading of simpletons that took this humanism for a "theological arithmetic." Finally, Levinas makes the claim that even though monotheism has always been a humanism and the Bible has always led toward the human tasks of man, the books in which this humanism was inscribed still await their humanists. The task of unlocking the true message of the Bible is one that still needs to be undertaken and must not be done under the aegis of religious orders but under that of a Jewish education that in no way betrays the ideals of the secular school.

Levinas's narrative runs counter to conventional historical accounts of the origins of humanism, and it is not difficult to accuse Levinas of retrofitting a later phenomenon, humanism in its twentieth-century variation, to justify his interpretation of the biblical mandate. Levinas's account, however, is essential to his construction of a Jewish humanism that is not derivative or dependent on the more familiar Western European variant of the term. This allows Levinas to conserve aspects of the larger humanist tradition as essentially Jewish, having been derived from Jewish sources instead. The origin answer to the question Levinas posed earlier: "How do such men become reality?" They do so by means of mitzvot, by acting morally and ethically. "For there to be justice, there must be judges resisting temptation. There must be a community which carries out the mitzvot right here and right now. The delayed effect of mitzvot carried out in the past cannot last forever" (OW 83, VM 177–78). This is to say, it is not enough to read about ethical action and responsibility or even to write about them. It is certainly not enough to claim affiliation with the people and texts Levinas sees as the model for such action. "That the mere fact of race is not a guarantee against evil, the Talmud saw and said better than anyone and with nearly unbearable force: the Jew without mitzvot is a threat to the world" (OW 83, VM 178). We are all commanded to act because without mitzvot, "being Jewish" devolves of humanism, to Levinas's mind, lies in the Bible and its commentaries and as such is fundamentally Jewish. But by "taking refuge in our old folios, the truths of Jewish humanism became the thought of an isolated people. The passion for justice that aroused the West after the Renaissance broke this isolation but made Jews lose the secret of their science, which they did not suspect beyond a few memories taken from translated writings. . . . Laid down in the Hebrew Bible, the Mishnah, and the Gemara, this civilization built on Justice unfolds in a science."[51] For Levinas, the task of Judaism and Jewish education is the restoration, though one might also say construction, of a Talmudic science which leads human actors not to the mysteries of God but "towards the human tasks of man."

In 1956 Levinas presented a lecture to the assemblée genérale of Le Fond Social Juif Unifié, an organization dedicated to the reconstruction and rejuvenation of the French Jewish community after the Holocaust. In this lecture, titled "How Is Judaism Possible?," Levinas reveals two other aspects of his educational program based on Jewish humanism that loom large in his Talmudic lectures. The first is his presentation of Judaism as a "spirituality that is foreign to the received category of religion" such that "the classical schema of an all powerful God helping or crushing men who place their confidence in Him or quake before Him does not express the essence of the phenomenon of Judaism."[52] The first part of the formulation is familiar, but the second into racialism or nationalism no different or less problematic than its most virulent strains. Hear this Israel: "Morality begins in us and not in institutions which are not always able to protect it. It demands that human honor knows how to exist without a flag (sans Drapeau)" (OW 81, VM 174). Each one of us must actively be doing good or else we are protecting the navel of nationalism or racism. "The privilege of Israel resides not in its race but in the mitzvot which educate it. The effect of mitzvot lasts beyond the practice, that is true. But as I have already said, not indefinitely" (OW 84, VM 179–80). It is not enough to be Jewish by birth, or because one attends synagogue, or keeps the ritual practices. Nor is it enough to *have done* the right thing, though the effect of such acts may last beyond the practice. Instead, it is by continuously *doing good*, as impossible as it may seem, that we come to what Levinas sees as part provides the template for a theology compatible with Levinas's post-Holocaust reality. A reality in which God does not, or at least did not, intervene in the everyday affairs of humans. For Levinas, the absence of intervention should not be equated with the absence of God who directs our action through the instruction of Torah and Talmud. On this reading, "moral purity" and "moral dignity are no longer played out in a tête-à-tête with God, but are sorted out between men." What's more, Levinas goes so far as to say that "the Jewish God *has never* tolerated theses tête-à-têtes. He was always the God of the multitudes. The Judaism in us should not be aroused on Yom Kippur, at the hour of prayer for the dead, but every day and for the living."[53] Levinas presents a shift in register where the relation between the individual and God is not best expressed through private acts of atonement but via the everyday relations between living human beings in the present. We will explore this further in the following chapter.

The second, and crucial, aspect revealed in the lecture is Levinas's invention of a postrabbinic chain of transmission. Levinas advocates for the creation of a "new type of Jewish school—a school that does not prepare you for any ecclesiastical role—" which would "assume a place at the forefront of the community." This was to be a . . .

> . . . full time school in which the teaching of the Hebrew language and the basic texts

new and different in his understanding of Jewish justice. "What Judaism brings to the world, therefore, is not the easy generosity of the heart, or new and metaphysical visions, *but a mode of existence guided by the practice of mitzvot*" (OW 84, VM 180, my emphasis).

Levinas turns to the story of Jacob and in this way returns to "even the good for nothings" who are nevertheless filled with mitzvot. "Jacob bore within himself all those who, in future generations, would rebel against the Law. . . . The scent of Paradise is Jacob bearing the weight of all that he will not do and that others will do" (OW 85, VM 181–82). Once again, Levinas points to the possibility and inevitability of moral failure that nevertheless does not short-circuit the need to act responsibly every day. This is a righteousness based on humility and realistic expectations rather than utopian ideals would be conducted by highly qualified teachers; in which the Jewish humanities would not be taught with a view to promoting historical criticism or cheap piety but for their intrinsic truth, whatever the path of their marvelous confluence. Teaching texts, not relics or alluvial deposits from the past.⁵⁴

Here again, much is familiar as Levinas seeks to chart a path between religious education founded on piety and the understanding of religion based on historical criticism. While the former results in the misguided tête-à-tête with God, the latter views Judaism as an ossified relic "that no more invites us to use these ancient texts than it asks us to cut wood with a stone age axe."⁵⁵ In contrast, the path between these two understanding leads to Levinas's understanding of Talmudic study in the Lithuanian tradition. What is novel here is Levinas's assertion that this "Jewish school, in which professional teaching staff can also be trained, must on the one hand rely on superior Jewish education, both traditional and modern, on research and scientific publications; and on the other on a Jewish intelligentsia, in possession of Jewish knowledge and nurturing that knowledge, whose pupils on leaving the school would expand such knowledge."⁵⁶ In effect, Levinas is calling for the creation of a modern Talmudic academy where the science of Talmud is taught in a modern way and disseminated by "Jewish intellectuals who know Hebrew and the basic Jewish texts; and attach vital importance to these texts."⁵⁷ The prototype for this endeavor

that inevitably cannot be upheld and in turn lead to cynicism and nihilism. Instead, "for the human world to be possible—justice, the Sanhedrin—at each moment there must be someone who can be responsible for the others. Responsible! The famous finite liberty of the philosophers is responsibility for that which I have not done" (OW 85, VM 182). Our freedom is not the freedom to do anything as we please, as if we existed in the center of the universe, it is the freedom to act responsibly in relation to others. "Even if you are free you are not the absolute beginning. You come after many things and many people. You are not just free; you are also bound to others beyond your freedom. You are responsible for all. Your liberty is also fraternity" (OW 85, VM 182).

Jewish education, on Levinas's reading, is what makes one a responsible being. It is the means by which we come to took the form of Levinas's Rashi course and his shorter-lived Talmud course, both held at the ENIO.

Soon after taking over the directorship of ENIO and commencing his studies with Shushani, Levinas began offering a course on Rashi held each Saturday at 11:00 a.m. in the oratory of the ENIO. Rashi (1040–1105), Rabbi Shlomo Itzhaki, also known as Salomon de Troyes, was a French rabbi who was the author of a comprehensive commentary on the Talmud and Tanakh. There is much one could say about Levinas's investment in the work and figure of Rashi, whose commentaries are essential reading for any study of Talmud. For our purposes, and while not making too much out of it, I think it worth noting Levinas's identification with the brilliant French Jewish commentator as well as the precedent set by Rashi in translating difficult Hebrew or Aramaic terms into the French language of his day. In the earliest days, Levinas offered two courses on Saturday: the morning course on Rashi's Talmudic commentaries and an afternoon course focused on works of literature such as Proust, Tolstoy, and Dostoyevsky. The afternoon course served as an attempt to foster an appreciation in his students of those works of literature he considered to be truly great, but over time it was the Rashi course that would endure.

The structure of the course was simple. On Friday, Levinas would designate a student to translate a chosen text from Hebrew or Aramaic into French and to understand the commandments we must follow and, crucially, the mitzvot we must all do. Not handing over the blame but accepting responsibility to do more . . . for the sins I did not commit . . . responsibility for the other. It is to act as if justice were at the center of the universe and in acting so, making it so.

"When someone from the first row of students goes up to take his place among the judges, the first place in the row is now empty and everyone moves up one place" (OW 87, VM 186). We are each eligible and responsible, even the good for nothings, but we do not acquire this elite privilege by birth or by proxy. We each move up one place as we learn and because we each move up, this ethical election is a "classification in which no one has a real place" (OW 87, VM 187). No one owns their place or can stake a claim to it. We each come after many provide a commentary on that text. On Saturday, the students and others would assemble at 11:00 a.m. From its inception the Rashi course was open to the public even if the target audience was students of the ENIO. The designated student would read the assigned passage in its original language before offering comment.[58] Catherine Chalier recalled that during her time in the course, the initial presentation would be followed by a second student who read Rashi's commentary; that second student would translate it and then provide their own interpretation. Levinas would sit at the head of a table and the interpreter would sit facing him at the other end. The participants would sit around the table while behind Levinas sat four or five elderly men who, according to Chalier, seemed to know Torah and Talmud by heart. On occasion, Levinas would ask them a question seeking clarification about a passage or translation, and one of the men would always have an answer.[59] Levinas directed the conversation, offering interjections, corrections, and his own thoughts on the passage, often citing Shushani or making a philosophical reference. Toward the end of the session, Levinas would close with a Talmudic apologue selected in relation to the theme of the text under discussion or the weekly Torah reading.[60]

Levinas described his weekly course like this: "In the sequence of each week, I choose some verses which I comment on in front of the students of the school and also

things and many people but neither is the order random or relative. It is an elitism open to all as a call to justice.

in front of a group of all kinds of people who come to listen, to prolong the spirit of Shushani."[61] The spirit of Shushani was pervasive throughout the course, and Levinas's tutelage under his Talmudic master was empowering.

> The capacity that M. Shushani had for amplifying or interpreting these passages [from *haggadah*] was very impressive. I don't know if I learned much from him about the manner in which purely juridical texts must be interpreted, but something remained, not the contents but the manner in which these haggadic stories must be approached. I worked on this a lot, first by returning to the Talmudic text and trying to understand it. I never expected to write a book about it, but I would know how to teach it.[62]

Shushani's interpretative method provided Levinas with carte blanche to bring his extra-Talmudic methods and skills to bear on sacred texts, and Levinas's study under a bona fide Talmudic master gave him the credibility and authority to do so.

> In all modesty really, because oneself isn't much, but next to [Shushani] one is nothing. I am extremely grateful for what I learned from him. In a hagaddic text from the *Pirke Avoth*, there is this phrase: "The words of the sages are like glowing embers." One can ask, why embers, why not flames? Because it only becomes a flame when one knows how to blow on it! I have hardly learned to blow. There are always

great minds who contest this manner of blowing. They say, "You see, he draws out of the text what is not in the text. He forces a meaning into it." But if one does it with Goethe, with Valéry, with Corneille, the critics accept it. It appears more scandalous to them when one does it with regard to Scripture. And one has to have met Shushani in order not to be convinced by these critical minds. Shushani taught me: what is essential is that the meaning that is found merits, by its wisdom, the research that reveals it. That the text had suggested it to you.[63]

The Rashi course provided the venue for Levinas to develop his own mode of interpreting and teaching sacred Jewish texts, to learn how to blow on the embers and rekindle the flames. The combination of interpretative audacity and filial devotion allowed Levinas the freedom to engage with Torah and Talmud in creative and even subversive ways but always under the cover of the master who taught him the proper means to do so. As Chalier put it in a talk at the ENIO in 1996, "In these Shabbat lessons, for Emmanuel Levinas, it was not a matter of 'taking' the floor in a magisterial fashion, but rather, as he liked to put it by citing his master Shushani, a matter of remaining faithful to one of the significations of the famous *lemor* which, in the Torah, so often concludes the divine address to Moses. He wondered: What does *lemor* mean? It must be understood as a call to transmit what is heard, because an utterance does not lose its infinite richness when it is transmitted."[64] Prosper Elkouby, who was a member of the first ENIO class, recalls the transmission in a different way. "You had the sensation of a discourse being constructed before your eyes. His thought would visibly grow with each sentence he spoke.... We were stuck on the letter of the text, we didn't go beyond it. And there, suddenly this knowledge that I thought belonged to another era found itself validated, actualized."[65] The weekly discussion of Talmud in the Rashi course, this constructed discourse actualizing a knowledge from a different era, this call to transmit what is heard, provided the early template for what would become his Talmudic lectures at the Colloque des intellectuels juifs de langue française.

In the early 1960s, at about the same time Levinas began giving his regular Talmudic lecture at the Colloque des intellectuels juifs de langue française, Levinas started teaching a Talmud course on Tuesday nights at the ENIO. The AIU schools in Morocco were in need of Jewish studies teachers with expertise in the study of Talmud to instruct students in the final year of high school, so the decision was made to select and train a small cadre of teachers: the "Talmud group." The sanctioned course at the ENIO was not taught by Levinas but by Rabbi Epstein outside of Paris in Livry-Gargan. In response, Levinas started his own Talmud course. Gabriel Cohen, who was a member of the group, recollects how

Levinas established a Talmud course on

Tuesday nights with Dr. Nerson, in addition to the Saturday lesson on Rashi. It was attended by auditors, some religious people, and the students of the Talmud group. I had the impression, moreover, that this Tuesday night course was partly born because of us. When [Levinas] saw that we went to Rabbi Epstein, he wanted us to be bound to him instead. What we got, of course, was a completely different view of the Talmud. What is expressed, what is explained, was a different world. I remember thinking that no one could argue with him, that he was a master without peers.[66]

Cohen's description of Levinas sounds strikingly similar to Levinas's description of Shushani: a master without peers next to whom one is nothing. The stakes were high for Levinas because, in his view, this completely different view of the Talmud was the only means by which to restore and retain the permanent values of Judaism, nurturing brains in order to nurture our souls.

Levinas could not leave the instruction of Talmud in the hands of the pious. He wanted to take control of the chain of transmission, to prolong the spirit of Shushani, and thus to fulfil the call to transmit what has been heard. In essence, Levinas sought to start a new tradition, a new chain of transmission, in keeping with his goals for Jewish education, his reformulation of Judaism as a humanism, and his post-Holocaust theology. As we have seen, such an approach opened Levinas up to the criticism that he was drawing from the text what was not there or imparting meaning anachronistically. Thus Levinas sought to find a way to sanction his interpretative freedom without also opening the door to pure perspectivalism or subjective musing. Levinas understood that his emphasis on the "amplification" of interpretation is always in danger of allowing everyone equal authority over the texts, and he combats it with comments that infer an appropriate or authentic course of training:

> The great books of Judaism do not in fact express themselves as parables that are open to the whims of poetic imagination or as concepts that are always schematic, but as examples that betray nothing of the infinite relations that make up the fabric of the social being. They offer themselves up as an interpretation that is as rigorous as parables are vague and as rich as concepts are poor. Whosoever has encountered the Talmud, especially if the encounter is with a real master, notices this immediately.[67]

The great books of Judaism cannot be made to say just anything, and the ability to find the meaning hidden in the text requires appropriate training. Levinas's model of Jewish education was designed to provide this training. While for Levinas "there was no such a thing as an expert in spirituality," he did believe that after the Holocaust each Jew needed to get back in touch with his or her inner life. To do so requires reading the great books of Judaism and to read, "a master is needed who guides the attention, who makes the letter a teaching experience, and who, in the image of Aaron's rod which began to bloom (Numbers 17, 23), enables words too long believed dead to begin living again."[68]

Despite his modesty and self-effacement, Levinas was fashioning himself as a master of Talmud replete with disciples. Ami Bouganmin, who studied with Levinas at ENIO, explains how:

> With the passing years, an entourage had gathered around this great Lithuanian, a court of faithful [followers] who respected and admired him . . . Come Shabbat, they all waited for the synagogue to open for study to take their seats around Levinas who, the Bible on his lap and his commentary books at hand, was setting out to share with his audience the Sabbatical delights which he managed to wrench from Rashi, in the best of the Pharisaic traditions, his commentary on the sidra (weekly section of the Torah) and, as if in passing, on the small domestic incidents of Israel and the major events of the world. [Homage and gratitude are rendered] to the Okar Harim Levinas was as a philosopher, a Talmudist, a pedagogue, and a master for his extreme intellectual richness"[69]

It is worth noting that Bouganim describes Levinas as an *Okar Harim*, the sage with a fiery mind who can uproot mountains, and not as a Sinai, the scholar with an encyclopedic mind.

In the end, Levinas's dream of establishing the ENIO as a center for Jewish learning based on his educational program did not come true. The reasons for the failure are varied but are, for the most part, the result of geopolitical changes after the war. To be sure, given the extant tensions between Cassin's commitment to the original goals and values of the AIU, Levinas's fixation on rejuvenating Jewish education based on his fashioning of the Lithuanian Talmudic academies, and the more traditional religious background of the ENIO students coming from North Africa, it is not evident that Levinas's plan ever could succeed. The two events that fundamentally altered the mission and profile of both the AIU and ENIO were the creation of the State of Israel and French decolonization. After the Arab-Israel War in 1947–48 and the establishment of the State of Israel the demographics of the Middle East changed dramatically. The war's outcome exacerbated Arab hostility toward Jewish communities living within their borders, and in response many of these Jews immigrated to Israel. After the departure of thousands of Jews from Iraq, the schools of the AIU closed. Soon after, the schools closed in Syria and Egypt. In Israel itself, the creation of the state and establishment of Hebrew as the national language made the need for education in French language and culture obsolete in a country that needed to teach Hebrew, Arabic, and increasingly English. Over time the AIU schools either merged with the Israeli school system or simply closed.

The rise of nationalism in Morocco and Tunisia ultimately led to independence from France, and this also led to a mass departure of Jews who relocated to France or Israel. The case of Morocco is striking because it had the greatest number of schools and students. Whereas in 1952 the schools of the AIU in Morocco had 24,788 students, by 1971 that number was 7,652. One can see similar declines across most of the schools.

These demographic shifts drastically reduced the demand for teachers and administrators trained by the ENIO to implement the Francophone curriculum mandated by the AIU. As a result, the ENIO never became the epicenter of Jewish education where future teachers of the schools of the alliance would be formed by and, presumably, disseminate the ideal of Jewish learning fashioned by Levinas. Over time, the ENIO increasingly took on the character of a Jewish private school,

TABLE Students enrolled in the schools of AIU from 1952 to 1971.

	1952–53	1963–64	1968	1971
Egypt	427			
Israel	3,997	5,253	4,828	5,044
Iran		5,933	5,158	4,034
Lebanon	1,260	1,301	1,109	
Libya	100			
Morocco	24,788	13,525	8,054	7,652
Syria	386	447	431	480
Tunisia	3,355	3,797	1,366	147

and it became clear that this was not the site where the call to "transmit what was heard" could be fulfilled. Instead, Levinas looked to transmit the call at the Colloque des intellectuels juifs de langue française where it would be heard not by the young students enrolled at the ENIO, but by the Jewish intellectuals of France and beyond.

CHAPTER 3

OUR SIDE

The Talmudic Lectures at the Colloque des intellectuels juifs de langue française

THE OTHER SIDE

Beyond Memory

The Colloque des intellectuels juifs de langue française was the brainchild of Edmond Fleg, Léon Algazi, André Neher, and Aron Steinberg, and the first conference was held in 1957 under the aegis of the World Jewish Congress.[1] Levinas was not among the initiators of the Colloque, but he was involved with the planning and organizing from the start. The impetus for the Colloque was to take up the question of Jewish existence after the Holocaust and in response to a French Jewish population that had changed dramatically since the war. This was an increasingly diverse Jewish population made up of refugee German and Eastern European Jews, Jews from Iraq, Syria, and Egypt who came to France after the Arab-Israel War in 1947–48, Magrebian Jews moving or returning to the metropole after the independence of Tunisia and Morocco in 1956 (and later from Algeria after 1962), and French Jews for whom per-

From the tractate *Berakhot*, 12b–13a:

> A man was going along and came upon a wolf—and got away. After that, he told nothing but wolf stories. He came upon a lion, and escaped: then he told the story of the lion. He encountered a snake—and got away. There he is, having forgotten both of them [the wolf and the lion] and telling nothing but the story of the snake. So with Israel: the most recent hardships eclipse the earlier ones.[1] (65) Gemara from Berakhot

89

secution under the Nazi and Vichy regimes was the occasion on which they discovered or came to acknowledge their Judaism.² The movement of Jews from Germany, Eastern Europe, North Africa, and the Middle East made France the largest and most vibrant Jewish community in Western Europe, and this created an intellectual environment that energized thinkers like Levinas who sought to mobilize this energy in the service of a modern renewal of traditional Jewish thought.

Equally important to the founders of the Colloque were French individuals who came to Judaism or Jewish identity as the result of persecution under Vichy or Nazi rule. Léon Algazi in particular had met many French Jews who came to him after the war searching for answers about Jewish identity, tradition, and learning. Some of these were people who knew their families to be Jewish but had fully assimilated or converted to Christianity. Others had lost track of their Jewish ancestry only to be confronted with it under racial law. Jean Wahl came to know he was Jewish when he was removed from his post at the Sorbonne and sent to the internment camp at Drancy.³ Levinas described what he saw as the futility of such assimilation in an essay for *Information Juive* from 1954:

> Assimilation failed because it did not placate the non-Jews, or put an end to anti-Semitism; on certain points, it stirred up heated reactions and arguments once more. Anguish and anxiety still surreptitiously alter apparently free behavior and every Jew

The conclusion to Levinas's commentary on *Berakhot*, 12b–13a, does not end with a discussion of traditional Jewish texts. Instead, he provides a sustained meditation on a text by Vasily Grossman titled *Life and Fate*. In this book, "cold and inspired," Grossman recounts "the Stalinian reality, in all its horror, blended with the Hitlerian horror." For Levinas, Grossman's account is indicative of the ways that, at the time, "the long-standing Western confidence in rational practices being generated from political and religious institutions and meant to foster man's being a neighbor to the other—belief in human institutions through which the *good* would succeed in *being*—is shaken. There is, in this book, a constant pessimism with respect to the possibility of saving humankind in this manner" (BM 77, AS 103). To confront the possibility of salvation after Stalin and Hitler, Levinas does not turn to the rational remains, in the largest sense of the word, a Marrano.[4]

The Colloquium in general, and Levinas in particular, sought to construct a positive understanding of Jewish identity to combat the more Sartrean variant in which one's identity as Jew is ascribed by the anti-Semite. This construction was complicated by the diverse understanding of Judaism and identity in a French Jewish community now numbering over 600,000. Levinas's Talmudic lectures at the Colloque sought to tap into that energy and serve to construct a positive understanding of Jewish existence and learning based on the educational ideals he had hoped to implement at the ENIO.

Levinas was not the only Jewish intellectual who sought to reenergize Jewish thought after the war, nor were the AIU or Colloque des intellectuels juifs de langue française the only organizations or events that sought to tap into the intellectual energy of the growing Jewish community in France. L'École d'Orsay, as it came to be called, was another such group initially formed during the occupation to produce a new "school of prophets" and to preserve Jewish learning and values in the face of persecution and threats of extermination. This resistance via learning led to the establishment of the École Gilbert-Bloch d'Orsay in 1946, which remained open until 1965. Founded by Robert Gamzun and Jacob Gordin, the École d'Orsay sought to formalize the clandestine educational format used during the occupation. As practices of the West but instead to the commandment to remember: Zakhor. "The proximity of God is experienced in Judaism through memory, and consequently in the prevalence of the past and of the events and imperatives foundational to Holy History, which is usually understood as elapsed time" (BM 65, AS 91). It is not any memory to which the Mishnah here refers but specifically to the "going forth from Egypt—the Exodus— and the evocation of that exodus in which freedom was given to a people, the coming to the foot of Mount Sinai where that freedom culminated in Law, constituted a privileged past, the very form of the past, as it were" (BM 66, AS 91). Specifically, it is the memory of enfranchisement and the granting of a freedom that is conditioned on acceptance of the Law creating a strange twinning of freedom and restriction, a freedom conditioned by restriction. It is "an such, the school maintained its ties to the Jewish Scouts, which were founded by Gamzun (also known as Castor) in 1923, as well as the related commitment to Zionism. The intellectual direction of the school was dictated by Jacob Gordin and Léon Askénazi. Jacob Gordin was born in Russia but moved to Berlin where he studied at the Akademie für die Wissenschaft des Judentums in 1924. Gordin was heavily influenced by Hermann Cohen and the neo-Kantian Marburg school but was equally committed to Midrash and Kabbalah.[5] After the death of Gordin in 1947, Askénazi (also known as Manitou) took over the school. Ashkénazi was the son of the Rabbi of Oran who, while in Algeria, had studied simultaneously in Yeshiva and French secular school and then went on to the University of Algeria before studying at the Sorbonne. Speaking of the two, Levinas described Gordin's influence as "drawing on the riches of the Midrash and Jewish mysticism, but sustained by a remarkable philosophical culture, his classes founded a tradition in the school [école d'orsay] that was brilliantly carried on by Leon Askénazi and his disciples, and determined a whole style of Jewish studies—recognized even in Israel, as due to the spiritual contribution of French immigration."[6] Other key members of the school were André Neher, Henri Atlan, and Liliane Atlan.

There are many similarities between Levinas's endeavor at the ENIO and the project of the École d'Orsay, especially insofar as each attempted to restore the vitality

intimacy that means obeying the commandments and serving God—but that remains freedom, or ensures freedom, by surmounting the very dependence that, formally, such a relation seems to imply" (BM 67, AS 92). Thus the dynamic relation between freedom and obedience must be one that does not tip too far in the direction of either. The memory of the exodus, and the command Zakhor, is essential if we are to comprehend the conditions of such a freedom, but blind adherence to memory is an obstacle as is the idea of total freedom. Contemporary understandings of freedom and memory lead us away from such a comprehension.

It is this combination of freedom and obligation rendered as the past of the Exodus and the Law that, Levinas tells us, forms the heart of Jewish weekday morning prayer, "or, more precisely perhaps, this memory is already prayer, morning of Jewish thought by bringing it into contact with modern ideas and especially into conversation with contemporary philosophy and philosophers. Both projects were keen to establish a link between French culture and their respective understandings of Judaism. But while Levinas was publicly supportive of the Ecole d'Orsay and welcomed its initiative as part of what he named the École de Pensée Juive de Paris, after the renowned Paris school of Jewish painters, there were also fundamental differences. The schools were two and not one. To begin, Levinas was not interested in the project of the Jewish Scouts with their rustic rituals and quasi-militaristic formations. Levinas also distanced himself from the more sentimental or emotional aspects of observance embraced by the École d'Orsay and its students. This included the emphasis on mysticism and Kabbalah. Instead, as we have seen, Levinas sought to promote and promulgate the methods of Shushani in the service of a rational and humanistic Judaism.

The Colloque des intellectuels juifs de langue française brought Levinas into close contact with the leading figures of the École d'Orsay both in the initial planning sessions and at the event of the colloquium itself. Edmund Fleg, like Gamzun, had been a key figure in the Jewish Scouting movement and also maintained a commitment to Jewish mysticism as a key component of modern Jewish education. The first colloquium took place in Versailles on May 24, 1957, and there were about twenty

prayer, prayer of awakening, awakening as prayer" (BM 66, AS 91). And yet, the first proposition of the Mishnah Levinas presents is an innovation that introduces this morning recollection of the Exodus into the evening liturgy:

> The exodus from Egypt is recalled also at night. (BM 66, AS 91)

Levinas asks what is the importance of this innovation, and here we enter into the delicate negotiation between memory and innovation that is also a negotiation between the past and the future. Commitment to the Law cannot arrest innovation in interpretation and practice as that would make the commandments a historical relic frozen in a bygone era and cut off from the issues of our present. At the same time, innovation cannot allow practice to become completely untethered from its source. Innovation is always in tension with the tradition or memory from which it is drawn. To square this people in attendance. Levinas was present at the colloquium but did not speak. The second colloquium was held in Paris on September 22, 1959, and at this event Levinas presented an intellectual biography of Franz Rosenzweig published in the colloquium proceeding as "Between Two Worlds." At the third colloquium held in Paris on September 25, 1960, André Neher presented a "biblical lesson" and Levinas a "Talmudic lesson," establishing a tradition that would define the Colloque des intellectuels juifs de langue française and that Levinas would continue until 1991. We should consider Levinas's Talmudic lectures at the Colloquium in the same light as his Talmud course at the ENIO offered in response to the one given by Rabbi Epstein. As in that case, and at roughly the same time, Levinas sought to take control of the chain of transmission and prolong the spirit of Shushani by offering his interpretation of Talmud to the audience of the Colloquium.[7] In this way, Levinas's lecture can be seen as a counter to the biblical analysis of Neher, or at least in competition with the teachings of the École D'Orsay. Ady Steg, who would serve as president of the Alliance Israélite Universelle from 1985 to 2011, recalled that the

> conferences were a real event because in that distress and despondency that gripped intellectuals immediately after the war, the conference functioned to reinvigorate them. This was a kind of defiance or revenge. And this presentation of Judaism

circle, Levinas turns to an anecdote on page 28a *Berakhot*. It is the story of Rabban Gamliel, head of the rabbinic academy, who was dismissed by force because he was too strict a master. He was replaced by Rabbi Eleazar ben Azariah who possessed wisdom, material independence, and nobility but was only eighteen years old and "without one white hair." "Can one teach without innovating? But can one innovate without reference to a tradition, without remaining the contemporary—real or apparent—of the discourse of the past? A miracle was needed! Eighteen rows of white hair appeared on Eleazar ben Azariah's head—who, at the age of eighteen, henceforth looked seventy, in order that all innovation should derive from earlier forms" (BM 68, AS 93–94). The miracle is the connection, real or apparent, between the innovation and the tradition from which it is drawn. For the past to affect the was altogether new in the sense that the Talmudic lesson was a particular genre.... The biblical lesson of André Neher was more traditional. The Bible was familiar to the intellectual world, to the non-Jewish world as well. But the Talmud was something totally ignored, reserved for those good Jews with long beards from Poland or Morocco. The idea that the Talmud could be studied in French, in public, and in the same manner that it was studied by the Jews from eastern Europe or from Maghreb, was extraordinary.... This was a completely different presentation, by someone who was a philosopher, but who in no way betrayed the teaching of the Talmud as I had known it.[8]

The conferences in Paris took place at the ENIO or at the Rashi Center, but as the event and Levinas became more popular it was moved to a series of Parisian auditoriums or the Sorbonne.

Scholars have often cast the movement Levinas labeled the École de Pensée Juive de Paris as built on the pillars of the École D'Orsay and the Colloque des intellectuels juifs de langue française but given the presence and influence of figures from the École D'Orsay in the organization and event of the Colloquium it strikes me that this division is not quite right. Instead, I would argue that the division is actually between Levinas's Lithuanian rationalist understanding of Judaism and Jewish thought as embodied by Shushani, and the more rustic, emotional, and mystical variant proffered by Neher,

present and have purchase on our future it cannot remain the past.

Interpretative innovations and modifications, such as those enacted by Levinas in the form of his Talmudic lectures at the Colloque des intellectuels juives française, are sanctioned when they tie the past to a greater future. To make this point, Levinas again looks to an innovative teaching of the meaning of the Exodus that liberates the event from its historical moment and context.

> As for our sages, they have taught: "The days of your life" means the entire duration of the world; "all the days of your life" implies the Days of the Messiah. (BM 69, AS 94)

Levinas explains that "the exodus from Egypt—original past—does not remain a memory dominating the time of persons and their finite duration. It punctuates the time of the total history of humanity,

Gordin, Askénazi, and the teachers of the École d'Orsay. The Colloque des intellectuels juifs de langue française was the intersection of these two competing strains of Judaism, but over time it was Levinas and his understanding of Judaism established in his Talmudic lectures that ultimately came to be dominant. This, especially after the École Gilbert-Bloch d'Orsay closed its doors in 1969 to reestablish itself in Israel. It is likely the success of Levinas's influence on the Colloquium that led to its retrospective assignation as one of the two pillars of the École de Pensée Juive de Paris.

Over the years, Levinas's Talmudic lecture became an event in itself with auditors from around the world coming to see him. Levinas told Claude Riveline that he chose the Talmudic page for each colloquium by looking over Maimonides's Mishna Torah for the subject closest to that year's theme and then traced Maimonides's Talmudic sources.[9] Just before the lecture was to start, "Levinas would distribute copies of the Talmudic passage to be commented on, in Hebrew and in French, so that even those who did not know Hebrew had the text before their eyes."[10] Levinas prepared the translation of the passage himself and after handing them out, he would then divide the passages into discrete sections and comment on each one. For Levinas, the event was participatory with the audience encouraged to come to their own conclusions in the tradition of *yesh omrim*, "there are those who say," signaling the importance of contradictory opinions.

right up to the point of its eschatological denouement." The story of the exodus is as important for the possibility of liberty in the future as for the particular story it tells about the past. "Their deliverance anticipated the salvation of humanity itself. The past of their memory carries the future within it. This would be the structure of history, and the foundation of the sages' position" (BM 69, AS 94). Two points are important to note. The first is that the memory need not correlate to an "actual" historical event. This is to say that the "memory" of the exodus from Egypt need not be a memory of something that actually happened but instead the memory must be such that it carries the future within it. The promise for the future is more important than the fidelity to the past. Related to this shift is an emphasis on the universality of the story for a future humanity that eclipses the

Levinas undoubtedly played the role of Talmudic master leading his students through the text but it was equally important to Levinas that the event be a dialogical relation between master and students, not an oratory. In the introduction to his lecture from 1963, "Towards the Other," Levinas instructs the audience:

> The passage to be commented on has been distributed to you. Perhaps you should not take it with you. The texts of the Oral Law that have been set into writing should never be separated from their living commentary. When the voice of the exegetist no longer sounds—and who would dare believe it reverberates long in the ears of its listeners—the texts return to their immobility, becoming once again enigmatic, strange, sometimes even ridiculously archaic.[11]

The lectures were given to be heard, discussed, and argued out.

This oral and aural component is an essential aspect of Levinas's Talmudic methodology. The desire to preserve the Talmudic lecture in its living moment translated even into his preparation of the written text. "When he was given a transcript of what he had said, which was recorded by a stenographer or tape recorder, he was incomparably scrupulous not to rework the thought he had expressed, but only the words he had said."[12] In this way, Levinas sought to limit the reach of his Talmudic lecture, pointing to the importance of living commentary and the dangers of particularity of the past event.

In this new light we find "a universality through Israel, more universal than the one that remains marked by the particularism of Jacob—though it is questionable whether Jacob's hardships will ever be effaced from history.... The greater universality is certainly what Ben Yoma intuits and what is about to be suggested by the mention of Abraham: a history beyond the one that is compounded by memories and could be contained therein. A history overflowing memory, and, in this sense, unimaginable. A history, as yet entirely novel, that has not yet happened to any particular nation" (BM 70, AS 95). Levinas presents us with a tangled web of temporalities insofar as a history that has not yet happened eclipses a history, Jacob's hardship, that may never be effaced. How can it be that an ineffaceable history can be eclipsed by another immobilizing the text in the written word. Nevertheless, he did publish faithful reproductions in the annual collections of essays from the Colloquium and also later in *Quatre lectures talmudiques, Nouvelles lectures talmudiques, A l'heure des nations, L'au-dela du verset*, as well as in *Difficile Liberté* and *Cahier de l'Herne*, creating something of a contradiction given that the reach of the books far exceeded that of the Colloquium. Indeed, it is as the author of these works that he secured his position as an authority on Talmud. A similar contradiction can be seen in the disparity between his repeated professions of modesty and naivete in his interpretation of Talmud, which he claimed to "pursue only as an amateur," and his equally repeated assertions that in order to understand the fundamental ideas in the Talmud underlying seemingly pedestrian discussions of "the right to eat or not to eat 'an egg hatched on a holy day,' or payments owed for damages caused by a 'wild ox,' *one needs to have encountered an authentic Talmudic master*" to be able to do so.[13] The modesty and circumspection stands in contrast to his claims to authority as the widespread dissemination of his commentaries stands in contrast to his request that the written version not be taken away from the lecture hall.

To understand Emmanuel Levinas as a reader of Talmud within the context of his lectures at the Colloque des intellectuels juifs de langue française, the reception of his books, and for us today, is to understand how he took his place in, or inserted

history that is yet to happen? Levinas explains that this

> does not mean that the exodus from Egypt "loses its place," but that the freeing from subservience to the empires will be the primary thing, and the exodus from Egypt the secondary one. In the same way that [Genesis 35:10]: "You will not be called Jacob, but your name will be Israel" does not mean that Jacob "loses his place," but that Israel will be his primary name and Jacob his secondary name. (BM 70, AS 95)

The emancipation from servitude and the enfranchisement of all (human or other) that we work toward should be the primary message, while the historical event of the exodus from Egypt is the secondary one. The past event is not lost, but guarding it is not sufficient because the singular focus on accomplishments of the past leads to complacency in the present. By contrast, himself into, a tradition. A tradition of reading Jewish scripture "across history going from pupil to master" enacted in "gatherings between colleagues questioning one another from century to century."[14] Two issues arise here involving (1) the entangled relation between oral and written texts that one must be able to properly "read" but also "write," and (2) the methodology and training to be able to do so properly. We have looked at many of the contributing factors, the strands of the braid, which led to the latter, but Levinas offers his own commentary on each in his discussions of how to "read" Talmud. Hence, in what follows I will work through these instances in an attempt to elucidate Levinas's own reading strategies, how these relate to the formative strands taken up in the previous chapters, what this tells us about his relation to the larger tradition of Talmudic commentary, and how it relates to Levinas's particular historical moment.

As we have seen, for Levinas the history of the Talmud was far less important than the Talmud's ability to communicate across time, that is, across history. This capacity is inherent in the structure of the Talmud itself, which is composed of two elements: Mishnah and Gemara. The Mishnah is the written collection of the Jewish oral traditions known as the "oral Torah," which was compiled in Palestine circa 200 CE. The Gemara is composed of rabbinic commentaries on the Mishnah that were themselves later redacted and compiled. It is the entangled relation of attention to the work that needs to be done in the future leads to action. In this way, the goal is no longer the liberation of the Jewish people but the liberation of all humanity. "There is a meaning of Israel that is broader than that of Jacob, but Jacob, a secondary or second name, remains the name of a living being" (BM 70, AS 95). The meaning and the message is larger, more universal, than the individual or event, even if it is the particular individual or event that provides the impetus, the memory, to inspire the action. It is innovation that liberates a meaning for the future from a tradition or memory of the past.

Thus "the memories of a prodigious past in which a parted sea let the freed tribes pass through and swallowed up their pursuers takes on an ambiguous meaning." The meaning is no longer determined solely by the historical event as it happened or how the Mishnah and commentaries on it that create the temporal dynamism that Levinas found so appealing. The Talmud is composed of a passage of the Mishnah that is put in dialogue with a long discussion of its comments by a series of interpreters from different times and different contexts. What's more, an essential component of its structure and content is the disagreement between commentaries that destabilize the authority of any one human voice.

The two elements are also composed in different styles and languages. The Mishnah, written in Hebrew, is declarative and flowing. The Gemara, written in Aramaic, is more abrupt and allusive.[15] The structure, style, and language of the Talmud signal to the reader the difference between Mishnah and Gemara as well as the hierarchy of authority because of the ways that the Gemara relies on Mishnah. It is worth noting that at Levinas's lectures he distributed the passages to be discussed in both the original language and in French translation, but because the lectures were delivered and published in French, the visible demarcation between Mishnah and Gemara is lost, creating a different sort of text in which Levinas appears as the sole author and authority. The shift in language also seems to run counter to his larger goals for Jewish education, which called for training in Hebrew. It is, however, in keeping with the shift of audience from Jewish students to French Jewish intellectuals. These French Jewish intellectuals were to be the recipients of Levinas's postrabbinic

it is remembered. "Zakhor (memory) ceases to indicate the meaning of History!" (BM 72, AS 97). This then leads Levinas to a parable in the text:

> A man was going along and came upon a wolf—and got away. After that, he told nothing but wolf stories. He came upon a lion, and escaped: then he told the story of the lion. He encountered a snake—and got away. There he is, having forgotten both of them [the wolf and the lion] and telling nothing but the story of the snake. So with Israel: the most recent hardships eclipse the earlier ones." (BM 72, AS 97)

At first glance, the story appears to be about forgetting rather than remembering. The man lives his life recalling only the most recent hardship while the past ones are forgotten, and so with Israel. "This is the form in which the *history* of Israel is forgotten," but Levinas chain of transmission and he their Talmudic master, a project of dissemination that required translation.

Here we arrive at a question provoked by the previous two chapters: is it possible to be a master of a tradition in which one has not been properly trained? I confess it is a question I will not be able to answer, although I believe that this, in itself, serves both a didactic and propaedeutic purpose. As we have seen, however, Levinas seems to imply that the answer should be "No."

> It is certain that, when discussing the right to eat or not to eat "an egg hatched on a holy day," or payments owed for damages caused by a "wild ox," the sages of the Talmud are discussing neither an egg nor an ox but are arguing about fundamental ideas without appearing to do so. *It is true that one needs to have encountered an authentic Talmudic master to be sure of it.*[16]

One must bring a critical eye to Levinas's statement, however, because while he may have studied with an "authentic Talmudic master" in the person of Shushani, his training in Talmud came late in life and was decidedly unorthodox. Thus, if Levinas's answer is "no," it must be a qualified "no."

As we have also seen, it was not until after World War II, after his training in Western philosophy and his extensive work on Husserl and then on/against Heidegger, and after the Holocaust, that Levinas came to the study of Talmud. Levinas's study with Shushani marked the beginning of also tells us that this is how "the future preceding the ultimate deliverance is announced" (BM 72, AS 97, my emphasis). There is something else at work here beyond a linear progression of events where each supplants, or eclipses, the other.

Levinas informs us that the triad of the wolf, the lion, and the snake is reminiscent of Amos 5:19, "It will be as when a man flees from a lion and finds himself face to face with a bear, enters his house and is bitten by the snake." In Amos, the wolf and lion are replaced by the lion and the bear, but the snake that ends the story is the same. The snake in Genesis 3:15 "comes crawling" and "attacks the heel." There is a difference between "The wolf and the lion, like the lion and the bear," which "are visible, foreseeable threats," and the snake that sneaks up on its prey" (BM 72, AS 97). On page 98b of the treatise Sanhedrin his own Talmudic readings and lectures, but his turn to Talmud is also inextricably linked to his education and training in the Western philosophical and literary traditions and commitment to the values of French Universalism/humanism. Thus we should understand Levinas's interpretation of Talmud in light of Richard Cohen's assertion that Levinas was "writing on the basis of the entirety of Western Civilization, from Athens to Jerusalem to Rome, and writing with all its greatest contributors and interlocutors in mind."[17]

Levinas is therefore at odds with what can be called the "traditionalist" approach to Talmud wherein "Rabbinic literature" is understood to have its origins at Mount Sinai and is guaranteed by direct instruction from teacher to teacher in an unbroken chain of transmission. This traditional approach follows the Mishna tractate (Mishna Avot 1:1), which teaches: "Moses received the Torah from Sinai and transmitted it to Joshua, Joshua to the elders, and the elders to the prophets, and the prophets to the Men of the great assembly." On this understanding, the oral Torah and its meaning remain stable as they are passed from Moses to Joshua and ultimately to the Men of the Great Assembly in an unbroken chain of transmission. Elizabeth Shanks Alexander presents a second source from the Babylonian Talmud (B. Eruvin 54b) that describes the means by which such an accurate preservation of the original meaning is possible. Alexander tells us that "one part of the process of securing tradition involves

Resh Lakish provides an interpretation of Amos as follows:

> I will show you an example of it in the world today. When a man goes to a field and meets a government surveyor, is it not as if he had met a lion? Here he is, back in the town, and he bumps into a tax collector. Is it not as if he had met a bear? He returns home and finds his sons and daughters dying of hunger. Is it not as if he had been bitten by a snake?" (BM 72, AS 97–98)

Of note is Resh Laquish's innovative reading of Amos, where the story is transformed to address the issues of his day: surveyors, tax collectors, hunger. The text is not left to the particular memory or history of Amos but is transported to Resh Lakish's moment in time. Even so, Levinas tell us that the text requires further deciphering. "The government surveyor challenges your title to the land you are working, the direct teaching from teacher to disciple (e.g., Moses to Aaron). Another equally important part of the process involves establishing witnesses as the teacher transmits to others (e.g., Aaron listening in as Moses teaches his sons). . . . The presence of the witnesses(es) ensures that the *material taught* remains the same from one lesson to the next. . . . This source, then, presents a very complex choreography between teachers and disciples, performers and audiences, that ensures the intact preservation of a discrete body of tradition."[18] Just as with the Mishna Avot, the oral transmission is an unbroken chain where the final transmission is indistinguishable from the original one. One point worth noting is that the written variant of the oral transmission should likewise record this fidelity. In any event, given Levinas's personal background and the historical event of the Holocaust, it was impossible for Levinas to claim access to such an unbroken chain of transmission.

Instead, Levinas's reading of Talmud and Jewish texts necessarily presupposes the rupture or breaking of the chain that was the result of Nationalist Socialist rule. It is both a confrontation with this rupture and an attempt to mend the chain or perhaps better, to bridge the chasm created by the destruction of the Talmudic academies and those who inhabited them. To do so, Levinas has to account for the break in transmission, and he does so in two ways. First, by arguing that the meaning imbued in the Torah is always available regardless of time or space. In his 1979 essay "On the tax collector always finds you owe money—these are civil servants of states questioning your illusory rights as a citizen. The Diaspora of Israel in lands that, always foreign, continually trample, beneath the tread of lions, wolves, and bears, the very legal order that made them inhabitable. But this is the domain of history, a structural realm in which it is possible to walk, to wander, to flee. Savagery and wasteland, the memory of which may yet fade" (BM 72–73, AS 98). The foreseeable threats are particular ones. Events that have occurred in history and are explainable, even if only in retrospect. Each of these hardships, be it savagery or wasteland, may fade from memory. Especially when confronted with a more recent hardship or savagery that takes its place.

"But the death of the starving children thrusts us into the snake pit, into places that are no longer places, into places one

Jewish Reading of Scriptures," Levinas refers to Rabbi Hayyim of Volozhin's interpretation of a passage from the *Sayings of the Fathers* where the rabbinical scholars compare the Torah to "glowing coals," and Levinas tells us that "Hayyim Volozhiner interpreted this remark approximately as follows: the coals light up by being blown on, the glow of the flame that thus comes alive depends on the interpreter's length of breath."[19] In Levinas's account, the reader is able to rekindle the coals through the force of their breath. The meaning remains in the coals, and what seems to matter most is not the direct chain of transmission but the individual interpreter's engagement with the coals. In Levinas's introduction to *Quatre lectures talmudiques* of 1968 (translated in English as the introduction to *Nine Talmudic Readings*) he states, "Our approach assumes that the different periods of history can communicate around thinkable meanings, whatever the variations in the signifying material which suggests them." The contemporary reference to rupture becomes clearer as Levinas continues: "For we assume the permanence and continuation of Israel and the unity of its self-consciousness throughout the ages."[20] Even in the face of the most horrible temporal disaster the "permanence" and "continuation" of Israel is guaranteed. What was lost can be found. What was destroyed can be rebuilt. The coals still hold the fire.

Such a move is consistent with tradition, and this leads to the second way in cannot forget, but that do not succeed in placing themselves in memory, in organizing themselves in the form of memories. We have known such pits in this [twentieth] century!" (BM 73, AS 98). The snake represents true evil, and here again we move beyond the realm of the particular into that of the universal. This is an evil that sneaks up on us in ways that are unforeseeable because they are unimaginable. For Levinas, the Holocaust is such an event, which one cannot forget but resides beyond the realm of particular memories in its magnitude and impact. Indeed, to dwell on the memory of the Holocaust at the expense of guarding against true evil in the present is to once again render true evil unimaginable and thus unforeseeable. The particular event in the past, in history, cannot be left in the past as though the danger is over and done with. Instead, it must punctuate the which Levinas accounts for the ruptured chain of transmission. By placing emphasis on the importance of the reader who is able to find the meaning in the text, Levinas adheres to a dynamic reading of Torah and Talmud. Here, the oral Torah is understood as the actualization of latent interpretative possibilities that lie dormant in the written text until they are activated by an engagement with the text traditionally in the form of the teacher's discussion of the text in the classroom.[21] Such interpretations can appear as novel or even contradictory but are sanctioned by the assumption that these meanings were waiting to be revealed. Levinas cites a story from the Babylonian Talmud where "the lesson taught at the school of R. Akiba is said to be incomprehensible to Moses, but yet is the very teaching of Moses."[22] The passage from B. Meahot 29b reads:

> When Moses ascended on high he found the Holy One, blessed be He, engaged in attaching crownlets to the letters. He said to Him, "Lord of the Universe, why do you bother with this?" He answered, "There is a man who is destined to arise at the end of many generations, named Akiva ben Yosef, who will expound upon each crownlet heaps and heaps of laws." [Moses] said before Him "Master of the Universe, show him to me." He replied "Turn around." Moses went and sat down behind the eighth row [of students listening to Akiva], but he could not understand what

time of the total history of humanity, right up to the point of its eschatological denouement. That is, it can only serve us if we look beyond its particularity as past and toward its guidance toward our future. The pure evil of the snake is the total abandonment of responsibility toward others. It is true evil, the snake, against which we must be vigilant rather than resting complacent with our escape from the lion or the wolf.

This leads Levinas to a painful question: "Might it be that the 'may the Eternal live' of the ultimate future will be announced by the inhumanity of the war that precedes it?" (BM 71, AS 96). Is the worst necessary that we may achieve the best? "Were all those woes— . . . those snake bites, that starvation of children, all that Passion of Innocents, that Passion of Israel— necessary in order for a reconciled humanity to be thinkable?" (BM 73, AS they were saying. His strength left him. But then they came to a certain topic and the disciples said to [R. Akiva], "Rabbi, how do you know this?" He replied, "It is a law given to Moses at Sinai." And Moses was comforted.

In this story, God reveals to Moses that some aspects of the Torah are destined for future interpreters, such as Akiva expounding heaps of laws from each crownlet, and Moses asks God to show him this future. God transports Moses to the academy of Rabbi Akiva, but on entering the school Moses is disconsolate to discover that he does not understand anything of the lessons being taught. His mood is lifted, however, when at the end of the lesson Rabbi Akiva attributes his teachings to the teachings of Moses at Mount Sinai. Here the eternal message is delivered within the context of temporal change, and the authority of Rabbi Akiva is not questioned despite the incomprehensibility of his teachings to Moses. There is something striking about the possibility that Moses, who received the written Torah from God, is unable to understand the interpretations of it derived in the oral tradition. In Levinas's presentation, however, it is principally the intellectual milieu of Akiva that is incomprehensible to Moses while the teachings are somehow constant. In either case, this reading strategy accounts for the instability of change over time. The meaning of the text is allowed to move and adapt to changing culture and context and in this maintains its relevance. Such a strategy also assures that the Torah

98). Was the Passion of Israel, the term Levinas uses for the Holocaust, necessary? The question borders on offensive when considered in regard to the particular event of the Holocaust. In what world could such an event be deemed necessary? Levinas warns us of remaining within the limits of "historical time. Does not the wisdom of the rabbinical doctor reach further, measuring the best in terms of the worst that will be transcended?" How can we understand the necessity of the "inhumanity" that precedes the "ultimate future"? How does one reach further than historical time?

Here again, innovation is the key. Levinas returns to the text:

> In I Chronicles 1:27: "Abram—the same is Abraham." He first became the father of Aram; he became in the end the father of the whole world. Sarai—the same is Sarah. She was first a princess

itself is generative, even if the chain of transmission is damaged or severed.

In this interpretative tradition, it is not necessary to think of the study of Talmud as an unbroken series of face to face oral transmissions. This is to say that the purpose of the oral tradition is not fidelity to the original ensured by face to face transmission as in the "traditionalist" mode but instead to bring to light hidden aspects of the written Torah through active interpretation making them available for human understanding. Active engagement with the written Torah becomes the means of retrieving or activating the oral Torah in a way that is "fluid, dynamic, and represented by the interaction between teacher and student as developed and amplified in the process of tradition."[23] The productive and transformative powers of this reading strategy are apparent in a parable from the Seder Eliahu Zuta 2:

> What is the difference between the Written and Oral Torahs? To what may the matter be compared? To a king of flesh and blood who had two servants. He loved them both with a perfect love. To one he gave a kab of wheat and a bundle of flax and to the other he gave a kab of wheat and a bundle of flax. What did the wise one do? He took the flax and wove it into a tablecloth. He took the wheat and made it into fine flour; he sifted it and he ground it. He kneaded it and baked it. Then he placed it on the top of the table and spread over the tablecloth. Then he left it for the king's return. The foolish among them did not do anything.

among her people; she finally became the princess of the whole world." (BM 73, AS 98)

In each case, we begin with a particular individual, Abram and Sarai, but their particularity is not what is most important, instead it is that in the change, the innovation, to "Abraham and Sarah a universal and united humanity is announced" (BM 73, AS 98). The change of names is an innovation that can be accounted for as an individual event, but to do so is to miss the way that this change transcends any particular time. It is a movement from the particular to the universal, from one person to one people, and which extends to all of humanity. Such a move is not obvious, especially when confined to a logic of historical progression that tells us that at a particular and definite moment in time, Abram became Abraham. As before, the text says more than it says

After some days the king returned to his house and said: My sons, bring me what I gave you. One brought out the bread of fine flour upon the table with the tablecloth spread over it. The other brought out the wheat in a box and the bundle of flax upon it. Alas for his shame, alas for his disgrace.[24]

One way to understand the passage is that it elucidates the difference between the static, fixed, and unchanging nature of the written Torah, which serves as the raw material for the dynamic, fluid, and malleable oral Torah. But beyond this it is indicative of a strategy that privileges an active, manipulative, and transformative reading of the text. The goal is to make the written text applicable and useful in its current context, and this aligns with Levinas's reading of Talmud and Jewish texts. "What is sought after, and often achieved in the incessant return to verses by the Talmudic scholars . . . is a reading where the passage commented upon clarifies for the reader its present preoccupation (which may be either out of the ordinary or common to its generation), and where the verse, in its turn, is renewed in the light of this clarification."[25]

But Levinas also sees his reading strategy as a violent endeavor. Levinas tells us a story from the Tractate *Shabbath* about a Sadducee who "saw Raba buried in study, holding his fingers beneath his foot so tightly that blood spurted from it."[26] Levinas interprets this passage as a template for his own Talmudic methodology when

and thus the meaning of the text requires further interrogation: "Here are some specifics: content incorporated to introduce Halakah: commandments and interdicts. To use the term Abraham is, according to Bar Kapra, a positive commandment. Not to call him Abram is an interdict, according to Rav Eliezer" (BM 73, AS 98).

There is a division between Abram and Abraham, Sarai and Sarah, that should not be taken lightly and can easily be missed. "Interdicts and commandments. Unless we are able to divine: Hear, through the relative present, bold anticipations of an absolute future! Hear, in the present's uncertainty, in Israel's misery, Abraham, the father of human universality, hailed as such, invoked as such! Time to accept universality!" (BM 74, AS 99). The text anticipates a universality to come that can be achieved but not if we are bound to either the he states: "to rub in such a way that blood spurts out is perhaps the way one must 'rub' the text to arrive at the life it conceals. Many of you are undoubtedly thinking, with good reason, that at this very moment, I am in the process of rubbing the text to make it spurt blood—I rise to the challenge!" This is not far removed from the violent manipulation necessary to transform the kab into bread and the flax into tablecloth to arrive at the form concealed in the raw materials. Levinas concedes and embraces the violent nature of such a task: "to the degree that it rests on the trust granted the author, it can only consist in this violence done to words to tear from them the secret that time and conventions have covered over with their sedimentations."[27] Levinas's self-proclaimed violent reading of the story of Raba is in tune with the dynamic interpretative Jewish tradition, but it also serves as the very justification for his methodology of Talmudic exegesis and his innovative interpretations. In essence, he grants himself authority based on his own reading of the Talmud.

Levinas's belief in the dynamic reading of Torah and Talmud is a conviction based in Jewish tradition, but for Levinas it is also a necessary post-Holocaust conviction. The dynamism is a mechanism for the recovery of what was destroyed in the Holocaust but also the means by which he is able to make sense of Jewish scripture in a post-Holocaust world and which bring his own interpretative methods to bear on the text. Levinas's violent manipulation of particularity of our relative present or the confines of our remembered past. Levinas implores us to be attuned to that for which we do not normally listen and in so doing to work toward the universality announced in Abraham and Sarah. "The anticipated is already irreversible! Israel—historians know it—has lived through its long centuries of persecution in this sort of ambiguity. Obligatory thoughts in waiting!" (BM 74, AS 99). The change from Abram to Abraham and Sarai to Sarah announces the shift from the particular to the universal as a commandment. "But here is the interdict: Do not conceive of Abraham in terms of Abram! Do not constitute the future from traces of memory, mistrusting new things and even the miracle required for universal peace" (BM 74, AS 99). To achieve human universality (and a universalism that extends beyond the human animal) we must be sacred texts, often inflected by Western philosophical or literary sources, enables him to bring these texts into his present. His "aim is to refer to a context which allows the level of discussion to be raised and to make one notice the true import of the data from which the discussion derives its meaning. The transfer of an idea to another climate—which is its original climate—wrests new possibilities from it."[28] The transcendent nature of this move certainly gives Levinas license to transport the Talmudic knowledge of prewar Vilna to the climate of postwar Paris. But given the violent and transformative nature of his interpretative reading, one must ask who or what is to keep this multiplicity of meanings from falling into pure perspectivalism or subjective musing? This is to ask, what keeps his hermeneutics from lapsing into relativism of one kind or another?

One answer returns us to the question we posed at the beginning of this chapter and Levinas's response that proper instruction and training in the reading and study of Talmud is required. In "On the Jewish Reading of Scriptures," Levinas further asserts that the reading processes for which he advocates "do not amount to identifying exegesis with the impressions and subjective reflections left by the word once it has been understood, nor to including them gratuitously in the 'outside' of meaning."[29] It is neither solely the intellectual genius of the reader nor interpretative happenstance that leads to discovery and innovation, but instead such innovation is evidence that prepared to jettison our prior and proper identity, even if it is that very identity that provides the template by which we seek human universality, as was the case with Levinas's Judaism. The future cannot be constituted from a frozen past that inhibits innovation and change. The paradox at play is precisely the way that the innovative change from Abram to Abraham, from Sarai to Sarah, can be arrested and frozen in the name of Abraham or Sarah whose names, once announced, cannot be changed if they are conceived of as the progenitors of a particular people or peoples. The template for change can become the very thing that inhibits it.

We seem to have strayed from the question, "Were all those woes— . . . those snake bites, that starvation of children, all that Passion of Innocents, that Passion of Israel— necessary in order for a reconciled humanity to be "in our reading of the Talmudic passage, inspiration and the exegesis that discovers it, we have discerned the spirituality of the spirit and the actual figure of transcendence."[30] Proper training may give one the tools to read the text but ultimately in what Levinas calls the paradigmatic modality of Talmudic reflection: "notions remain constantly in contact with the examples or refer back to them, whereas they should have been content as springboards to rise to the level of generalization, or they clarify the thought which scrutinizes by the secret light of hidden or isolated worlds from which it burst forth; and simultaneously this world inserted or lost in signs is illuminated by the thought which comes to it from outside or from the other end of the canon, revealing its possibilities which were awaiting the exegesis, immobilized in some way, in the letters."[31] To return to the relation of God on God's own side and God on our side, for Levinas the sacred book or text holds more weight than any individual interpreter or school of interpretation, and thus it is the text that serves as the conduit or pathway to God on God's own side. Techniques of reading that have only recently been made available in the present on our side, such as phenomenology, can be used to pry meanings from the text that somehow have always been present on God's own side, silently waiting to be revealed.

As noted, Levinas's reading technique serves several purposes: it maintains connection with the divine source of the text, thinkable?" (BM 73, AS 98). Levinas turns to an example where the name or event is not forbidden or forgotten.

> But what of he who continues to call Jacob Jacob? [Answer: Here there is a difference! The Scripture itself returns to [this name of] Jacob [Genesis 46:2]: "And God spoke unto Israel in a vision during the night and He said: Jacob, Jacob." (BM 74–75, AS 100)

Israel retains the name of Jacob in such a way that the past, the memory, is conserved in the futural gesture of the change.

"God speaks to Israel but calls him Jacob as formerly." Here there is a difference. "The language of accomplishment [Israel] reverts to that of pure promise [Jacob]. It is memory surviving forgetfulness. A tired man, opposing the violence and lies of the earth, having had many misfortunes, continues the struggle. The greatness of Israel it allows for innovative interpretations of the text that make it relevant to the present context, it allows Levinas to employ his training in Western philosophy as one of the means to interrogate the text, and it allows Levinas to insert himself into the Talmudic tradition to which he came late. There is a definite tension between the secular post-Enlightenment tradition of philosophical inquiry in which Levinas was trained, the French Universalist doctrine he values, and the Talmudic tradition he later adopts. Much of Levinas's originality lies in the ways he strives to maintain the three strands of the braid in his reading of Jewish scriptures. This is to say that Levinas's reading of Talmud and Jewish scriptures accepts the existence and importance of the divine often associated with antirational strains of thought but without devolving into irrational acceptance of myth or ecstatic mysticism by simultaneously privileging the rationalist approach to thought most often associated with secular scholarship.

In "A Religion for Adults," first published in 1957, Levinas makes it clear that he considers such a position consistent with the "oral tradition of exegesis which crystalized in the Talmud and its commentaries."[32] For Levinas, what makes Judaism a "religion for adults" is that it does not assume God to be a divine parent intervening in worldly affairs via miracle or material intervention. Nor does it assume humans to be actors directed entirely by Divine will. Instead, on Levinas's reading,

is still in Jacob!" (BM 75, AS 100). Greatness is still yet to be achieved and the struggle is not behind us. Indeed, God's call to Jacob takes place at the moment when "leaving the Holy Land, Jacob leads the children of Israel toward slavery in Egypt" (BM 75, AS 100). The promise of universal humanity is announced in the names of Abraham and Sarah but "henceforth the promise made to the Patriarchs will be kept only as a hope of the exiled" (BM 75, AS 100). The greatness of Israel is to be realized in the Exodus and after the hardship of slavery. The best is to follow the worst, and this could be one answer to the unseemly question as to whether the Passion of Israel, the Holocaust, was necessary? This is not where Levinas lets things stand. He asks: "Is Scripture, then, only a historical work concerned with seeing that the rights of certain subjects are respected?" (BM 75, AS 100). Is all of this a history for Judaism, the goal of education consists in instituting a link between humans and the saintliness of God and in maintaining the human in this relationship. But all its effort—from the Bible to the closure of the Talmud in the sixth century and throughout most of its commentators from the great era of rabbinical science—consists in understanding this saintliness of God in a sense that stands in sharp contrast to the numinous meaning of the term, as it appears in the primitive religions wherein the moderns have often wished to see the source of religion.... Judaism has disenchanted the world contesting the notion that religions apparently evolved out of enthusiasm and the sacred.[33]

There is a distinction and a divide between the saintliness of God and our understanding of that saintliness, and thus while we work toward it we must also be distrustful of what we take it to be. For Levinas, the proper reading of Jewish texts is one that conserves the critical spirit of humanism questioning any ascription of divine power or intervention insofar as "the numinous annuls the links between persons by making beings participate, albeit ecstatically, in a drama not brought about willingly by them, an order in which they founder." What's more, "this somehow sacramental power of the Divine seems to be contrary to the education of humans, which remains *action on a free being*. Not that liberty is an end in itself, but it does remain the condition for any value humans may attain."[34] Levinas refuses to relinquish concerned with the trials, tribulations, tragedies, and triumphs of a particular people? Are we to remember the snake bite of the Holocaust so as to conserve the particular name of Jacob as the basis to retain the particular people of Israel? Levinas's answer is "no." "In the Talmudic page we have just examined I have been especially sensitive to a Judaism that overflows memory, that attempts to conceive of it beyond the Exodus, and sees an unforeseeable future ('no eye has seen it'), but also a future opening up through a new mode of trial, new dimensions of suffering" (BM 75, AS 100–101). This is a Judaism that is not beholden to the memory of the exodus, even if the enfranchisement of the Jewish people provides the template for universal emancipation. The emphasis on innovation means that such a Judaism cannot be complacent with past victories or accomplishments nor can it remain locked in the perceived gains that the Enlightenment, advances in science, and innovations in modern philosophy have bequeathed to humanity. He does not want to return to animism, fatalism, or mysticism. It is also clear that he views secular humanism as inadequate and even harmful when left to its own devices.

In his 1964 Talmudic lecture on "The Temptation of Temptation," Levinas tells us that the "temptation of temptation" of which he speaks "may well describe the condition of the Western man." As we have seen, this temptation of temptation is the temptation of philosophy, the seduction of reason as a tool by which humans can master and control the world around them. We are aware that this temptation of temptation is one that seduced Levinas himself in the years before World War II, leading him from his studies in Russian literature and then Western philosophy to his tutelage under Martin Heidegger.[35] In his 1963 Talmudic lecture "Toward the Other," Levinas makes explicit his regrets about following the course of study that led him into the orbit of a philosopher who enthusiastically embraced National Socialism. He also makes clear his explicit condemnation of Heidegger, his political choices, and what he sees as the solipsistic nature of his philosophy.[36] Indeed, in the figure and philosophy of Heidegger, Levinas detected the limitations and ultimate paucity of the Western philosophical tradition, which, absent any Divine connection, became completely unmoored from ethical direction.[37]

a preconceived idea of identity. Just as Abram became Abraham and Sarai became Sarah, we cannot remain beholden to a previous concept of identity. Our identity may conserve the memory of its past, as Jacob become Israel, but we must also be prepared to overflow such a memory and such an identity. In this way, Judaism has always been a humanism insofar as it holds the possibility for a universal humanity within itself.

As we have also seen, Levinas is unwilling to completely forsake this tradition. Instead, Levinas argues for a link between Judaism and the Western tradition of philosophy; the realization of the universal aspirations of philosophy is manifest through the particular tradition of Judaism: "It is not by virtue of simple chance that the way towards the synthesis of the Jewish revelation and Greek thought was masterfully traced by Maimonides, who is claimed by both Jewish and Muslim philosophers; that a profound respect for Greek knowledge already fills the wise men of the Talmud; that education for the Jew merges with instruction and the ignorant man can never really be pious."[38] Thus the goal of Levinas's Talmudic lectures and then writings on Jewish scripture is to lead educated and intelligent men and women through their training in Western philosophy back to Revelation and back to Ethics. Levinas's primary audience was likely the intelligent men and women educated at the ENIO, though the audience expanded and changed with the success of his Talmudic lectures at the Colloque des intellectuels juifs de langue française. In either case the move requires initiation into the proper reading of Talmud.

In "On the Jewish Reading of Scriptures," Levinas attempts to instruct the reader in the multilayered process of dynamic interpretation. Such a reading leads us back to the meaning inherent in the Talmud but that "would not be possible for us without recourse to a modern language—in other words, without touching on the problems of today."[39] But making the texts and issues of the past speak to the problems of today is no easy task, because what a Talmudic text "intends to do is not immediately apparent in terms which, for an inexperienced reader, may seem unusual, and which in fact allow for several levels and dimensions."[40] Levinas tells us that to "move toward a meaning which is retained despite an apparently antiquated language, it is necessary first of all to accept patiently—as one accepts the conventions of a fable or a stage stetting—the particulars of the text in their specific universe."[41] Levinas asks the reader to suspend the critical impulse granted by modern reading techniques in order to access the divine inspiration hidden in the text, which "breaks through from beneath the immediate meaning of what is meant to be said, another meaning which beckons to a way of hearing that listens beyond what is heard, beckons to extreme consciousness, a consciousness that has been awoken."[42] By means of this suspension one opens oneself up to the transcendent meaning hidden in the text. Such a suspension runs counter to the convictions of a person educated in the post-Enlightenment Western tradition. Levinas asks, "will the person today not resist such readings by reducing the transcendence of inspiration, exegesis, and the moral message to man's interiority, to his creativity or his subconscious? Is not ethics basically autonomous?"[43] This is to suggest that modern secular views are by and large naturalist, rationalist, or both, and that modern intellectuals tend to reject or oppose transcendence or anything like it. To answer this question Levinas turns to a section of a Talmudic extract when R. Eleazar presents a particularly audacious exegesis of a number of passages from Genesis, from Samuel, and from Kings in order to substantiate his reading of Makkoth 23b. "One interlocutor, Raba, questions such extravagance: there is no need to have voices intervening in discourses where reason is sufficient. But it is R. Eleazar's lesson that the Talmud retains. It retains it without discussion, in the name of tradition. Inspiration is thus said to be in the exercise of reason itself!" Levinas argues that inspiration is not the domain of independent and autonomous human thought but the conduit to the transcendent domain of the divine. It enables the text to say more than it says and more than reason left to its own devices can discern. Even so, Levinas continues, "it should be emphasized that despite tradition, the redactors of the Talmudic text recorded the opinion that was rejected: Raba's skepticism. It is still written down."[44] Reason is not to be rejected outright but conserved.

Just as the suspension of reason does not come easily or without danger, the conservation of reason and the Western intellectual tradition is also fraught. This is because the very language in which Levinas finds the opening to transcendence is also the object of philology, and in the view of philology "the transcendence that is expressed through it would be just an illusion, the prestige of influences to be demystified by History."⁴⁵ At first blush, this move appears as the negation of the transcendent power inherent in the text, but Levinas tells us that it is also this move that conserves the text for modern readers. Indeed, the conservation of sacred texts by philologists and historians cannot be undervalued after the destruction of the Talmudic academies during Nazi rule. The rule of reason may have led to the conservation of the texts but it cannot contain the sacred meaning held within the text, which gains power through the incorporation of the very reason that calls it into question. "Monotheism surpasses and incorporates atheism, but it is impossible unless you attain the age of doubt, solitude, and revolt. . . . One wonders, in fact, whether the Western spirit, philosophy, is not in the last analysis the position of a humanity that accepts the risk of atheism, if it must be held to ransom by its majority, but overcome it."⁴⁶ The acute reader must make his or her way through the doubt that leads to atheism, but then there is a movement back, a return or Teshuvah: "from history and philology to the understanding of meaning coming from behind the literature of letters and anachronisms, an understanding that again affects and wakes, forcing us out of the bed of the preformed and customary ideas that protect and reassure."⁴⁷ For Levinas, the power of Judaism lies in its ability to maintain the critical tools of doubt and skepticism that release human kind from a fatalist and dependent relation with God or gods, thus fostering autonomy and personal responsibility but without succumbing to atheism and the hubris of anthropocentrism.[48] "It is a great glory for the Creator to have set up a being who affirms him after having contested and denied Him in the glamorous areas of myth and enthusiasm; it is a great glory for God to have created a being capable of seeking Him or hearing Him from afar, having experienced separation and atheism."[49]

To make this move, Levinas turns to the work of Hayyim of Volozhin, and in this work many of the connections between Levinas's life, his inscription into the chain of transmission, and his reading of Jewish texts are made apparent. My argument is not that Levinas claims to be expert on the work of Hayyim of Volozhin, or even faithful to it, though Levinas's appeal to Hayyim of Volozhin does make sense on intellectual grounds.[50] More important, the affiliation allows Levinas to insert himself into the lineage of Lithuanian Talmudists that began with Rabbi Elijah, the Gaon of Vilna (1720–97), and that was disseminated through the Yeshivah founded by his disciple Rabbi Hayyim of Volozhin (1749–1821). It also allows Levinas to align himself with the Mitnageddic school of interpretation, which saw itself as the counter to what Levinas calls the miraculous, mystical, and ultimately charismatic powers of the Hasidic rabbis. The tradition into which Levinas inserts himself comes from the land of his birth and conserves his own antimystical convictions. There is, therefore, something of revisionist autobiography in the qualities and positions Levinas finds in the work and influence of Hayyim of Volozhin, especially as it relates to Enlightenment thought and the place of the divine. Levinas tells us that:

> The influence of Rabbi Hayyim Volozhiner and the Talmudic studies that were renewed by the *yeshivah* of Volozhin, and the houses of study that were created after its example, perhaps also shows through in the way that the "Age of Enlightenment," the rationalism of the *Haskalah*, had been assumed by the Jewish communities of Eastern Europe. From the nineteenth century onwards they in fact found themselves progressively led towards studies that were different to those of the Torah, and towards which Western European Jewry had voluntarily been entering since the eighteenth century. This movement towards so called modern life really became apparent with the Russian, Polish, and Lithuanian Jews almost concurrently with the influence that can be attributed to the *yeshivah* of Volozhin. *But while undergoing the seduction of the West and its rationalist culture, Eastern Judaism, for the greater part, remained immunized against the temptations of pure and simple assimilation to the surrounding world.*[51]

The historical accuracy of the statement is less important to me than the way it confers a special place to Eastern European Jews, and thus to Levinas himself, as uniquely positioned to navigate between rational

Western discourse and the study of Torah. Most notable is the fact that Levinas's characterization of the simultaneous appropriation and resistance to the West and its rationalist culture is one that I would argue can only be applied to Levinas retrospectively. Nevertheless, Levinas does insert himself into the Lithuanian Talmudic chain of transmission as both an authority on Hayyim of Volozhin and as the embodiment of an Eastern European Jew who moves progressively "toward studies that were different to those of the Torah."[52]

The connection to the chain of transmission, even absent Levinas's actual participation in yeshivah during his youth, is further enforced in passages such as this one from a writing on Spinoza: "It would be a mistake to think that Jewish communities—and even their Rabbis—are at all times and all places the authentic interpreters of Talmudic tradition."[53] The essential point is that while arguing for the privileged place of the Talmudic interpreter who maneuvers between rational Western discourse and transcendent Talmudic meaning, he simultaneously authorizes himself as the inheritor and embodiment of that tradition. "The Judaism of the Talmudic schools—*or the memory of this Judaism as it persisted in families*—," and this is Levinas's relation, "was to protect the Jewish masses from assimilation," such as into secular Western culture, "as it had protected the Hasidic movement from schism" by curtailing the overemphasis on mysticism and charisma.[54]

As if to emphasize the particularly Jewish credentials of Levinas's position despite his own training in Western philosophy, status as a philosopher, and director of a school founded on the principals of French Enlightenment thought, Levinas makes clear that the writings of Hayyim Volozhin contain "absolutely nothing of the philosophy or the science of the new times. No Descartes, no Leibnitz, no Spinoza and—although only a few hundred kilometers away from Königsberg, Jena, and Berlin—no sign of Kant, Fichte or Hegel."[55] "But" Levinas continues, "if the proof remains exegetic from beginning to end, it is moreover, a question of an exegesis conducted according to the rabbinical mode, the mode of the *Midrash* which solicits the letter of the text in order to seek out, above and beyond the plain meaning, the hidden and allusive meaning."[56] This is a move away from Western philosophical sources and toward rabbinic authority but toward such an authority that embraces studies different from Torah and rejects mysticism or numenism.

From this position, Levinas is able to assert a humanism that is not atheism. This is to say, a confidence in the intellectual abilities of humankind that does not veer off into the hubris of atheism but achieves an understanding of our connection with God as revealed in sacred Jewish texts. "The whole course of the universe is decided at the bottom, in humans. . . . Consequently, the system of *mitzvot* acquires a cosmic import and, in its universality, confirms its ethical significance: to practice the commandments is to endure the being of the world."[57] For Levinas, the power of God is not as a miracle worker, puppet master, or disciplinarian but as the inspiration for good, for Ethics. "The Bible . . . is a book that leads us not towards the mystery of God, but towards the human tasks of man."[58] It is the conduit between God on God's own side and God on our side. Levinas looks to Hayyim of Volozhin and the Talmud to give divine credence to an argument he presents in *Totality and Infinity* but that also articulates a theology compatible with his post-Holocaust reality. As noted, on Levinas's reading God is not a direct actor in the world, although one might say that God directs our action through the instruction of Torah and Talmud. This is tied to Levinas's understanding of the human's role before God. "Associated with the world, God would not exhaust his religious significance, for he would thus represent only God from the human viewpoint—God 'on our side,' as *Nefesh ha'Hayyim* expresses it. But God also has a meaning in the Tetragrammaton, signifying something that man cannot define, formulate, or even name. . . . It is 'God on his own side.'"[59] God on its own side is characterized by the term *En-Sof* or Infinity while God on our side can only be understood within the limitations of the finite. Humanism and the tradition of rational secular historical understanding resides in the finite and is restricted by the limits of human comprehension. This comprehension can be pierced from without by the idea of God. "The human, therefore, would not be just a creature to whom revelation is made, but something through which the absolute of God reveals its meaning. This human impossibility of conceiving the Infinite is also a new possibility of signifying."[60] The absolute of God is revealed as a surplus that pierces the finite nature of our being revealing an opening to the Other. "The human finitude that it determines is not a simple psychological powerlessness, but a new possibility: the possibility of thinking of the Infinite and Law together, the very possibility of their conjunction."[61] The presence of God on God's own side guarantees the divine and permanent meaning of the text, while our understanding of God on our side allows that meaning to change and shift so as to remain relevant to our current context. Levinas's description of a God on God's own side, removed from and unmoved by human actions, is one that places responsibility squarely on human action.[62] While this is where Levinas wants it to reside in his ethical model, it also allows Levinas to account for a God that did not intervene during the Holocaust, and this too must be factored into our assessment of Levinas's reading and understanding of Talmud and Jewish texts.

As we saw in both the story of Moses-Akiva and of the glowing coals, Levinas's emphasis on the transcendence of meaning and dynamism of the text enabled him to restore life to a tradition, the Lithuanian Talmudic tradition, that was lost during the Holocaust, but it also allowed him to do so in a way that conserved his own particular talents and interests. Perhaps on entering one of Levinas's Talmudic lectures at the Colloque des intellectuels juifs de langue française, the Gaon of Vilna would have had the same reaction as Moses entering the academy of Akiva? Levinas forges a forced continuity based on transcendence and justified by his reading of the Talmud that enabled him to insert himself into the rabbinic chain of transmission following the Gaon of Vilna and Hayyim of Volozhin. It was also a move that allowed him to understand and account for this tradition in his modern context and in a post-Holocaust world. All of this returns us to the question posed at the beginning of the chapter: is it possible to be a master of a tradition in which one has not been properly trained? Levinas's initial answer implied "no," and while his reading and use of Talmud allowed Levinas to work through his own understanding of Judaism in a post-Holocaust world, he did not initially set out to be a Talmudic master, and thus the "debt to Torah" of which Levinas speaks in *Beyond the Verse*, for example, is one that he did not attempt to pay in the years before the war. Despite his own statements in many of his writings, Levinas also acknowledges the limits of his training, telling his audience that "one should not think after hearing me that the Jewish intellectuals of France now know what the Jewish tradition thinks of forgiveness. This is the danger of sporadic explanations of Talmudic texts, like ours, the danger of premature bad conscience, by the very sources of Jewish thought."[63] Perhaps Levinas's acknowledgment of his limits is a clue in itself reminding us that the genius of the reader or the writer is not where inspiration lies or where we should look to understand Levinas as a reader of Talmud and Jewish texts. Instead, we should look to the transcendent meaning of the text, the opening to the Other that always retains the potential to say more than it says.

CHAPTER 4

OUR SIDE

Hebrew into Greek

Translation and Exemplarism

THE OTHER SIDE

Contempt for the Torah as Idolatry

In his work for the ENIO through the Alliance Israélite Universelle and then via his lectures at the Colloque des intellectuels juifs de langue française, Levinas sought to construct a positive and authentic understanding of Jewish identity attuned to the realities of his contemporary world. As we have seen, such an authentic Judaism is not one of excessive piety, nor a mystical or emotional relation with God, but neither is it assimilated secularism. Instead, for Levinas, an authentic Judaism is one that conserves the rationalism of the Enlightenment yet moves beyond it in pursuit of what Levinas calls a religion for adults. This is an understanding of Judaism that relies on, and thus conserves, the three strands of the braid we have been weaving: Western philosophy, French Enlightenment Universalism, and the Lithuanian Talmudic tradition. For Levinas, it is a move past the tenets of atheism that brings one back to God

From the Tractate *Sanhedrin*, 99a and 99b:

> Rabbi Yehoshua ben Korha said: "Whoever studies the Torah without repeating the lesson is like a sower who does not reap." Rabbi Yehoshua said: "Whoever learns the Torah and forgets it is like a woman who brings a child into the world only to bury it."

> Rabbi Akiva said: "To each day its song, to each day its song." (44)[1]

The topic of this lecture is the relation of the Torah

purged of those aspects of religion or worship that he considered juvenile or overly exuberant. In this way, the move is reminiscent of Kant's process of maturation but in Levinas's model, the exemplary or authentic Jew is the one who has progressed through religion to scientific rationalism culminating in atheism and then found their way *back* to Judaism via Talmud. Yet, while this developmental process is undoubtedly at work, Levinas also contends that this sense of rational and enlightened humanistic thought was always already at play in Talmudic exegesis when properly performed.

For Levinas, it is because Judaism presupposes European humanism that its precepts and teachings are available to be translated to a larger and more diverse audience, as he attempted to do in his Talmudic lectures. This is one meaning of Levinas's oft-stated, and even more often cited, claim that in his Talmudic lectures and his confessional writings in general, his purpose was to translate "Hebrew into Greek." For the sake of clarity, Levinas's Talmudic lectures refer to the lectures he gave almost annually at the Colloque des intellectuels Juifs de langue française in Paris from 1960 to 1989, whereas Levinas's confessional writings are the occasional pieces written on topics that concern questions surrounding Judaism, many of which appeared in publications of the Alliance Israélite Universelle. As we have seen, a number of his writings published in books such as *Difficult Freedom* are more or less internal documents about the future of Jewish education, while others take up a to idolatry, and Levinas begins by directing us to the prohibition of idols, images, and other gods as the dominant message inscribed within the text. "I would like to speak of the Torah itself, the book of anti-idolatry, the absolute opposite of idolatry! A wisdom that does not permit itself to share the category of the religious with the non-religious or non-gods—whatever may have been their reality, their sociological and ethnographic extension" (CTI 46, MPI 70). The import and impact of this message is not dependent on the historical or sociological conditions and context in which the book was written. It is the message, the prohibition that Levinas wishes to interrogate, and one question we must ask is what, if anything, is problematic about the worship of idols? Is the prohibition against idolatry an axiomatic condition of Judaism, a commandment that simply must be obeyed? Or is there some deeper more philosophical approach to the question of what it means to be a Jew after the Holocaust. Because many of Levinas's collections include writings from both genres they have often been grouped together, and certainly Levinas himself places them in the same category or genre in relation to the project of translating Hebrew into Greek.

The statement, "translating Hebrew into Greek," has been interpreted in myriad and disparate ways from Annette Aronowicz's very positive understanding of the statement as making universal what is or was particular (which she does in the introduction to her translation of Levinas's first two books of Talmudic lectures, *Nine Talmudic Readings*), to the very critical analyses of Andrew McGettigan in "The Philosopher's Fear of Alterity," or John Drabinski's rehabilitative *Levinas and the Postcolonial*, in which the McGettigan and Drabinski pieces each see the statement and Levinas's endeavor as a privileging of European or Western thought. The stakes of such an understanding are high because whether employed by critics or disciples, "there is something presupposed in Levinas's conception of Europe that not only make . . . racist and xenophobic utterances possible, but even makes them necessary."[1] McGettigan argues that "those who have sought resources in Levinas for a project of anti-racism have been confounded by some of his [negative or disparaging] comments about non-Western cultures. . . . My strong claim [is] that the problematic of implication toward which Levinas directs us?

Levinas continues: "I wish to speak of the Torah as desirous of being a force warding off idolatry by its essence as Book, that is, by its very writing, signifying precisely prescription, and by the permanent reading it calls for—permanent reading or interpretation and re-interpretation or study; a book thus destined from the start for its Talmudic life" (CTI 46, MPI 70–71). Here we have a clue, as the Torah, itself, cannot ward off idolatry but instead does so by means of its status as a book that not only contains prescriptions but also demands interpretation. This call for a permanent reading links the Torah to the Talmud. From the start, the Talmud or oral Torah was required to not only activate the written Torah but also to keep it from ossifying into a hardened and fixed state, like a statue or an idol. The Torah does not ward the face [of the Other] is at root mobilized in a valorization of the Judaeo-Christian legacy against those who come from outside 'the West.'"[2] This leads McGettigan to a stinging and total critique of Levinas and his work because to his mind "the two problems—metaphysical apparatus and unpalatable comments—are fundamentally connected through Levinas's conception of transcendence."[3] For McGettigan, what one might call Levinas's psychological attitudes toward Europe, European culture, and non-European cultures or practices are inextricably bound to his philosophical understanding of the human condition, sociality, and ethics. On this reading, Levinas's promotion and elevation of a particular ethics or face (Jewish, European/Greek) impeaches the possibility that such an ethics could be truly universal.

Fred Moten responds to this claim in *The Universal Machine* (the conclusion to his trilogy in which he explores the relation between blackness and phenomenology via a suite of essays on Levinas, Arendt, and Fanon) when he asks: "How does Levinas's arrival at the cusp of a clear vision of the end of philosophy as decolonization, as an abolition both internally and externally directed in its relation to what he will come to speak of under the rubric of 'escape,' turn into another version of the same (racism), however unintended?"[4] These are the questions we will take up in this chapter in relation to Levinas's Talmudic lectures and the project of translating Hebrew into Greek.[5]

off idolatry because it is divine, which it is, but because it is a book. The call to interpretation of the Book also provides the means for the Torah to move in time and place. "The Talmudic life and destiny of the Torah, which is also an endless return, in its interpretation of several degrees, to particular cases, to the concreteness of reality, to analyses that never lose themselves in generalities but return to the examples—resisting invariable conceptual entities" (CTI 46, MPI 71). The reading of the Torah, which Talmudic life demands, forces the reader to place the writings within the context of their particular time and place. The reader must come to understand how the commandments held within the Book make sense in light of their "concrete reality" and "particular cases." The general or universal rule is never enough and must be brought into contact with the actualities of the day.

First, it is worth noting that Levinas himself saw the project of his Jewish or confessional writings as separate or distinct from his philosophical writings, going so far as to make sure that he had a different press for the publication of each. Now, whether he saw his philosophical writings as falling under the category of Greek and his writings on topics of Jewish concern as Hebrew is itself an open and important question related to the ones already posed. What we can say is that Levinas never stated the need for translation in reference to his philosophical writings, whereas it is something like the raison d'être for the confessional ones.

So what does it mean for Emmanuel Levinas to translate "Hebrew into Greek"? A common place to look is in his Talmudic lecture "The Translation of the Scriptures," which he presented at the Twenty-third Colloque des intellectuels juifs de langue française in 1983.

> I have proceeded on my own, of course, in attributing to the Greek language the order, clarity, method, desire to move from the simple to the complex, and especially the unbiased quality of the language of Europe—or at least the language of the university such as it should be, the language a European university professor cultivates and speaks, even when denouncing the language of the university and rehabilitating the "savage mind" [a reference to Lévi-Strauss's *La pensée sauvage*]. I say it again a bit differently—and, for me, this is

Invariable conceptual entities are to be avoided, perhaps, as one resists an idol. "Thus to base one's Jewishness on the teaching of a book is to see oneself above all as a reader, i.e., as a student of the Torah, and to turn away from idolatry by true reading or study. The reading or study of a text that protects itself from eventual idolatry of this very text, by renewing, through continual exegesis—and exegesis of that exegesis—the immutable letters and hearing the breath of the living God in them" (CTI 46, MPI 71). It is the reading and study of Torah that keeps one from idolatry and from worship of the physical object that the Torah is. A temptation that can become more powerful than the golden calf. On Levinas's reading, the Torah too, can become an idol.

This is not to deny or resist the divine origin and power of the Torah. Instead, it is to resist the beauty of Greece that must dwell in the tents of Shem: the language of deciphering.[6]

In this quote we can see the basis for the disparate understandings of what it means to translate "Hebrew into Greek" based on whether one emphasizes the order, clarity, and method of Greek as the language of deciphering or the assumption that there is a direct lineage from Greek to European thought that distinguishes it from the "savage mind." I will come back to these understandings, but first I'd like to point out that for Levinas, translating Hebrew into Greek refers both to a need or desire for philosophy to express what is essential in Jewish thought (which is also a desire for proximity to Europe and European thought) and to the translation of the Hebrew Bible into Greek, this is the Septuagint. In regard to the translation of the Hebrew Bible into Greek, in the same lecture Levinas tells us that "the Greek Bible very quickly replaced the Hebrew one, which was read without being understood in the synagogue. Philo knew no other." The two types of translation are of course related as the reference to Philo suggests, and Levinas asserts that in the Talmudic portion he is discussing in that lecture, there is the "sense of a sign of divine approval given to the undertaking itself of translating the Pentateuch into Greek—that is, [in the text] the approval of Rabbi Shimon Gamliel's position. . . . Do we not have here at least some indication of the sense in which rabbinic Judaism wishes to be a part of Europe? . . . a certain 'assimilation

ascribing physical qualities to God in the medium of the Torah: "A God not incarnate, surely, but somehow inscribed, whose life, or a part of it, is being lived in the letters: in the lines and between the lines and in the exchange of ideas between the readers commenting upon them—where these letters come alive and are echoed in the book's precepts—ordering without enslaving, like truth—to answer in justice to one's fellow, that is, to love the other" (CTI 47, MPI 71). The qualities of God are inscribed, not ascribed, and to study the commandments is to wrestle with the commitments in regard to actual others (be they human or not) that one encounters. This is "a liturgy of study as lofty as obedience to the precepts," but one that does not stop at precepts because it is "a never-ending study, for one is never done with the other" (CTI 47, MPI 72). One cannot stop or rest content with what has to Europe' not rejected by the Talmudic doctors as purely negative."⁷

The reference to the Septuagint is important because it points to the possibility of making the ancient texts accessible to a modern audience and also a larger audience. The reference to philosophy holds equal weight for Levinas because it is a call to rigorous and careful thought, "the language of deciphering." The two aspects converge in relation to Levinas's own goals for Judaism and Jewish thought after World War II. We see this in the makeup of the audience for his Talmudic lectures at the Colloque des intellectuels juifs de langue française, which at its inception in 1957 consisted of many assimilated French intellectuals of Jewish heritage, such as the philosopher Jean Wahl, whose self-identification as a Jew was bound up with the Vichy-era policies of persecution. Here, translating Hebrew into Greek was a strategy for making a positive Jewish identity available and accessible to assimilated Jewish intellectuals with little or no background in Jewish ritual practice let alone knowledge of Torah or Talmud. For many, though not all, of the initial participants at the Colloque, the language of philosophy was far more familiar than the language of Torah or Talmud. They were disciples of Bergson and Husserl rather than Maimonides and the Gaon of Vilna. This leads to a second equally important point. In these lectures and in his writings, Levinas sought to establish himself in the Mitnageddic tradition of the Lithuanian

been revealed or done or said in the past. It is this "incompleteness that is the law of love," and as such "it is the future itself, the coming of a world that never ceases coming, but also the excellence of that coming compared to presence as persistence in being and in what has always been" (CTI 47, MPI 72). The incompleteness is a sign of the dynamism that propels us toward a better future, which Levinas contrasts to the stasis of persistence in being and what has been. Thus one way to understand the problem of idolatry is as a belief in a static object worthy of adoration and adulation that will either tell one what to do or do those things that one tells it.

Levinas makes reference to a midrash quoted earlier at the Colloque "according to which the entire Torah would signify nothing but the forbidding of idolatry, so that the various ways of 'scorning the Torah,' of which the text

Talmudic academies, which saw itself as counter to what Levinas calls the miraculous, mystical, and ultimately charismatic powers of the Hasidic rabbis. The tradition into which Levinas inserts himself as reader and teacher of Talmud came from the land of his birth and conserves his antimystical convictions. As we have seen, there is something of revisionist autobiography in the qualities and positions Levinas finds in the work and influence of the famous Lithuanian Talmudists, the Gaon of Vilna and Hayyim of Volozhin, given that Levinas did not attend a Talmudic academy or study Talmud during his youth in Lithuania but came to it in France after World War II. It is not difficult to draw a correlation between Levinas's emphasis on the Gaon of Vilna's call for a rational Talmudic science and dialectic, in opposition to the "sentimental mysticism" of the Hasidic movement,[8] and Levinas's own training in philosophy with his preference for close textual analysis and the contemplative life over and above claims to direct experience, sentimentalism, or mysticism. This is one strand of the braid.

The other strands can be seen in Levinas's desire to reach his intended, assimilated, audience via rational philosophical argument based on close textual analysis in which we see Levinas's allegiance to Europe, the project of the Enlightenment, and thus in some sense to Christianity. It is equally important to note that this allegiance is not an uncritical one. The Universalism and rationalism that Levinas we are now considering speaks, would indicate various ways of incurring the risk of idolatry or of succumbing to it, falling to different depths" (CTI 48, MPI 72). This is a different though related issue where to scorn the Torah is to invite, if not commit, idolatry. In particular, Levinas is interested in the "various ways of no longer hearing, or wrongly hearing, the monotheistic Revelation" (CTI 48, MPI 72). The prohibition against the worship of actual idols is low-hanging fruit, it is the scorn for the Torah inherent in misreading that poses a more pernicious problem. "The latent birth of its nature must already be detectable in Israel's wavering faithfulness to the Torah, and in what is said to be contempt for the Torah, and even in the faulty reading of it" (CTI 48, MPI 72). Fidelity to the Torah lies in the proper reading and rereading of its contents, but the possibility of misreading and misunderstanding ascribes to Greek and thus to European thought is attractive, powerful, and seductive, but as such Levinas also sees it as problematic. This is one way to understand his 1964 Talmudic lecture on "The Temptation of Temptation." As we have seen, in the figure and philosophy of Heidegger, Levinas detected the limitations and ultimate paucity of the Western philosophical tradition whose origins he places in Greece, which, absent any Divine connection, became completely unmoored from ethical direction.[9]

In his Talmudic lecture, "Model of the West," from the seventeenth Colloquium in 1976, Levinas states that "Greek wisdom is an opening but it is also the possibility of speaking through signs which are not universally understood and which, as signs of complicity, thus have the power to betray. Greek wisdom, inasmuch as it is enveloped by ambiguity in a certain language, is thus a weapon of ruse and domination. In philosophy, it is the fact that it is open to sophistry; in science, that it places itself in the service of strength and politics."[10] For Levinas, the ultimate and most damning proof of the inadequacy of Greek or European thought was the Holocaust, the extermination of six million Jews including Levinas's immediate family in Lithuania. In his 1961 piece "Jewish Thought Today," Levinas wrote: "Many Jews continue to think that the rational aesthetic and political values of Graeco-Roman humanism are the true foundation for the understanding between Jews and Christians, just as they has always been an issue. Contempt for the Torah is the result of this wavering faithfulness. Levinas turns to the proposition from Mishna 90a, which is the source of the discussion in 99a and b of the tractate Sanherin: "Among those who have no share in the world to come, there is the one who says of the Torah that it is not from heaven" (CTI 48, MPI 73). Levinas provides two cases: "You do not have your share in the future world when you doubt the heavenly origin of the Torah, violating its prohibitions if you are an *apikoros*, or if you interpret the Torah in a way contrary to the Halakhah—contrary to the practical law of conduct that is applied traditionally. These are various manners of dejudaization!" (CTI 49, MPI 73).

In regard to the first, Levinas tell us that "the identification of one who scorns the Torah with the *apikoros* requires an explanation. In its accepted form the basis for understanding all religions," but "the extermination of the Jews signified a crisis for the world that Christianity had modeled for twenty centuries."[11] To Levinas's mind, Greek thought, and the Christian European tradition he takes to be its heir, lacks Ethics and thus, despite his affinity and attraction to this tradition, he believed it must be challenged in the name of ethical responsibility. What's more, the events of World War II and his own internment in a German camp for Jewish Prisoners of War made him keenly aware that the European tradition was one to which he did not entirely belong and from which he could be excluded.

As demonstrated, Levinas was unwilling to completely forsake this tradition. He goes so far as to reference "the Greek wisdom which the Talmudists admired."[12] Instead, Levinas argues for a link between Judaism and the Western tradition of philosophy, the realization of the universal aspirations of philosophy made manifest through the particular tradition of Judaism: "It is not by virtue of simple chance that the way towards the synthesis of the Jewish revelation and Greek thought was masterfully traced by Maimonides, who is claimed by both Jewish and Muslim philosophers; that a profound respect for Greek knowledge already fills the wise men of the Talmud; that education for the Jew merges with instruction and the ignorant man can never really be pious."[13] Thus the project of translating "Hebrew into Greek" is to serve as a corrective to meaning today, this word designates the unbeliever" (CTI 49, MPI 74). In regard to the second, he explains that: "One who interprets the Torah in a sense contrary to the traditional rules of conduct takes the Torah as a product of culture available for intellectual jousting matches, drawing-room amusement, 'purely theoretical' views devoid of responsibility" (CTI 50, MPI 74). The obvious references here are to: (1) unbelievers or *apikoros*; and (2) those scholars and modern thinkers who take the Torah to be a product of purely human origins, which is to say as a historical artifact. Of course, the two can be related as in the secular academic use of the Torah or perhaps the privileging of a modern vantage point that assumes our position in the present to be more advanced and thus superior to anything smacking of the past. Such interpretations attempt to translate the Torah from a divine register the Greek or European tradition wherein the ethical imperative revealed by the study of Talmud is to be disseminated via the universal language of philosophy. An essential goal of Levinas's lectures and writings on Jewish scripture was to lead educated and intelligent men and women through their training in Western philosophy back to Revelation and through them back to Ethics.[14]

This is one reason that Levinas refers to Judaism as "A Religion for Adults," because his understanding of monotheism is shorn of mysticism and direct divine interface or intervention. Indeed, he goes so far as to claim that secular explanations for phenomena that have no recourse to the divine are more proximate to his understanding of Judaism than most conventional understandings of religion. As we saw in chapter 2, Levinas tells us that "atheism is much closer to the One God than the mystical experiences and horrors of the Sacred to be found in the supposed religious revivals of our contemporaries," and in one of his first Talmudic lectures he claims, "Judaism adores its God while remaining acutely aware of all of atheism's reasons or Reason."[15] Levinas saw the interventions and innovations of European philosophy as a necessary step in human intellectual development leading us away from an understanding of God and religion based on folklore or mythology, where fantastic deities intervened miraculously, to an understanding of God established on rational human action and human choices:

into a secular one either as an object of scorn or of purely academic interest which, Levinas tells us, "is the attempt to seek for them a translation that the properly religious surplus of truth already presupposes" (CTI 49, MPI 74).

We should dwell on this "surplus of truth," for it is this aspect of the Torah that maintains its dynamism and its connection between the past and the future. "The Torah is transcendent and from heaven by its demands that clash, in the final analysis, with the pure ontology of the world." Any attempt to turn the Torah into an immanent object is an attempt to deactivate its dynamism, but beyond this, it renders it an ontological object rather than an ethical teaching. "The Torah demands, in opposition to the natural perseverance of each being in his or her own being (a fundamental ontological law), care for the stranger, the widow and the orphan, responsibility. "It is a great glory" he writes "for the Creator to have set up a being who affirms Him after having contested and denied him in the glorious areas of myth and enthusiasm; it is a great glory for God to have created a being capable of seeking Him or hearing Him from afar after having experienced separation and atheism."[16] This is a world understood through the lens of rational secular thought but open to a relation with the divine that provides an ethical ground or backstop that keeps reason from devolving into sophistry or the will to power. From this position Levinas is able to assert a humanism that is not atheism. "The whole course of the universe is decided at the bottom, in humans. . . . Consequently, the system of *mitzvot* acquires a cosmic import and, in its universality, confirms its ethical significance: to practice the commandments is to endure the being of the world."[17] For Levinas, the power of God is not as a miracle worker, puppet master, or disciplinarian but as the inspiration for good, for Ethics. In this light "The Bible . . . is a book that leads us not towards the mystery of God, but towards the human tasks of man."[18]

This is where Levinas's retrospective refashioning of himself as inheritor of the Lithuanian Talmudic tradition is essential for understanding his project of translating Hebrew into Greek without succumbing to either the temptation of assimilation or regression to an irrational form of religious belief, specifically Hasidism. In reference to the Lithuanian Mitnageddic tradition, a preoccupation with the other person. A reversal of the order of things! We do not have as much awe as we should at this reversal of ontology into ethics, and, in a sense, the dependency within it of being on the dis-interestment of justice" (CTI 49, MPI 74). The dis-interestment of justice implies an ethics untethered from the essence or identity of any given being, and yet Levinas is well aware that in the practice of everyday life there is no such thing as a perfect or unconditional disinterestedness. We are all, at some level, bound to identity, but our identity cannot be the basis of our ethics or actions. The ethics or justice we are called to enact must be one without any interest in the parties involved, especially proximity to oneself or one's "people." It is a precept that commands justice for the eternity of the present, and thus it is a commandment that must continuously be fulfilled. We should also recognize

Levinas tells us that the Gaon of Vilna resisted the spread of Hasidism because this "popular movement, demanding more fervor than knowledge, denied Talmudic science and dialectic their primary place in Jewish religious life, and that by grouping the communities around spiritual personalities with charismatic power—the *Tsadikim* or the 'miraculous Rabbis' who did not refuse the adoration of the faithful—it changed the true relations between disciple and master, and undermined the fundamental principles of Jewish monotheism."[19] For Levinas, Jewish monotheism cannot be achieved through charismatic personalities or miraculous rabbis. But neither can it be achieved solely by adopting the principals of Enlightenment thought, for he also tells us:

> The influence of Rabbi Hayyim Volozhiner and the Talmudic studies that were renewed by the *yeshivah* of Volozhin, and the houses of study that were created after its example, perhaps also shows through in the way that the "Age of Enlightenment," the rationalism of the *Haskalah*, had been assumed by the Jewish communities of Eastern Europe. From the nineteenth century onwards they in fact found themselves progressively led towards studies that were different to those of the Torah, and towards which Western European Jewry had voluntarily been entering since the eighteenth century. This movement towards so called modern life really became apparent with the Russian, Polish, and Lithuanian Jews almost concurrently with a disconnect from an ontology Levinas associates with the Greeks, and this should in turn condition any understanding of what it might mean to translate "Hebrew into Greek." "Incompleteness that is the law of love: it is the future itself, the coming of a world that never ceases coming, but also the excellence of that coming compared to presence as persistence in being and in what has always been. A world to come, to be conceived in a way different from that of the Greeks" (CTI 47, MPI 72).

This "world to come" marks an important pivot in our understanding of contempt for the Torah as idolatry. For in such idolatry the transgressor makes the Torah an object of the past or an object in the present and in so doing disregards its power to shape the future. The tractate references Numbers 15:31 and Levinas directs us to the citation: "'Cut off he shall be, cut off'—this means cut off from this the influence that can be attributed to the *yeshivah* of Volozhin. *But while undergoing the seduction of the West and its rationalist culture, Eastern Judaism, for the greater part, remained immunized against the temptations of pure and simple assimilation to the surrounding world.*[20]

As stated earlier, the historical accuracy of the statement is less important to me than the way it confers a special place to Eastern European Jews of the Mitnageddic tradition, and thus to Levinas himself, as uniquely positioned to navigate between rational Western discourse (Greek) and the study of Torah (Hebrew). Most notable is the fact that Levinas's characterization of the simultaneous appropriation and resistance to the West and its rationalist culture is one that can only be applied to Levinas retrospectively. Nevertheless, Levinas does insert himself into the Lithuanian Talmudic chain of transmission as both an authority on the Gaon of Vilna and Hayyim of Volozhin and as the embodiment of an Eastern European Jew who moves progressively "toward studies that were different to those of the Torah" in ways that conserve his particular interest and training in European philosophy.

Thus there is much that is laudable in Levinas's translation project, which is in line with Aronowicz's assessment, but the special relationship that Levinas articulates between Hebrew and Greek, between a certain conception of Judaism and Europe, also serves to create a formidable and I would say double blind spot in his project.

world and cut off from the world to come" (CTI 51, MPI 76), and then he explains that "to the eschatological sanction—which may not be perceived as particularly disturbing—there is therefore added a sanction threatening this present world!" (CTI 51, MPI 71). When one is cut off from the world to come, one is also cut off from the world in which one lives. By deactivating the possibility of justice in the future the idolater threatens not only their future but their present as well. Indeed, the act of cutting oneself off from the future is in itself an act of cutting oneself off from the present. Levinas asks whether such an injunction is indicative of the "jealousy and violence of an Old Testament? Or the danger of a form of idolatry that worships visible certainty?" (CTI 51, MPI 76). It is the latter that correlates to the secular world in which definitive evidence produced by human intellect is the sole arbiter of certainty, a form

This is because, as we have seen, Levinas buys into the fantasy that European culture and philosophy is the privileged direct inheritor, and thus proprietary owner as it were, of Greek thought and by extension the claim to "Universalism," though as we have also seen not without caveats and correctives. This leads to the second blind spot, which is Levinas's emphasis on an *even more* privileged place for the tradition of Jewish thought, and specifically Jewish texts, in which he designates the Jew as the "other" par excellence, the exemplary other, to the likely exclusion of all other others. Thus, firstly, as per McGettigan and Drabinski, Levinas privileges the Jewish and Greek/European traditions to the exclusion of all other cultures, which leads to the "unintended racism" detected by Moten. These excluded cultures are what Drabinski calls "the other Other."[21] Secondly, Levinas privileges Judaism above Greek/Europe.

This returns us to the problematic issues of authenticity and exemplarity with which we concluded chapter 1 and began this chapter. The complexity of the problem can be seen in Levinas's presentation of the idea of election. "Hence the idea of election which can deteriorate into pride but which originally expresses the awareness of an indisputable summons which gives life to ethics and through which the indisputability of the summons isolates the personal responsibility."[22] On the one hand, such a summons is a call to personal responsibility, which gives life to ethics. On the other hand, the election is a moment of idolatry that worships visible certainty.

Levinas returns to the tractate:

> Another baraita: "For having scorned the word of the Lord"—this refers to one who says: "The Torah is not from heaven." And even if he says: "The whole Torah is from heaven except this verse, which Moses said on his own initiative," that still means: He has scorned the word of the Lord— And even if he says: "The whole Torah comes from heaven, except this deduction, except this a fortiori or this 'proof by analogy'" it is still: He has scorned the word of the Lord. (CTI 52, MPI 76)

Levinas explains that, "Obviously we may read here, on the first level, an absolute negation of all human intervention in the writing of the Torah, and hence a condemnation in advance of all critical exploration of the biblical text on grounds of idolatry" (CTI 52, MPI of separation, of hierarchical elevation, and of the temptation to assume such an election implies an exemplary and privileged position.[23]

In *The Universal Machine*, Fred Moten identifies some of the most troubling aspects in Levinas's thought where privilege and exemplarity trample on the ethical message. It is worth reproducing the portion of the interview between Levinas and Christoph von Wolzogen with which Moten begins his chapter.

> E. L.: I always say—but under my breath—that the Bible and the Greeks present the only serious issues in human life; everything else is dancing. I think these texts are open to the whole world. There is no racism intended.
>
> Q. "Everything else is dancing"—one could naturally think of Nietzsche.
>
> E. L.: Yes, but you know, television shows the horrible things occurring in South Africa. And there, when they bury people, they dance. Have you seen this? That is really some way to express mourning.
>
> Q. It too is an expression.
>
> E. L.: Yes, of course, so far I am still a philosopher. But it supplies us the expression of a dancing civilization; they weep differently.[24]

In a separate interview cited by Moten, Levinas replies to a question about structuralism by stating: "It [structuralism] certainly responds, from a moral perspective, to what 76–77). At first glance, this appears to be an injunction against critical scholarship, which borders on censorial anti-intellectualism. "But," Levinas asks, "are we not, in reading the text in this way, being too impatient? Everything depends on how we understand the unity of a spiritual work, and the spiritual unity of a people who are the bearers of such a work, even if the human may have to intervene in the very formulation of the word of God. Is the human not the very modality of the manifestation and resonance of the Word?" (CTI 52, MPI 77). Critical human intervention finds its place because humans have to interact critically to make the word of God intelligible, and yet it is imperative that the interpreters do not place themselves above the word of God with which they are engaging. This is about translation. Translating the word of God into the language of human beings.

one calls decolonization and the end of a dominating Europe, but my reaction is primary—it is, I know worse than primitive: can one compare the scientific intellect of Einstein with the 'savage mind' . . . ? How can a world of scientific thinking and of communication through scientific thinking be compared to it?"[25] Even if one brackets the reference to Lévi-Strauss, the sentiment expressed in both cases displays a hierarchy of thought and culture in which European superiority is simply beyond compare. This problematic line of thinking is especially pronounced in Levinas's dismissal of all peoples and religions that are not monotheistic. These peoples are often described as underdeveloped, irrational, and thus at some level primitive. In "Jewish Thought Today," a scant two pages after Levinas extols the possibility of Jewish thought engaging with universal humanity of every faith and nation, he asks whether "the rise of the countless masses of Asiatic and under-developed peoples threaten this new found authenticity?" His answer further betrays his own prejudices and fears as he frets that "under the greedy eyes of these countless hordes who wish to hope and live, we the Jews and Christians are pushed to the margin of history."[26]

Moten asks: "How does a kind of sneering dismissal of 'what one calls decolonization and the end of a dominating Europe' (reduced here to a mere object for structuralist thought) emerge from the thinker of the terrible interplay of universalization and force? . . . How does Levinas's arrival at the cusp of a clear vision of the end of

In this light, Levinas seeks to recuperate and rehabilitate the critical or scholarly reading of Torah and Talmud from its idolatrous conclusions. "'To be the Torah from heaven': is this its origin going back to a kind of transcendental dictation, or the affirmation of this life in the Torah? And whatever may be the vicissitudes and divisions and traces of 'histories' that the historian's eye discerns in the contributing elements of inspiration, the confluence into a unique, coherent message (one sole Judaism through the millennia) of the many human meanderings of prophecy and rabbinic discussions—*is not that confluence as miraculous, as supernatural, as a common origin of sources, imagined to be as unique as the voice of an oracle?*" (CTI 52, MPI 77, my emphasis). Levinas tells us that even if the Torah and Talmud are historically determined and developed, its existence is no less miraculous than had an oracle received it philosophy as decolonization, as an abolition both internally and externally directed in its relation to what he will come to speak of under the rubric of 'escape,' turn into another version of the same (racism), however unintended?"[27] Moten, McGettigan, and Drabinski are surely right to point to Levinas's privileging of the Bible, the Greeks, and Europe as the likely source for this view. In doing so they also point to the influence of Franz Rosenzweig on Levinas as an equally likely source.

Levinas's first public lecture at the Colloque des intellectuels juifs de langue française, "Entre Deux Mondes (Biographie spirituelle Franz Rosenzweig)," translated as "Between Two Worlds," was focused on Rosenzweig and the privileged relation between Jewish and Christian/European thought. In *The Star of Redemption*, Rosenzweig makes clear his reasons for privileging this axis over all others. Rosenzweig tells us that "it is no coincidence that the Revelation, when it went out into the world, did not take the path of the East but that of the West. The living 'gods of Greece' were worthier opponents for the living God than were the phantoms of the Asiatic East. The godheads of China and India are immense edifices built from the blocks of ancestral times; like monoliths, they still tower up to this day in the cults of the 'primitives.'"[28] For Rosenzweig, as for Levinas, the West is the source of Revelation while the Asiatic East is the source for the cult of primitives. "India and China, the people that dream with

directly from God. What is most important about the Torah is not the fact that Moses received it, which would result in a fetish for Moses and a Revelation given in the past, but its continuing existence as a living Revelation that propels us into the future. "I have always admired a midrash that traces back to the voice heard at Sinai all that will be said in the way of expositions and lessons, objections and questions, the entire future accumulation of study of the Torah from the Decalogue to our own time, including the questions that the children in elementary school would ask their schoolmasters teaching them the Hebrew alphabet. Revelation in its fullness of life!" (CTI 52–53, MPI 77).

By contrast, "Idolatry would be the reduction of these sources to the histories and anecdotes lived by the individuals of the past, instead of sensing in them the prophecy of persons and the genius of eyes closed and the people that dream with eyes open—are the heirs of man of primitive times who takes refuge in the delirium of the world because he lacks the courage to observe the world; and once again the Greeks, the people of discoverers, are the guides of our breed on the road of clarity."²⁹ Rosenzweig sets up a historical trajectory of development where "India and China which stopped on the way before reaching the goal, never reached the tragic neither in the dramatic work of art nor in the prefiguring of the folk-tale."³⁰ By contrast, Europe and the West guided by the Greeks took the road to clarity on which Rosenzweig finds the Jewish-Christian axis of Creation, Revelation, and Redemption.

In a speech delivered to the French Students' Union at the Mutualité in the winter of 1959, "Monotheism and Language," Levinas groups all three monotheistic religions together, extolling "the long historical collaboration between Jews, Christians and Muslims, their geographical proximity as Mediterranean neighbors, the way in which they intermingle throughout in our world of homogenous structures, the real world that mocks anachronisms, creates, whether we like it or not, a *de facto* community between Jews, Muslims and Christians—even if serious misunderstandings separate them and even if they are opposed to one another."³¹ While Levinas presents an alliance of the three religions against the world of homogenous structures, it turns out to be the relationship between monotheism and Greek thought, not between Jews, Muslims, and a people, and hearing in them the birth of the message for all, and the voice of God in its extreme straightness through the appearance of the tortuous paths it takes" (CTI 53, MPI 77). The divine source becomes an idol, a motionless statue when it is robbed of its futural movement. As a history, all that is legible is the torturous path of one particular people while what is effaced is the message for all, the voice of God in its extreme straightness. If this is so, "then our baraita is right after all. It criticizes the historian who, in the voice of Moses, hears only an everyday, private discourse, and who is content to reduce the meaning of a biblical verse to its hither side—the circumstances, dictated by events, leading to its coming to mind; content to seek in the logical configurations themselves in which the verse is developed nothing but the trace of I know not what social or ideological condition of

Christians, that is the essential factor. "It is because the monotheists have enabled the world to hear the word of the one and only God that Greek universalism can separate in humanity and slowly unify that humanity."³² The emphasis on a community of monotheists is deceptive as it pertains to Islam because its importance is confined to the role it plays in conveying Greek thought to modern Europe. "The memory of a common contribution to European civilization in the course of the Middle Ages, when Greek texts entered Europe via the Jewish translators who had translated Arab translations . . ."³³ Here again, it is notable that Levinas follows the influence of Rosenzweig in creating a Jewish-Christian axis and not a Jewish-Muslim or Jewish-Christian-Muslim one. Whereas Rosenzweig differentiated Judaism and Christianity from the nonmonotheistic "Eastern" cultures, which he took to be the source of the cult of primitives, he saw Islam as inferior to Judaism and Christianity in terms of its originality and relation to paganism. "Mohammed," Rosenzweig writes, "found and took over the idea of Revelation as one picks up a find, that is to say without producing it from out of its presuppositions." As such, Islam is a "remarkable case of world historical plagiarism . . . what a belief in Revelation would necessarily look like when springing directly from paganism so to speak, without God's will, without the plan of his providence, that is, in 'purely natural' causality."³⁴

The demotion of Islam is surprising and disappointing not only because of the affinities between the religions of monotheism nonnarrative historical analysis" (CTI 53, MPI 77–78). Of course, as we saw in our discussion of "The Temptation of Temptation," this is one way to understand the history of Moses, the Torah, and the Jewish people. But as we also saw, this can be a limiting understanding. "Respect for the Torah depends on the way it is read" (CTI 53, MPI 78). It is not the context in which the Torah was given that is important nor its status as a religious object. It is the act of reading and interpreting the Torah that brings Revelation to life.

One must, of course, know how to read and wrestle with the Torah in the correct way, and this is why any discussion of reading is also one of education, of teachers and students. "The student, being both other and, generally speaking, younger, must come with questions, in the name of the future, and boldly, despite the respect due to the master. The student and the interconnections of the three in the transmission of Greek philosophy but also because of Levinas's work for the Alliance Israélite Universelle and the École Normale Israélite Orientale where he was charged with the education of Jewish youth from predominantly North African countries who came to Paris for their training before the axis of education shifted to Israel. Of course, the mission and reach of the Alliance Israélite Universelle (including the use of French as its language of instruction) also points to the privileging of European values and the *mission civilisatrice* that accompanied them. While the engagement or relationship with European Christianity is prevalent throughout Levinas's writings, the possibility of a relationship with Islam, or what this relationship could mean, is sparse at best. The issue becomes increasingly problematic not only over time given the historical realities of French decolonization and the Algerian conflict but also, and more visibly, in terms of Levinas's evaluation and allegiance to the State of Israel.

"Between Two Worlds" is what one might call Levinas's proto-Talmudic lecture, in which he affirmed the special relation he saw between Judaism and Christianity in his discussion of Rosenzweig's return to Judaism through his pursuit of Christianity. "This double movement," Levinas tells us, "towards Christianity and then Judaism, is not of interest to us only as a psychological curiosity. It bears witness to the destiny of modern European Judaism, which can no longer ignore the fact that for two thousand

will ask questions based on what the Torah will mean tomorrow" (CTI 54, MPI 78). Teaching, in this sense, is not only about what happened in the past. It is not solely a list of things that were done, it is also a call to take up what still must be done. "The Torah not only reproduces what was taught yesterday, it is read according to tomorrow; it does not stop at the representation of what yesterday and today goes by the name of the present" (CTI 54, MPI 78). The Torah engenders a relation between teacher and student that is itself a relationship with the future that is open to change and, as such, open to the other. "The Mishnah is the tradition of the oral Law which was added at Sinai to the written Torah. But it is also the non-written with all its possibilities—it is that which is beyond the verse, awakening it" (CTI 54, MPI 79). The relation between the oral Law and the written Law, years now Christianity has been a determining force in Western life."³⁵ From the outset, Levinas pairs these two forces and cites Rosenzweig to explicate the nature of this special relationship: "The exceptional position of Judaism and Christianity consists precisely in the fact that, even when they become religious, they retain within themselves the power to free themselves from the *nature* of this religion, and rediscover themselves to return to the open field of reality" in a "New Way of Thinking."³⁶ Unlike the religions of the East or even Islam, Levinas, following Rosenzweig, sees Christianity and Judaism as holding within themselves the ability to move beyond the initial constraints of those religions. Levinas goes so far as to say that,

> We therefore owe to Rosenzweig (I think this is self-evident, but the word 'religion' provokes so much violent reaction as soon as we utter it that it is best to recall) the fact that he reminds us of a notion of religion that is totally different from the one that secularism combats and is put forth, as though emerging in the economy of being, at the very level on which philosophical thought emerges. No one is more hostile than Rosenzweig to the unctuous, mystical, pious, homiletic, clerical notion of religion and of a religious person, a notion that reformism, attacking the integral nature of the ritual, has never managed to surpass, and whose immodesty it even emphasized through its open display of the so called religious soul.³⁷

enacted in discussion and disputation, opens interpretative possibilities for the Torah, which would remain closed should the Holy Book be treated as a static set of proscriptions and commandments. The ceaseless movement maintains the living Revelation. "It is the Torah fed by its own flame through time" (CTI 54, MPI 79).

There is a right way and a wrong way to engage with the Torah. The right and productive way sees that the Torah must be studied, argued, and debated to be maintained. The wrong way is to take the Torah as a finished product worthy of worship in itself. "Rabbi Nehorai said: 'It is whoever has the opportunity to study the Torah and does not do so' [who has rejected the Torah]" (CTI 54, MPI 79). Levinas interprets this as saying that "it is one for whom the Torah's entering the world has not transformed the latter drastically. One for whom the Torah exists,

Here we see how Levinas's dependence on Rosenzweig coincides with his own understanding of "Judaism" as having surpassed both the conventional understanding of religion and also the secular reaction against it put forth by science and philosophy. "[Rosenzweig] successfully moves from a position that had been until then philosophical to a religious position, and the great revealed religions enter into a sphere of his meditation. Let us retain their theme: the web or reality is religious history. It commands political history. That is Rosenzweig's anti-Hegelian position."[38]

Samuel Moyn has artfully and convincingly demonstrated the ways that Levinas's initial encounters with the work of Rosenzweig occurred in the context of the interwar discovery of Kierkegaard in France as well as the lasting impact that Levinas's initial Kierkegaardian reading of Rosenzweig had on his philosophical work. On Moyn's account, "it is ultimately impossible to understand the shape of Levinas's intersubjective theory except as a secularization of a transconfessional, but originally Protestant, theology of encounter with the divine."[39] There is no doubt that the influence of Kierkegaard played an outsized role in what Henry Corbin described as the "insertion of divine transcendence into the flux of history."[40] In Kierkegaard's presentation, the story of Abraham and Isaac is as meaningful to us today as it was to the first Hebrews, because "no generation begins other than where its predecessor did, every generation begins from the beginning, the self-enclosed like an institution or a sacred object, whereas its essence is opening" (CTI 54, MPI 79). In the latter account, the Torah has become an idol, and "here idolatry can also be taken as idolatry of the Torah" (CTI 54, MPI 79). This gives another meaning to the title of the lecture where contempt is reserved for those who revere the Torah as an idol rather than as a book.

This leads Levinas back to the tractate:

> Rabbi Yehoshua ben Korha said: "Whoever studies the Torah without repeating the lesson is like a sower who does not reap."

"Not repeating the lesson means not remembering the Torah; but it also means denying what the first reading—which opens but at the same time covers up—has already hidden. The first reading hides the horizons of the gaze as well as its relativity. It is succeeding generation comes no further than the previous one, provided the latter was true to its task and didn't betray it."[41] On this account, one need only read the text because the meaning held within transcends time and place, but one must read closely and critically. Thus the close and skeptical reader (a philosopher like Levinas?) is particularly suited to the task of coaxing meaning from sacred texts, but they must be willing to accept that there is meaning beyond their intellect, evolution, or historical development. This is what Levinas refers to in his Talmudic lecture *Towards the Other* as the "paradigmatic method" where "the transfer of an idea to another climate—which is its original climate—wrests new possibilities from it."[42] One could also point to Kierkegaard as the template for Levinas's privileging of the return to religion following the contemplation and mastery of philosophy and science as a higher or more authentic understanding. In the pseudonymous works of Kierkegaard we witness a similar progression through life's spheres: from the aesthetic understanding predicated on appetite and desire, to the ethical understanding based on reason, to the realm of Religiousness (a), which is that of resignation, or ultimately to Religiousness (b), which is the sublime realm of the Knight of Faith.

By the time of Levinas's first lecture at the Colloque des intellectuels juifs de langue française in 1959, however, Levinas was more interested in the separation of Judaism from Christianity than their

satisfied with the first word, the first impression, first-level truths. It takes metaphorical meaning literally, which is the negation of the spiritual and the source of all idolatry. To sow without reaping is also to cease sowing, increasing and renewing the harvest" (CTI 55, MPI 79). This is how Levinas understands idolatry of the Torah: It is an essentialism that makes the first reading also the last, thus covering up all that may be revealed in the future. When metaphorical meaning is taken literally, interpretative dynamism is replaced by dogmatism. This results in a harvest that cannot be consumed because the sowing has ceased.

The tractate continues:

> Rabbi Yehoshua said: "Whoever learns the Torah and forgets it is like a woman who brings a child into the world only to bury it."

"A striking image, not only because of its dramatic

proximity. Levinas's use of Rosenzweig in the lecture is intended to disavow the influence or importance of Kierkegaard. In this text, Levinas tells us that "[Rosenzweig] knows . . . A simple spontaneity is no longer possible after so much knowledge, and the anarchy of the individual protestations of subjective thinkers, as he calls them, such as Kierkegaard or Nietzsche, threatens us with every kind of *Schwärmerei* and every kind of cruelty."[43] For Kierkegaard and for Levinas, it may take only one man to restore meaning to a sacred text, but whereas Kierkegaard is content to allow the Knight of Faith to bask in the ultimately subjective position of his personal salvation, Levinas is not. "In order for love to be able to penetrate the World, which is Redemption, in order for Time to move into Eternity, Love must not remain at the state of individual enterprise, it must become the work of community."[44] For Levinas, the figure of emulation is not Abraham, who cannot explain his act and therefore must necessarily act alone, but Moses who is given the daunting challenge of translating Divine will into human law: translating God's word into Hebrew. This move is later replicated in the Septuagint when Hebrew is translated Greek.

Levinas proposes a move toward Judaism and not Christianity. Despite the proximity Levinas discerns between the two religions, following Rosenzweig, it is Rosenzweig's journey through philosophy toward Christianity, which ultimately led to his decision *not* to convert evocation of the suffering mother. The image suggests the idea that study is not just any activity but a giving birth—and that the result of study is an other me, who answers me, tearing me away from my solitude, and for whom I am answerable" (CTI 55, MPI 79–80). Study is indicative of a dynamism that is also a dislocation of sorts. It is an understanding of oneself completely dissociated from essentialism in regard to a people, a religion, or even the seemingly primary unit of the self or ego. Studying must not be devotion in the sense of piety to an immobile code or rote memorization but a motion forward that reveals the way that such a self is always a work in process, a construction, an other me that can be a better me. As such, it is also an opening to the other. This is a constitutive dissymmetry that never lets the self or ego rest in isolation or satisfaction. "Torah and permanence, Torah and all time. An extraordinary to Christianity, and his *return* to Judaism that serves as a template for Levinas's narrative of development and progress toward authentic Judaism. In "Franz Rosenzweig: Une pensee juive modern," from 1965, Levinas explains that "what characterizes contemporary Jewish thought after Rosenzweig is that special new experience of the Return. It touches even those formed by tradition, but who rethink that tradition as if returning from some remote West, needing to learn everything. We must turn to Rosenzweig to learn what force can resist the seduction of Christianity and the wisdom of philosophy."[45] For Levinas, the lesson to be learned from Rosenzweig is not only about the return to religion from a secular, scientific, philosophical understanding of the world but also a turning away from Christianity toward Judaism. This must be a Judaism sufficiently robust and modern to resist the seduction of Christianity (assimilation) and the wisdom of philosophy (the temptation of temptation). As such it is a Judaism that has engaged with and understands philosophical thought and progressed beyond it so that it can understand the crucial differences between Judaism and Christianity.

In "Between Two Worlds," Levinas differentiates between the temporal registers in which each Judaism and Christianity operate. Whereas, Levinas tells us, Christianity is experienced as a march through time, "the Jewish community, on the other hand, is a community that bears Eternity in its very nature."[46] In this sense, and book, calling for the toil of effort, tension—a book distrustful of all leniency toward oneself" (CTI 59, MPI 83–84).

And yet, this toil is not without joy.

> Rabbi Akiva said: "to each day its song, to each day its song." (CTI 55, MPI 80)

As we have seen, such a singing must be more than a "text being learned by heart, it's ever increasing familiarity," it must also reveal the "possibility of its being gone over daily without the boredom of repetition" (CTI 55, MPI 80). Rashi, "also commenting on the word 'song,' also sees it as a 'promise of joy for the world to come'" (CTI 55, MPI 80). The joy is not only in the act of singing but also joy in the promise of a world better and different from the one in which we sing. This does not lift the text to the level of funk, perhaps, but neither is it entirely devoid of it. Still, one unlike Christianity, Judaism stands outside of history, because for Levinas, "The Jews are strangers to the history that has no hold on them" and thus they are in a position to "judge history—that is to say, to remain free with regard to events, whatever the internal logic binding them."[47] In this way, Levinas follows Rosenzweig's anti-Hegelian and antihistoricist move by asserting that the position of the Jewish people "outside of history" is a positive rather than a negative attribute. What's more, for Levinas, such a stance outside of history gives Judaism an ethical valence that, he implies, Christianity lacks. "Independence in the face of history affirms the right possessed by human consciousness to judge a world that is ripe at every moment for judgement, before the end of history and independently of this end—that is to say, a world peopled by persons."[48] One aspect of this claim is evidently anti-Hegelian insofar as it is opposed to a speculative philosophy of history or any argument wherein the ends justify the means. Ethical judgment and action should not be grounded on an outcome to be achieved in the future but should be instead applicable at every moment and for every person.

Levinas's assertion that this position outside of history is one particular to Judaism, however, indicates that Jewish thought holds a particular and privileged position over and above Christianity. Christianity is bound by time and history, whereas Judaism is an eternal project. Levinas and Rosenzweig are both metahistorical insofar must be wary of taking the joy of singing for the joy to be received from the work to come. This is perhaps "a problem that haunts the Jewish religious consciousness, the repercussions of which can be perceived in Hasidism, in the form in which it entered into a certain eighteenth-century Jewish piety" (CTI 55–56, MPI 80).

This leads us to the crux of the lesson, which turns on the question as to whether one finds joy in the act of having done something or in the reasons for which one does it. "Nothing is ever definitely gained in it [the Word or lessons of the Torah], beyond the living attention of the gaze, which may become weary. The Torah is not simply part of a cultural treasure, like song and the arts. The Word of God, supreme meaning, is without insistence—it flies away like a dream. Perhaps Judaism is, after all, nothing but an accident of history or the as they each present Judaism as external to history. Nevertheless, a historical logic of progress remains at work in Levinas and Rosenzweig that in some respects mimics the Hegelian journey of spirit. Levinas admitted as much responding to questions at the end of his lecture when he states that, "Rosenzweig remains Hegelian on one point, for him subjective protest is powerless against historical necessity" and "in this sense, religion is the event that follows the end of history."[49] The common thread that allows both Rosenzweig and Levinas to privilege European and ultimately Jewish thought/culture is a logic of progress and intellectual development over time.

This logic of historical progress or development can be mapped onto the discussion of Levinas's educational goals and understanding of Judaism as presented in the first three chapters and with which we began this final one. In response to the events of World War II and the Holocaust, Levinas sought to construct a positive and authentic understanding of Jewish identity that was to be formed by his vision of Jewish education. This authentic Judaism is one derived in the light of both philosophical and scientific advances and, as such, eschewed excessive acts of piety and mystical or emotional relations with God. In rejecting this form of religiosity this Judaism was not seduced by the promises of assimilated secularism. Instead, authentic Judaism is one that has traveled the historical road through the rationalism of the Enlightenment and ultimately beyond it. As stated,

miracle of an unflagging attention. Idolatry is real reality, natural reality" (CTI 56, MPI 81). While Judaism in its particular configuration as a people or an identity may be nothing more than an "accident of history," the "unflagging attention" that the Torah demands is a miracle. It is the command to pay attention and work unceasingly for a better future. Idolatry, in this understanding, is a condition of inattention. It is the anaesthetization of ethics that occurs when one's attention is consumed by what is or by what has been rather than on the work that needs to be done to make this world better. It is enjoying the act of singing, as if that was enough, without paying attention to the reason one sings. The lessons one obtains by the study of Torah and Talmud do not just remain, they must be continuously achieved and renewed.

This attention to reading, this constant

Levinas's understanding of Judaism relies on, and thus conserves, the three strands of the braid we have been weaving (Western philosophy, French Universalism, and the Lithuanian Talmudic tradition) but does so because of the historical development that allows Levinas, and modern Jewry, to move past atheism and back to a relation with God now purged of those aspects of religion or worship that Levinas considered juvenile or overly exuberant. The move is akin to Hegel's journey of consciousness insofar as the exemplary or authentic Jew is the one who has progressed through religion to scientific rationalism culminating in atheism and then found their way back to Judaism via Talmud. It is in this sense that Levinas says religion, and here I take him to present Judaism as its most elevated form, is the event that follows the end of history. Despite or because of the way that Levinas affirms the special position afforded Jews as external to world history, his logic of progress nevertheless embraces a hierarchy of development wherein certain cultures or belief systems are further along than others.

To return to Moten's question about the troubling contradiction in Levinas's project, a different answer can be found in Levinas's dismissal of "dance." Moten presents Levinas's dismissal of dance and his denigration of affect as a boundary-building move that elevates the cold, calculating, and invasive stillness of rational philosophy while demoting, to the point of exclusion, other rhythms, moods, or interrogation, is certainly akin to the practice of philosophy, and Levinas asks whether it can be achieved through the study of logos in the Greek sense. "Is idolatry excluded from the logos? Is Greek intelligibility sufficient for the human? And is what we have already caught a glimpse of in the intelligibility of the covenant and of sociality as participation in the future world already assured by language?" (CTI 58, MPI 83). The answer can be found in the story of Manasseh, the son of Hezekiah. Levinas tells us that Hezekiah, a king from the lineage of David, was "the most faithful to Torah" or "the most learned in Torah" who lacked only one gift, the ability to sing (CTI 59–60, MPI 84). Hezekiah, however, was unable to educate his son, Manasseh, who would become the "most idolatrous king among the kings of Judea!" (CTI 60, MPI 84). Manasseh was educated and cultured but this only led him to "try his hand at interpreting the Torah movements of thought. Moten wants to avoid the conclusion that "Levinas was as devoid of funk as Hendrik Verwoerd" and turns to Levinas's early work in which Moten detects "a refusal of the denigration of affect that is almost as striking as that of the denigration of tonalities, a refusal that will disappear in the late interviews when singing joins dancing as the very figures of the nonserious and, when weeping differently, when degraded mourning, will have marked the unruly irruption of ascented, affective spectacle back into the nexus of Europe/Man/The Bible/The Greeks from which they had been (always unsuccessfully) banished."[50] Moten sees a shift from Levinas's early work to the later, which he characterizes as from "resistance to enforcement of the ban."[51] Moten believes it is possible to read "a resistance to racism in some early" and thus, seemingly, uncontaminated "texts of Levinas that is prior to and critically anticipatory of the racism in his later interviews."[52] Moten holds an ambivalent attitude toward the work of Levinas and is searching for a mechanism to redeem it, but I would argue that his exculpatory turn to Levinas's earlier work cannot outrun the exclusionary mechanism, the exemplarism, that manifests so prominently in the later interviews. This is because Levinas's early thought contains the germ of the later prejudice in the form of Levinas's distrust and dismissal of Eastern European Jewry.

As we saw in chapter 2, such a prejudice appears counterintuitive given Levinas's in a shameless way" (CTI 60, MPI 84). Manasseh's is "the denial of the Torah by one who says that the Torah is not from heaven, but who also denies its intrinsic value. He denies it in a fundamental way. It is the prototype of a whole attitude—with which you are quite familiar—and even of an entire modernism of good humor" (CTI 61, MPI 86). We may see Manasseh as an extreme case because of his insolence and arrogance; nevertheless, his denial of the Torah on such grounds does not stand far apart from the modern secular interpretation. Manasseh denies that the Torah came from heaven instead attributing it to Moses or to other authors, dismissing or demoting its messages and value on those grounds. Whether the Torah is dismissed out of hand or treated like a philosophical treatise, human interpretation is not enough because it assumes that one can master the text. That one can tell the text what it own place in rehabilitating Jewish learning centered on the reading of sacred texts in the Mitnageddic tradition. To revisit the claims of chapter 2, Levinas's understanding of Jewish learning was aligned with his commitment to the guiding principles of the Alliance Israélite Universelle as well as the influence of Franz Rosenzweig's educational project in his *Lehrhaus*. As such, Levinas's understanding of authentic Judaism and Jewish teaching emphasizes a highly intellectual study of Talmud, in opposition to the miracles and wonders that characterize the Hasidic movement with its emphasis on prayer. I want to emphasize Levinas's distrust of, and distaste for, the miraculous, the mystical, and the enchanted, which should surely include the ecstatic emotional connection to God brought on by song and dance. Levinas saw these as juvenile fantasy or inebriated indulgence opposed to the sober work of Judaism as a religion for adults. This is not to say that Levinas was totally devoid of funk or humor but that his understanding of authentic or exemplary Judaism is defined against the Eastern European or Hasidic Jew who is, for Levinas, the initial other Other. To be sure, Levinas finds proximity to the rustic, emotional, and mystical variants of Judaism whose practices he hopes to correct through education, as we saw in chapters 2 and 3. He does not afford such a connection to non-European cultures or traditions. One could argue that the "civilizing" educational mission in each case follows the same template aligning with the project of the AIU.

means once and for all. By contrast, the divinity of the Torah is enacted in the dissent, dispute, and discussion that enables a living Revelation. Philosophy and the Greek logos remain idolatry, at least insofar as they assume human and/or individual mastery over the text. The constitutive dissymmetry resulting from the constant work of reading implies that there is no mastery, only learning. This all turns on our ability to read the Torah in a way so as not to scorn its contents or to turn it into an idol worthy of worship all alone.

There is a final lesson to be learned from the story of Manasseh. A final example of contempt for the Torah as contempt for idolatry, and it is likely the most important one. The lesson is drawn from a statement that Manasseh makes:

> He would say: Didn't Moses have anything else to write besides "and Lotan's sister was

The unintended racism of which Moten speaks has its origins in a logic of authenticity based on a hierarchy of intellectual development in which we find an order ranking from the "primitive" to the "pagan" to the "Eastern European Jew" to the "enlightened European" to the "enlightened European Jew" and ultimately leading to the "authentic Jew" as defined and cultivated by Levinas's educational program. It is at the end of this developmental road, this history of intellectual progress, that the Bible and the Greeks are "open to everyone" and yet closed to all who have not reached the terminus of this historical journey. For those who have not, the Bible and the Greeks remain closed . . . "there is no racism intended." Thus, in a way, the authentic Jew for Levinas is the authentic European, and this sheds light on Moten's conclusion that "such recoveries of original Europeanness are always put forward as the answer to the question of our problematic, fallen contemporaneity. . . . It's as if Jewish intellectuals in Europe are given the task of saving a culture that has, on the one hand, disavowed itself, no longer knows itself and, on the other hand, never knew itself, never recognized this moment of fallenness and disavowal as its most authentic possibility."[53]

The priority and privilege afforded to the European and the Jew in Levinas's translation project, Hebrew into Greek, seem to undercut the message of responsibility toward the Other that is the basis for his Ethics not only in the confessional

Timna?" [Genesis 36:22] (CTI 60, MPI 85)

One need not have the arrogance of a Manasseh to question the import of Moses's reference to Lotan's sister. Such a statement could easily be dismissed. After all, "there was no need for her to be mentioned in the series of important individuals among Esau's descendants" (CTI 62, MPI 87). Levinas asks us to delve deeper and to read more closely. "The Gemara says what the text of the Torah does not say: that Timna [who was of royal blood] had gone to Abraham, Isaac, and Jacob to ask for a husband from among Abraham's descendants" (CTI 63, MPI 87). When they turned her away she became the concubine of Eliphaz, Esau's son. The Gemara states: "She must have said to herself: 'It is better to be a servant in this nation than to have lordly rank in another'" (CTI 63, MPI 87). Levinas tells us that Timna preferred to be a servant works but also in his philosophical ones. If the account rests on what is, in the end, a journey of historical development where rational thought in the West then leads to Ethics on the basis of a Jewish reason that is "beyond reason in rational truth itself: a personal relation in the universal and truth" (BTV 30) that "surpasses and incorporates atheism," then we are talking about a modified Enlightenment narrative similar in structure to the progress narratives of Whiggish history, French Enlightenment Universalism, or Hegel's journey of the spirit.[54] This logic of progress creates what Dipesh Chakrabarty has called a waiting room of history where some peoples are destined to lag behind others in the hierarchy of progress until they are deemed sufficiently caught up to enter the game.[55] As such, Levinas's project would at worst be impeached (McGettigan) or at best require serious modification (Drabinski) or recalibration (Moten).

Perhaps history is precisely the problem and, given Levinas's own distrust of history as an explanatory or meaning-making device, I think it worth revisiting the project of translation shorn of its contextual baggage and the implied historical teleology. I say this not to rehabilitate Levinas or exonerate him and his work but because there is an alternative logic at work in Levinas's project of translating Hebrew into Greek that is completely at odds with the more historical one even if both are available. I would also say that this alternative logic is one less apparent to the historian whose

in the spiritual greatness of that line rather than to retain membership in a great nation in which there are wars, victories, and conquests. Timna was forced into servitude because Abraham, Isaac, and Jacob refused her request to join them on equal footing. Thus the teaching that Amalek, the son of Timna and Eliphaz, caused Israel so much suffering. Levinas takes the moral of the Gemara to be clear: "Timna should not have been turned away" (CTI 63, MPI 88). The admirable teaching of the Torah and Talmud is for naught if the openness exuded is only reserved for a chosen few. "To this admirable rigor, this superb spirit, a movement of openness must be joined. Failing which the high-mindedness of the Torah becomes haughtiness of spirit" (CTI 63, MPI 88).

Such an openness moves beyond the particularity of a chosen people or specific history, and here, tools of chronological contextualization and narrative explanation favor the sort of account with which I began this chapter. Given the critique at the heart of Levinas's use of Greek-European-Christian philosophy, let's see if we can tackle translation at a different level to liberate it from the presumption that reason belongs to Greek and ethics belong to Hebrew. This would be the uncanny translation of the word of God into the language of humanity.

Levinas seems to suggest that our modern understanding of history, one to which at least in some aspects he ultimately subscribes, creates blind spots by obscuring what is important and meaningful in texts. As argued in the introduction, secular historical scholarship and interpretation overplays our interpretative abilities at the expense of the text to be interpreted. In his lecture from 1982, "For a Place in the Bible," Levinas asks, "Is it not perhaps the case that the ideas of a thought worthy of the name rise above their own history, royally indifferent to their historians? There are perhaps more constants through time than one is led to believe by the difference of language, differences that in most cases come only from the variety of metaphors. And perhaps modernity, that is, the claim of deciphering all the metaphors, is but the creation of metaphors whose wisdom can already be grasped in ancient ways of speaking."[56] Levinas asks us to reconsider the privileged place we assign ourselves based solely on the historical contingency that we live at a later moment in time than those who came before us. Elsewhere he states following Levinas, we can take the translation of Hebrew into Greek as a metaphor. The literal interpretation would not register a shift from the particular to the universal because the very ideal of the universal is ascribed to a particular people be they "Greek" or "European." The task is to translate the word of God into the language of humans in such a way as to resist stasis, surety, or mastery. Contempt for the Torah as idolatry is contempt for those who idolize the Torah because to do so is to ossify the words in the form of a statue. Idolatry does not allow for the translation of God's words into our own. For Levinas, the move from Revelation to Elevation is done through textual analysis, but the reading of texts is not limited to what has been written. For Levinas, the Torah (which is the translation of the divine into human language) is composed of the written books of Moses and also the oral tradition that

that "it is necessary to consider these texts from various epochs as contemporaneous," lamenting that "the lucid work of historians and Jewish and non-Jewish critics—who can reduce the Jewish miracle of Revelation or that of national spirit to a multiplicity of influences that they have undergone—loses its spiritual importance at the critical hours which have frequently struck in the course of 2000 years for post-exilic Judaism."[57]

One must in a sense step out of time to enter the Talmud, and in doing so one suspends what we might call the bias of the modern that includes the presumption that we now know more and better than those who came before us. The suspension, however, must be done in such a way that the texts from then can speak to us now. When discussing the Exodus, the point is not to recount a story of long ago for its own sake or to champion a triumph over adversity indicating our superior position in the present. Instead, the reader must inhabit the position of the text as their point of departure: "The trauma I experience as a slave in the land of Egypt constitutes my humanity itself" and should in some way instill an ethical imperative though not in any Kantian sense of the term. On such an unstable temporal scaffold there is not one definition of ethics for all time even though there is an Ethics that is eternally available. The act of translation is not from Hebrew into Greek per se but from the word of God into the language of humankind. This is a destabilization of the logic of universal and particular as each can be seen to be inside the other.

allows what was written to be unpacked for our moment. This is the translation of an ethical ideal (universal) into a practical application (particular). Strangely, it is the inverse movement of the more literal understanding of "translating Hebrew into Greek" at least insofar as the movement is from universal to particular.

One final point is worth examining. Hezekiah, who was unable to teach his son the reading of Torah, is also the one who lacked the ability to sing. Could Hezekiah's failure as a teacher be linked to his inability to engage with the joy of song? And could that inability be cast back on Levinas despite him being "the most faithful to Torah" or "the most learned in Torah"? "A refusal of the denigration of affect that is almost as striking as that of the denigration of tonalities, a refusal that will disappear in the late interviews when singing joins dancing as the very figures of

Thus for Levinas, "The Scriptures have a mode of being that is quite different from the exercise material for grammarians, entirely subject to philologists; a mode of being where the history of each piece of writing counts less than the lessons it contains, and where its inspiration is measured by what it inspires."[58] What counts, or should count, is not the particular historical context in which the writing occurred but instead the inspiration it imparts for the present. The study of Talmud is essential to his endeavor because it is composed of both the written Revelation at Mount Sinai, which was codified in the Pentateuch or Old Testament and of the oral Revelation, which Levinas tells us holds equal weight but was given so as not to be codified. To be sure the oral portion was eventually written down as the Jerusalem and Babylonian Talmud but, in Levinas's words, "its writing down came late." For Levinas, "Writing is immediately bound to an 'oral Torah' at once preliminary and renewing. This is not an historical contingency but an essential possibility of Spirit, one of its vocations. The Jewish reading is anything but unbiased, although here being a biased reader means, not the sterility of dogmatic prejudices, but the possibilities and risks of transcending the given; and probably the extraordinary trace that Revelation leaves in a thought that, beyond the vision of being, hears the word of God."[59]

To answer Moten's question of how "a kind of sneering dismissal of 'what one calls decolonization and the end of a dominating the nonserious and, when weeping differently, when degraded mourning, will have marked the unruly irruption of ascented, affective spectacle back into the nexus of Europe/Man/The Bible/The Greeks from which they had been (always unsuccessfully) banished."[2]

"To each day its song, to each day its song."

Europe' (reduced here to a mere object for structuralist thought)" can "emerge from the thinker of the terrible interplay of universalization and force?" The dismissal is based on a logic of progress that, in the end, deems some people more advanced than others. This is why, for Levinas, the thought of Einstein cannot be compared to the "savage mind." This is how "Levinas's arrival at the cusp of a clear vision of the end of philosophy as decolonization, as an abolition both internally and externally directed in its relation to what he will come to speak of under the rubric of 'escape,' turn[s] into another version of the same (racism), however unintended."[60] The place to read "a resistance to racism" is not in the early texts of Levinas but through the competing and contradictory project of translating God's word into human language.[61]

It is significant for Levinas that "the Talmud is the other form of Revelation distinct from the Old Testament which Christians and Jews have in common" because the Talmud is a site of understanding uncoupled from historical development.[62] The distinction should not be seen in terms of exemplarism (though that would fit with our prior contextualist narrative) but instead in the way that the lessons of the Talmud do not derive from historical development (OT-NT-Koran-Enlightenment) and are not bound to any moment in time or place, but must be seen instead as a continuous Revelation. The Revelation of oral tradition is, in a sense, timeless, as it is open to perpetual contestation where "consequently, the Talmudic texts, even in the physiognomical aspects that their typography takes on, are accompanied by commentaries, and by commentaries on discussions of these commentaries."[63] It is perhaps ironic that Levinas here calls for the need to read these texts in their original Hebrew and Aramaic, which appears to be the inversion of the mandate to translate "Hebrew into Greek," but we should be aware that any project of translation carries the risk of codifying or freezing the translated text into forms that themselves become relics short-circuiting the possibility of renewal. The return to the ancient language is not a fetish for origins but a further destabilization of any one hegemonic meaning: "With its ellipses, the unpredictable behavior of its vocables, its figures foreign to all rhetoric, its ostensible non-sequiturs, [the Talmud] seems to be a medium marvelously well suited to permanent interrogation, through which various eras can communicate."[64]

On this reading, Talmud is always in need of translation into the present context and into living language by means of exegesis, wherein the dialectic or contestatory relation of written and oral Revelation in Talmud excludes the idea of doctrinal authority. This is a continuous Revelation permanently engendering new meanings that each speak to their own time because they are attuned to the Other, and this for Levinas is the meaning of Election.

CONCLUSION

Constitutive Dissymmetry

The question that vexes me and has vexed me throughout the writing of this book is one Fred Moten posed in *The Universal Machine*, why can't we let ourselves go?[1] Why couldn't Levinas let himself go? Clearly, his turn to the study of Talmud was marked and motivated by the issues of Jewish existence and identity after the Holocaust. The three strands of the braid—Western philosophy, Enlightenment Universalism, and Lithuanian Talmud—were woven together for the purpose of ensuring the survival of Judaism in the post-Holocaust world. In Levinas's Talmudic lectures, however, we encounter the ways in which the lessons he taught encourage us to let go of essentialist notions of identity based on a particular history or people. As we saw in Levinas's lecture "Beyond Memory," the primary lesson to be taken from Exodus is that we must work toward the future emancipation from servitude and enfranchisement of all humanity while the historical event of the exodus from Egypt is the secondary one. The emphasis is not on the self but on the other. Yet even here, the names of both Jacob and Israel are conserved as is the particular history: "'You will not be called Jacob, but your name will be Israel' does not mean that Jacob 'loses his place,' but that Israel will be his primary name and Jacob his secondary name" (BM 70, AS 95). In our everyday existence, is it even possible to let go of identity, character, personality, or nationality?

The particular history of Levinas's turn to Talmud in the years after the Holocaust and following World War II demonstrates the myriad ways that Levinas's Talmudic lectures and his related category of "being-Jewish," conceived in the confinement of a German prisoner of war camp, conserve an emphasis on identity, essentialism, and exemplarism that is in tension with the teachings of his Talmudic lectures and his philosophical works in general.[2] As we saw at the end of chapter 1 and throughout chapter 4, this tendency created a blind spot in which Levinas conserved aspects of the authentic/inauthentic distinction inherited from the philosophy of Heidegger, which in turn enabled Levinas to afford a privileged and exemplary status to Judaism by emplotting its historical journey past religiosity, past atheism, and then back to a relation with God purged of immaturity or hubris. These retentions cannot be taken lightly because in the aftermath of the Holocaust, Levinas realized all too well the potential and actual danger of these constructs in both the Hegelian and Heideggerian form. And yet, it is because of the Holocaust that Levinas could not let go of Judaism for fear that the very annihilation assigned to the Jews by the Nazi final solution would come to be fulfilled by assimilation into the "modern" world.

This same desire to maintain Judaism and what he calls the ontological category of being-Jewish simultaneously motivate Levinas's commitment to ethics as first philosophy and the concomitant deposition of the self in favor of the other. For Levinas, Jewish Scriptures and their interpretations are what make such an ethics of alterity possible. "Alterity becomes proximity. Not distance, the shortest through space, but initial directness, which extends as unimpeachable approach in the call of the face of the other, in which there appears, as an order, an inscription, a prescription, an awakening (as if it were a 'me'), responsibility—mine, for the other human being."[3] Here we reach a seemingly intractable problem. The basis for the ethical lessons that Levinas asserts should apply to all humanity are only to be found in the reading of particular sacred texts and on the basis of a particular tradition of textual interpretation.

> The role played by ethics in the religious relation allow us to understand the meaning of Jewish universalism. A truth is universal when it applies

> to every reasonable human being. A religion is universal when it is open to all. In this sense, the Judaism that links the Divine to the moral has always aspired to be universal. But the revelation of morality, which discovers a human society, also discovers the place of election, which, in this universal society, returns to the person who receives this revelation. This election is made up not of privileges but of responsibilities.[4]

Any access to the universal ethics, of which Levinas writes, must be drawn from Judaism and from the reading of sacred Jewish texts.

Not just any reading of these texts but the strategy of interpretation offered by Levinas himself in what we can call the postrabbinic Lithuanian tradition. As we have seen, Levinas's dynamic reading of Torah and Talmud, based in Jewish tradition and his tutelage under Shushani but also his particular training in philosophy, is the mechanism by which he attempts to recover what was destroyed in the Holocaust: the very academies and practitioners of the Lithuanian Talmudic tradition. It is also the means by which Levinas employs his own interpretative methods to make sense of Jewish scripture in a post-Holocaust world.

The problem of exemplarism, essentialism, and identity is further complicated by the creation of the State of Israel, the instantiation of an actual political state as opposed to a diasporic relation with God. In a short piece, "From the Rise of Nihilism to the Carnal Jew," written for the edited volume *D'Auschwitz à Israël, vingt ans après la Libération* from 1968, Levinas ties these two historical events together.[5] "The Nazi persecution and, following the exterminations, the extraordinary fulfilment of the Zionist dreams of a State in which to live in peace is to live dangerously, gradually become history."[6] Levinas is aware of the problem inherent in entering into "history," the danger that "Israel, by dint of insisting on its significance as a State, has been entirely reduced to political categories."[7] Judith Butler takes up this issue in *Parting Ways: Jewishness and the Critique of Zionism* when she attempts to disentangle the conflicting definitions and registers that Levinas attributes to "Israel."

> If Jews are considered "elect" precisely because they carry a message of universality, and what is "universal" in Levinas's view is the inaugurative structuring of the subject through persecution and ethical demand, then

the Jew becomes the model and instance for this preontological persecution. The Jew is, accordingly, no longer historical. In fact, the problem is that the Jew is a category that belongs to a historically and culturally conditioned ontology (unless it is the name for the infinite itself); so if the Jew maintains an "elective" status in relation to ethical responsiveness, then a full confusion of the preontological and the ontological is thereby accomplished in Levinas's work. The Jew is neither part of ontology nor history—the Jew cannot be understood as belonging to the order of historical time—and yet this exemption becomes the way in which Levinas makes claims about the role of Israel, itself historically formed and maintained, as forever and exclusively persecuted and, by definition, never persecuting.[8]

Butler concludes that this construction enables Levinas to attribute the "timeless suffering" of a universal Israel to the historical political state of Israel, thus denying that this state is itself a product of a particular history that includes the persecution of Palestinians, a present that includes the producing of displaced peoples as well as a set of possible futures. It is worth looking at Levinas's text in relation to this analysis not to discount Butler's lucid and cutting indictment but to see the ways that Levinas's dynamic reading of Torah and Talmud is at work here.

As Butler observes, Levinas does at times conflate the two meanings of Israel. She refers to these as preontological and ontological, but we could also think of them along the registers of an authentic and inauthentic Judaism as discussed in chapter 1.[9] The inauthentic variant pertains to the understanding of Judaism as the particular history of a people, whereas the authentic understanding is conditioned by the living Revelation of Torah and Talmud. In his essay considering the State of Israel twenty years after Auschwitz, Levinas tells us that "what is proclaimed at the end of this twenty-year evolution is the return of the forces to which in reality we have been exposed since our Emancipation. They are not the forces of Evil. The danger of the assimilation—if it retains some meaning—does not stem from the value inherent in any nationalism. It comes from the essential ambiguity of an admirably free thought to which we cannot refuse to give ourselves, but which is not protected against tyranny—that is to say, against nihilism."[10] The danger facing the Jewish people may no longer be the forces of Evil encountered at Auschwitz, but the Jewish people are not free from danger. The creation of the State of Israel marks the Jewish people's entry into the modern political world, and in this regard they are no different from any other nation.[11] The danger Levinas detects, the same danger facing the Jewish people since their Emancipation, is that of assimilation. As we saw in chapter 2, "The Sanhedrin believes itself to be the navel of the world, but every nation believes it is at the center of the world! The very idea of nation arises each time that a human group thinks it dwells at the navel of the world. It is precisely because of this that it wants sovereignty and claims every responsibility" (OW 78, VM 167). Levinas considers the idea that one resides at the center of the universe to be the source of tyranny. It is a selfishness that manifests itself as nationalism but that Levinas also associates with the nihilism of free thought completely unrestrained. Here, the contingencies of history are taken as justifications for the status quo.

In contrast, Levinas instructs us that "the prophets of Judaism do not philosophize within the traces or predictions of the conquerors. They separate victory from truth. They designate good and evil without worrying about the meaning of history."[12] Victory is not a sufficient condition for truth, whereas the timeless truth of Judaism provides answers unhinged from the contingencies of history even if they speak to any given historical moment. To return to Levinas's lesson on the Sanhedrin, he presents it as a mode of justice that does not exemplify any particular nation. Instead, it is the instantiation of the ethical responsibility of individual humans who have been given divine guidance (the relation with God on God's own side) but who, as humans, are prone to weakness, temptation, and failure (our side). With this in mind, we can turn to what is a particularly difficult passage, a particularly difficult conflation.

> Without abjuring logic, we can recall that besides the Israel that is interrupted spiritually, where there is an obvious equation between Israel and the Universal, there exists an Israel of Fact, a particular reality that has traversed history as a victim, bearing a tradition and certainties that did not wait to win acclaim from the end of History. Israel equals humanity,

but humanity includes the Inhuman, and Israel then refers to Israel, the Jewish people, its tongue, books, Law, earth.[13]

Levinas makes it clear that there are two Israels: the Israel interrupted spiritually, which he claims is obviously universal, and the "Israel of Fact," which he tells us has traversed history as a victim. The former is the realm of divine guidance as revealed in Levinas's understanding of Jewish education, while the latter references the particular history of the Jewish people. It is of note that Levinas sees the Israel of Fact as having traversed history as a victim, had he chosen to reference the book of Joshua it could equally be considered a history of persecution, of perpetrators. Butler is surely right to call Levinas out on this point in reference to the extant State of Israel, his conflation of persecution and victimhood as both preontological and ontological conditions. The end of the passage, however, may give us means to think about another conflation, which may be the one on which the prior rests.

Levinas cautions us against taking the "Israel of Fact" to be a victim who is akin to Hegel's slave or bondsman who is the secret victor of History. Instead, in the final sentence Levinas equates Israel with a humanity that *includes* the Inhuman. On the one hand such an equation is to be taken as the remedy against the danger of assimilation and as such retains access to the divine teachings and through them, ethics. The danger facing the State of Israel is that it has lost touch with authentic Judaism, it has lost touch with God on God's own side, rendering it a nation-state no different from others, including the most egoistic, selfish, and tyrannical tendencies. "The destiny of a Jew who is not one only according to spirit, who remains the detestable carnal Jew vomited forth by Pascal, is still more mysterious. Since the Emancipation, he has increasingly freed himself in Europe from the letter of the texts. He has regarded as outmoded everything that was seemingly contingent in the traditions he inherited."[14] The moral guidelines for any given nation, the nation of Israel included, are not instantiated in the particular history of that nation but are accessed through the traditions inherited: the study of Torah and Talmud. "This indicates the degree to which the notion of Israel can be separated in the Talmud from any historical, national, local, or racial notion."[15]

On the other hand, Levinas's conflation also assumes the privileged position of the nation of Israel as the conduit to the divine. After all, it is not a matter of inheriting any tradition. As we saw in chapter 4, it is the privileged or exemplary position afforded the Jewish tradition as conduit to the ethical that creates the blind spot in Levinas, which allows for the worst tendencies of essentialism. This is how Levinas can reach the conclusion that "this 'position outside nations,' of which the Pentateuch speaks, is realized in the concept of Israel and its particularism. It is a particularism that conditions universality, and it is a moral category rather than a historical fact to do with Israel, even if the historical Israel has in fact been faithful to the concept of Israel and, on the subject of morality, felt responsibilities and obligations which it demands from no one, but which sustain the world."[16] In this formulation, the State of Israel is afforded an exemplary moral status that by definition denies the Palestinian the status of victim or Other.

In this way, Levinas finds himself at odds with himself, at least if one can accept the transcendent logic of his Talmudic lessons. Levinas tell us that

> perhaps the ultimate essence of Israel, its carnal essence prior to the freedom that will mark its history, this manifestly universal history, this history *for all*, visible to all, perhaps the ultimate essence of Israel, derives from its innate predisposition to involuntary sacrifice, its exposure to persecution. . . . To be persecuted, to be guilty without having committed any crime, is not an original sin, but the obverse (*envers*) of a universal responsibility—a responsibility for the Other (*l'Autre*)—that is more ancient than any sin. It is an invisible universality![17]

There is a distinction between the public everyday existence of the State of Israel marked by its universal history "for everyone to see" and the ultimate essence of Israel derived from its innate predisposition to involuntary sacrifice, which is ultimately a private individualized existence. The everyday public existence of a nation, made up of social, political, and economic aspects, bears no obvious mark of "being-Jewish" (they are just another painting or literature).[18] The predisposition to involuntary sacrifice, however, is the obverse of a universal responsibility visible to all. It is an Election. Thus the emphasis must be on the nature of the involuntary sacrifice (the invisible universality), which presupposes the exposure to persecution (which is visible to all). The exposure to persecution may be a consequence of involuntary sacrifice but it cannot become the justification for self-beneficial actions or claims if it is to mean anything. This seems in keeping with Butler's call to move beyond "the infinitely self-legitimating claims of being persecuted" and "toward a new notion of relationality that does not presume and reinforce persecution as its precondition."[19] This responsibility for the other begins with me and as such is an invisible universality dependent on the realization that every self is guilty prior to committing any crime. It also correlates to another definition that Levinas gives to the term *inhuman*, in which it does not reference the divine but instead the worst acts that humans can do: "Might it be that the 'may the Eternal live' of the ultimate future will be announced by the inhumanity of the war that precedes it?" (BM 71, AS 96). The inhuman is our potential to transgress, which is a part of what makes us human, but, for Levinas, the relation to the Inhuman points us toward our potential to do good. As in the quote from *Beyond Memory*, at some level the achievement of what is best in us is built on our admission that we can also do the worst, the realization that every self is "guilty without having committed any crime." Levinas's reference here is not to Talmud or Torah but to Dostoyevsky's *The Brothers Karamazov*, though in either case it is surely the self, the "me," who is called on, elected, to sacrifice oneself in deference to the other.[20] This is an election made up not of privileges but of responsibilities, and as such it is an election oriented toward the future.

Even at this more intimate register, there are reservations. Jacques Derrida for one, and despite his close proximity to Levinas both in terms of the call to responsibility and also in announcing the privileged place of the Other, is uneasy with this call, with this election:

> every time I have had to address seriously, if in a different mode, within the history of philosophy and of onto-theology, for example in Nietzsche, Heidegger, or Levinas [I want to note that Derrida includes Levinas], and in many others as well, this theme of an originary guilt or incrimination, a guilt or a responsibility, the theme of a debt, an indebtedness, a being-indebted, all originary, prior to any contract, prior to contracting anything; well then, every time I have addressed this great philosophical

> problematic, I would see returning, from the bottomless ground of memory, this dissymmetric assignation of being-Jew, coupled immediately with what has become, for me, the immense and most suspect, the most problematical resource, one before which anyone, therefore the Jew among others, must remain watchful, on guard, precisely: the cunning resource of *exemplarism*.[21]

The problem for Derrida, as in a different way for Butler, is the coupling of the dissymmetric assignation of what Derrida calls "being-Jew" with the cunning resource of exemplarism. On the one hand the call to and from the Other announced in the call to and response from Abraham is the exemplary moment of putting oneself before the Other, of giving oneself over to the hospitality of the other, the revelation of the dissymmetric assignation of what both Levinas and Derrida refer to as "being-Jewish." On the other hand it is a moment of separation, of hierarchical elevation, and of the temptation to assume such an election consists of having been "chosen a guardian of a truth, a law, an essence, in truth here of a universal responsibility." This is the paradox and contradiction that Derrida sees inherent in "being-Jewish" and by extension in Levinas's self-proclaimed authority as a Talmudic master.

The solution, for Derrida, lies embedded in what we can call the constitutive dissymmetry imposed by the law of what announces to the Jew their own identity and the perpetually futural nature of this identity that is always to be determined. The "here I am," the "I am Jewish," is itself a response to the order or injunction of the other "to whom the 'I' of the 'I am Jewish' is held hostage" and to whom it must respond. The "I" of the "I am Jewish" is not the first to know that "I am Jewish," and thus the logic of Jewish identity is necessarily built on a displacement of the self in relation to the other. It is an identity that does not coincide with itself.[22] Derrida is quick to assert that one should recognize "in this heteronomous dissymmetry of the hostage that I am, the very traits, the universal features that Levinas gives to ethics in general, as metaphysics or first philosophy—against ontology." The visibility of these universal features should give us pause, but in the work of Levinas, Derrida finds a counter to the logic of essentialism and exemplarism. This is so in the way that Derrida's noncoincidence of identity mirrors Levinas's understanding of election structuring personhood wherein "there is a contradiction in the notion of 'ego' ['*moi*'] that defines this notion."[23] It is also so in the way that Derrida's temporal construct of "being-Jewish" conserves Levinas's presentation wherein "being-Jewish" eschews completion in that it is always situated in the "not yet" of an "infinite time behind us" and the promise of a messianic future to come.

Still, we must be vigilant to the ways that Derrida *includes* Levinas in the lineage of "the most problematical resource" that he begins with Nietzsche and Heidegger. Despite Derrida's laudatory words regarding Levinas's ethics he concludes his statement by cautioning that here "again is posed the great question of an *exemplarist* temptation."[24] Derrida seems to imply that in Levinas's attempt to overcome the temptation of temptation, Levinas himself has given in to the *exemplarist* temptation instead. The promise and problem that Derrida finds in Levinas's stance can be seen in "the Temptation of Temptation." Whereas one can certainly reconcile Levinas's statement that "the world is here so the ethical order has the possibility of being fulfilled" with Derrida's own pronouncements about "messianicity" and the "not yet" of a Judaism/Jewishness to come, there is divergence with the statement that conditions Levinas's remark: "The meaning of being, the meaning of creation, is to realize Torah . . . the question of ontology will thus find its answer in the description of the way Israel receives the Torah."[25] Derrida is at home with the possibilities he finds on the secular side of Levinas's construction but not with the divine Revelation that Levinas considers the source of those possibilities and the related problem of the ways that such an election still addresses a people chosen by God and thereby elevated above all others.

While both Derrida and Butler find much of value in the writings of Levinas, they each take issue with his exemplarism as announced in the problematic construct of election. For Derrida, this manifests in having been "chosen a guardian of a truth, a law, an essence, in truth here of a universal responsibility." For Butler, this same tendency becomes the basis for Levinas's unwavering support of the State of Israel as the instantiation of those truths, those laws, that universal responsibility. For Moten, it is the source of Levinas's racism, however unintended. To be clear, there is no doubt that the faults each find in the writings of Levinas are there. It is also the case that they each find these faults on "our side" of the secular-theological divide. As Butler states, "In fact, the problem is that the Jew is a category that belongs to a historically and culturally conditioned ontology (unless it is the name for the infinite itself)."[26]

For Butler, as for Derrida, and in a certain way for Levinas as well, history is precisely the problem. Unless the Jew is the name for the infinite itself. This is the possibility that I want to take up. Why can't we just let go? Why can't we address the Jew, being-Jewish, Israel, in relation to the name of the infinite itself? Why can't we move beyond the particular history of Levinas or the particular history of a people? Why can't we take this up from the other side to see if the category of the Jew, or what Levinas calls "being-Jewish," Israel, can maintain its elective status in relation to ethical responsiveness, the predisposition to involuntary sacrifice as the invisible universal, without succumbing to the temptation of exemplarity, which enables the privileging of one nation or people or self over another? Can we tear the lessons of Levinas's Talmudic lectures from the particular context or historical circumstances in which they were given?

Butler suggests that the only remedy for Levinas's thought is the possibility that the category of the Jew is the name of infinity itself. To ask this is to ask too much, but to dismiss the name of the infinite on these grounds results in "reducing the transcendence of inspiration, exegesis and the moral message to man's interiority, to his creativity or his subconscious." On such grounds, "Is not ethics basically autonomous?"[27] For Levinas, the Jew, being-Jewish, Israel, is not the name of the infinite but that name reveals the relation with the infinite, the relation between God on God's own side and God on our side. Such a formulation conserves the possibility of Butler's reading because humans are finite creatures and, in Levinas's understanding, God is not a direct actor in the world. "Associated with the world, God would not exhaust his religious significance, for he would thus represent only God from the human viewpoint—God 'on our side,' as *Nefesh ha'Hayyim* expresses it. But God also has a meaning in the Tetragrammaton [the Name of that which cannot be named], signifying something that man cannot define, formulate, or even name. . . . It is 'God on his own side.'"[28] God on God's own side is characterized by the term *En-Sof* or Infinity, while God on our side can only be understood within the limitations of the finite. For Levinas, the category of the Jew, being-Jewish, Israel is this relation between humans and God, between the finite and the infinite as instantiated in the Tetragrammaton, the name of the infinite. "The human, therefore, would not be just a creature to whom revelation is made, but something through which the absolute of God reveals its meaning. This human impossibility of conceiving the Infinite is also a new possibility of signifying.'"[29] What interests me here is the way this relationship implies that there exists something that comes before (and after) me, something other than me. The question that follows is, how might one have access to such a relationship?

For Levinas, this occurs through the book, through the instruction of Torah and Talmud. "The Torah is received outside any exploratory foray, outside any gradual development. . . . Its urgency is not a limit imposed on freedom but attests, more than freedom, more than the isolated subject that freedom establishes, to an undeniable responsibility, beyond commitments made, for in them the absolutely separated self can put itself into question, claiming to hold the ultimate secret of subjectivity" (TT 46, TTf 100). It is in relation to this Book received and revealed that the self is placed in question, but the means by which its meaning is transferred is metaphor. At one level we are talking about the interpretative opportunities that metaphor offers. Levinas tells us, "What is sought after, and often achieved in the incessant return to verses by the Talmudic scholars . . . is a reading where the passage commented on clarifies for the reader its present preoccupation (which may be either out of the ordinary or common to its generation), and where the verse, in its turn, is renewed in the light of this clarification."[30] The meaning travels and is transferred from one time or place to another so that "notions remain constantly in contact with the examples or refer back to them, whereas they should have been content as springboards to rise to the level of generalization, or they clarify the thought which scrutinizes by the secret light of hidden or isolated worlds from which it burst forth; and simultaneously this world inserted or lost in signs is illuminated by the thought which comes to it from outside or from the other end of the canon, revealing its possibilities which were awaiting the exegesis, immobilized in some way, in the letters."[31] Whereas, in "Contempt for the Torah as Idolatry," Levinas warns that when one takes metaphorical meaning literally it is the negation of the spiritual and the source of all idolatry.[32] As suggested in the first passage, however, we are talking about the transportation of meaning from one time to another and from one specific set of historical concerns to another. We may be more comfortable assuming such metaphors to be literary but we must also remember that for Levinas, it is a transfer or transportation from the word of God on God's side (the infinite) to the word of God on our side (the finite). The presence of God on God's own side guarantees the divine and permanent meaning of the text, while our understanding of God on our side allows that meaning to change and shift so as to remain relevant to our current context. Meaning can be transferred not only from the past to the present but also to the future. It is the emphasis on metaphor as a site of contested meaning that maintains the dynamism, and thus it is this aspect that interests me most. The Torah is transcendent and from heaven by its demands that clash, in the final analysis, with what Levinas calls the pure ontology of the world. This relation points to something beyond us and beyond all the means by which we seek to deem ourselves more special than others. It refers to something beyond our selves, beyond our "people," and even beyond our time (we moderns).

Levinas recognizes that there is a danger inherent in "the idea of election which can deteriorate into pride but which originally expresses of an indisputable summons which gives life to ethics and through which the indisputability of the summons isolates the personal responsibility."[33] This, of course, is Butler's and Derrida's concern as well. What is to keep such a move, and such a historically particular relation, from descending into exemplarism, essentialism, nationalism, or racism? The answer lies in the constitutive dissymmetry between the call to responsibility or election required to assume such an identity and the identification with the calling itself. Just as there is a dissymmetry between God on God's side and God on our side or between the finite and the infinite which constitutes the relation that is Judaism, being-Jewish, Israel, there is a dissymmetry announced in the calling itself. The relation is such that it places the nature of the relation, the calling, the election in question whether it concerns a person, a people, or even the book itself.

Derrida takes up this issue in "Abraham, the Other" when he (following Franz Kafka) instructs us to think of "another Abraham" and concludes by articulating that this possibility, "that there should be yet another Abraham," is "the most threatened Jewish thought, but also the most vertiginously, the most intimately Jewish one that I know to this day."[34] This is because for Derrida, this possibility of another Abraham, the possibility of a mistaken election, that "perhaps I have not been called, and that perhaps I will never know it is not me who has been called. Not yet. Perhaps in a future to come, but not yet" threatens the origins and identity of Judaism and as such instantiates the constitutive dissymmetry of being-Jewish.

Derrida presents the ontology of "Being-Jewish" as the "experience of appellation and responsible response" where "any certainty regarding the destination, and therefore the election, remains suspended, threatened by doubt, precarious, exposed to the future of a decision of which I am not the masterful and solitary—authentic—subject."[35] For Derrida, the oscillation and undecidability that condition the noncoincidence of Jewish identity and thus permanently resist the temptation of exemplarism are what is revealed as *exemplary* about "being-Jewish." In relation to the Book, study can be seen as indicative of a dynamism that is also a dislocation of sorts. A constant questioning enabled by the structure of Torah and especially Talmud that disallows for a final answer or completed subject. The inability to reach a definitive answer about what is exemplary is what is exemplary about the study of Talmud. An essential component of its structure and content is the disagreement between commentaries that destabilize the authority of any one human voice. This is the content of the form. Levinas addresses this when he shows us that the isolated and complete self or identity is a fiction derived from the temptation of temptation. If one succumbs to such a temptation, the relational aspect of Election and Revelation is lost in self-reflection and the quest for self-certainty. "Overcoming the temptation of temptation would then mean going within oneself further than one's self" (TT 34, TTf 75). Here again, we see the emphasis on a self that surpasses itself. One must give up, defer, question one's place as the portal through which all meaning and value flows. "To be a self" on this reading is not to be the arbiter of what one can know based solely on what one can hold in their grasp, it "is to be responsible beyond what one has oneself done. *Temimut* consists in substituting oneself for others" (TT 49, TTf 107). The constant work of reading implies that there is no mastery, only learning.

This righteousness is founded on humility and realistic expectations rather than utopian ideals that inevitably cannot be upheld, leading to cynicism and nihilism. This is a calling to involuntary sacrifice that is intimately aware of the ways we humans are prone to failure. The understanding that we are guilty before committing any crime stands in stark contrast to the demands and expectations of utopianism or the teleology of Enlightenment, whose master narratives and normative values are announced as available to all, but never offered to most. The humility is conditioned by the realization that "nothing is ever definitely gained in it, beyond the living attention of the gaze, which may become weary. The Torah is not simply part of a cultural treasure, like song and the arts. The Word of God, supreme meaning, is without insistence—it flies away like a dream" (CTI 56, MPI 81). The Torah presents commandments without insistence, and as such the relation with the book is a twinning of freedom and responsibility. The responsible act is one that must be maintained.

I think we can follow Levinas away from Levinas insofar as we can mobilize the constitutive dissymmetry of Judaism, being-Jewish, Israel toward an understanding of ethics and responsibilities that does not allow itself to rest on its historical past or its status in the present. As we have seen throughout this book, Levinas was not particularly interested in what one could call "religious" authority or with an orthodox keeping of sacred texts. Modern Judaism appeared to him as indistinguishable from other religions in regard to piety, faith, services, and leadership. Levinas wanted to return to the Talmud in order to restore Judaism to life. He sought to make the past present for the future by blowing on the coals and reigniting the fire that he believed lives within the sacred texts of Judaism. It is in the relationship that we each can have with the text and not through the institutions that guard them. "Morality begins in us and not in institutions which are not always able to protect it. It demands that human honor knows how to exist without a flag (sans Drapeau)" (OW 81, VM 174). Such a move was at times in conflict with the concerns, biases, and priorities that occupied Levinas's historical moment and the historical events that conditioned his life. But the promise made to the future is more important than the fidelity to the past if one is not to end up worshiping the Torah or the flag of Israel as one might the golden calf.

There is a firm distinction between Israel understood as a relation with the Infinite and Israel understood as a modern state or a particular people. Israel as relation with God or the Infinite is on our side but as such is the opening to the other side. The means by which this relationship occurs for Levinas is through the study of Torah. "A God not incarnate, surely, but somehow inscribed, whose life, or a part of it, is being lived in the letters: in the lines and between the lines and in the exchange of ideas between the readers commenting upon them—where these letters come alive and are echoed in the book's precepts—ordering without enslaving, like truth—to answer in justice to one's fellow, that is, to love the other" (CTI 47, MPI 71). Israel conceived as a modern political state or particular people exists only on our side and as such it is nonrelational and solipsistic. This Israel is akin to what Levinas calls idolatry. As in the discussion of the Exodus, the relational understanding of Israel should be the primary lesson while the state or people of Israel must be the secondary one. The Israel of state or people takes the Jew to be a category that belongs to a historically and culturally conditioned ontology. Israel as relation takes the Jew to be the relationship with the name for the infinite itself.

This is a shift in temporality from the past to the future and in emphasis from the particular to the universal even if the constitutive dissymmetry that is its condition will not allow for either to fully unfold. The past is always in the future and the future is always in the past. The meaning and the message is larger, more universal, than the particular individual, even if it is the particular individual or event that provides the impetus, the memory, to inspire the action. Each pushes the other forward wherein the good for the one is directed to the good for all but the good for all must always account for every one. It is innovation that liberates a meaning for the future from a tradition or memory of the past. To achieve human universality (and a universalism that extends beyond the human animal) we must be prepared to jettison our prior and proper identity, even if it is that very identity that provides the template by which we seek human universality, as was the case with Levinas's Judaism. The invisible universality of which Levinas speaks is a universality that begins and ends with the individual (it is enacted by the individual) but directed toward the other (a particular subject in a particular place and time). If all commit to such an ethics of deferral, we are in the kingdom of heaven on earth and it is in this sense that we are each the Messiah. "The Messiah is Myself; to be Myself is to be the Messiah. . . . Who finally takes on the suffering of others, if not the being who says 'Me.' The fact of not evading the burden imposed by the suffering of others defines ipseity itself. All persons are the Messiah."[36] Messianicity. Of course, the humility at play recognizes the inhuman as well as the Inhuman, which undergirds the predisposition to self-sacrifice.

It is not enough to read about ethical action and responsibility or even to write about them. It is certainly not enough to claim affiliation with the people and texts Levinas sees as the model for such action. "That the mere fact of race is not a guarantee against evil, the Talmud saw and said better than anyone and with nearly unbearable force: the Jew without mitzvot is a threat to the world" (OW 83, VM 178). Actions are what count. It is not enough to recognize the grounds on which our institutions have been built and the peoples displaced or enslaved to do so. We must actually do the work to repair the future. This, of course, brings one perilously close to the "inaugurative structuring of the subject through persecution and ethical demand," but in the act of repair we are always close to identifying the subject as victim. The ethical imperative of constitutive dissymmetry destabilizes any such essentialist logic through the emphasis on self-sacrifice that conditions the vulnerability but the emphasis on the work, the mitzvot, that need to be done, the not yet. When one is cut off from the world to come, one is also cut off from the world in which one lives. By deactivating the possibility of justice in the future the idolaters threaten not only their future but also their present as well. By contrast, attention to the work that needs to be done in the future leads to action now.

The history of Emmanuel Levinas's Talmudic lectures is about identity and authority on one side or the other. The story can be told on our side by looking to the contextual circumstances, influences, and relations that led him to Talmud or in relation to the other side by accepting the possibility of a transcendent relation between God and Humans made manifest in a text. Working through this history on both registers forces one to think twice, to think differently. While this applies to the specific case of Levinas, asking one to think differently about Levinas is also asking one to think differently about everything. It is to consider an alternative logic of what makes sense and how the world works, which in turn questions the logic and stability of the assumptions we hold dear. It makes one uncomfortable and uneasy because it dislodges our sense of what we consider to be essential. The goal is to imagine what happens when we let ourselves go to think about the past and the future in accord with a totally different logic. This means letting go of all the coordinates by which we find ourselves privileged so as to dissociate from essentialism as much as we can, in regard to how we comport ourselves as a person, a people, a religion, or a temporal vector. This would truly be an opening to the other.

Notes

INTRODUCTION

1. Ady Steg, "Apologue," in *Emmanuel Levinas: Philosophe et Pédagogue*, ed. Nelly Hansson and Anne Grynberg (Paris: Éditions du Nadir de l'Alliance Israélite Universelle, 1998), 7.

2. David Banon is director of the Département des études hébraïques et juives at the Université de Strasbourg; Ami Bouganim is a philosopher who was director of L'institut de recherche et de développement du département de l'Éducation de l'Agence juive until 2010; Catherine Chalier is professor emerita of philosophy at the Université Paris Ouest Nanterre La Defense.

3. Judith Friedlander, *Vilna on the Seine* (New Haven, CT: Yale University Press, 1990), 3.

4. Stuart L. Charmé, "From Maoism to Talmud (With Sartre Along the Way): An Interview with Benny Levy," *Commentary* 78, no. 6 (December 1984): 50.

5. Emmanuel Levinas, *Nine Talmudic Readings*, trans. Annette Aronowicz (Bloomington: Indiana University Press, 1990), 5–6; *Quatre Lectures Talmudiques* (Paris: Les éditions de minuit, 1968), 14–16.

6. Brad Gregory, "The Other Confessional History: On Secular Bias in the Study of Religion," *History and Theory* 45, no. 4 (December 2006): 132–49.

7. Emmanuel Levinas, *In the Time of the Nations*, trans. Michael B. Smith (New York: Continuum, 1994), 13–14; *A l'heure des nations* (Paris: Les éditions de minuit, 1988), 33.

8. Constantin Fasolt, "History and Religion in the Modern Age," *History and Theory* 45, no. 4 (2006): 21.

9. Emmanuel Levinas, *Beyond the Verse*, trans. Gary D. Mole (New York: Continuum Press, 1994), 159; *L'au-delà du verset* (Paris: Les éditions de minuit, 1982), 195.

10. Emmanuel Levinas, "The Name of God According to a Few Talmudic Texts," in *Beyond the Verse*, 119; *L'au-delà du verset*, 148.

11. Levinas, *Beyond the Verse*, 161; *L'au-delà du verset*, 198.

12. Notable authors to consult on the subject include Dan Arbib, Robert Bernasconi, Catherine Chalier, Joseph Cohen, Simon Crtichley, Sarah Hammerschlag, Anabel Herzog, Robert Gibbs, Claire Katz, Martin Kavka, William Large, Diane Perpich, Jill Stauffer, Hent de Vries, and Edith Wysograd. In particular see Robert Bernasconi, "Who Is My Neighbour? Who Is the Other? Questioning the 'Generosity of Western Thought,'" in *Ethics and Responsibility in the Phenomenological Tradition* (Pittsburgh: Simon Silverman Phenomenology Center, Duquesne University, 1992), 1–31; Bernasconi, "Strangers and Slaves in the Land of Egypt: Levinas and the Politics of Otherness," in *Difficult Justice: Commentaries on Levinas and Politics*, ed. Asher Horowitz and Gad Horowitz (Toronto: University of Toronto Press, 2006); Howard Caygill, *Levinas and the Political* (London: Routledge, 2002).

13. Lawrence Kaplan, "Israel under the Mountain: Emmanuel Levinas on Freedom and Constraint in the Revelation of the Torah," *Modern Judaism—A Journal of Jewish Ideas and Experience* 18, no. 1 (February 1998): 35, https://doi.org/10.1093/mj/18.1.35.

14. Kaplan, "Israel under the Mountain," 35.

15. Kaplan, "Israel under the Mountain," 43.

16. Martin Kavka, "Is There a Warrant for Levinas's Talmudic Readings?," *Journal of Jewish Thought and Philosophy* 14, no. 1 (January 2006): 153–73; Martin Kavka, "For It Is God's Way to Sweeten Bitter with Bitter: Prayer in Levinas and R. Hayyim of Volozhin," *Levinas Studies* 13 (2019): 43–67.

17. Levinas, *Beyond the Verse*, 161; *L'au-delà du verset*, 199.

18. Ethan Kleinberg, *Haunting History: For a Deconstructive Approach to the Past* (Stanford, CA: Stanford University Press, 2017).

19. Jacques Derrida, *Positions* (University of Chicago Press, 1981), 56; Derrida, *Positions*, 2nd ed., trans. Alan Bass (New York: Continuum, 2002), 41.

20. Emmanuel Levinas, *In the Time of the Nations*, trans. Michael B. Smith (London: Continuum, 2007), 8; *A l'heure des nations*, 27.

21. In her book *Levinas's Politics: Justice, Mercy, Universality* (Philadelphia:

University of Pennsylvania Press, 2020), Annabel Herzog also pursues the possibility of understanding Levinas's work by employing the *double geste* but does so quite differently. Herzog contends that Levinas's Talmudic lectures can be seen as "literary" in contradistinction to, and in dialogue with, his philosophical writings. To my mind, this argument follows from Sarah Hammerschlag's analysis in *The Figural Jew: Politics and Identity in Postwar French Thought* (Chicago: University of Chicago Press, 2010) and to a lesser extent in *Broken Tablets: Levinas, Derrida, and the Literary Afterlife of Religion* (New York: Columbia University Press, 2016). Herzog uses the distinction between the philosophical and Talmudic writings as the basis for her *double geste* such that the Talmudic writings challenge the philosophical ones. On Herzog's account, the Talmudic writings represent the political and the philosophical represent the ethical. The philosophical writings are thus universal while the Talmudic writings are particular. I find the book and the approach incredible, but in the end, Herzog restricts her analysis to one that rests entirely on "our side." In short, the philosophical texts are allowed to take the place of Revelation, and as such any dissonance between the two bodies of texts remains a matter of human interpretation within the bounds of conventional academic scholarship.

22. Readers interested in issues pertaining to theory of history should note that the double session also reveals the ways that aspects of each tendency are always already at work in the other. The "secular" historical frame retains aspects of Christian, thus confessional, belief from its means of dating events on a calendar to the Protestant underpinnings of its methodological apparatus. In this light, the second session emerges from and is necessitated by the first and vice versa. This makes clear the necessity of an interminable analysis wherein the historical investigation turns on itself as the hierarchy is constantly reestablished, each undermining the definitive status of the other. For an in-depth discussion of what I call the theologico-historical hold, see my *Haunting History: For a Deconstructive Approach to the Past* (Stanford, CA: Stanford University Press, 2017), chap. 3, 72–114.

23. This is a literal undertaking of the content of the form. Hayden White, *The Content of the Form* (Baltimore: Johns Hopkins University Press, 1991).

24. As noted, the two sessions of each chapter are designed to be in dialogue and dispute with each other, although each can also stand on its own.

25. Emmanuel Levinas, *In the Time of the Nations*, trans. Michael B. Smith (New York: Continuum, 1994), 3–4; *A l'heure des nations*, 22.

26. John Drabinski, *Levinas and the Postcolonial* (Edinburgh: University of Edinburgh Press, 2013), 6.

27. Emmanuel Levinas, "Contempt for the Torah as Idolatry," in *In the Time of the Nations*, 55; "Mépris de la Thora comme idolâtrie," in *A l'heure des nations*, 80.

28. Fred Moten, *Universal Machine* (Durham, NC: Duke University Press, 2018), xi.

CHAPTER 1

1. For an overview of the intellectual and religious climate in Lithuania, see Judith Friedlander, *Vilna on the Seine* (New Haven, CT: Yale University Press, 1990).

2. Marie-Anne Lescourret, *Emmanuel Levinas* (Paris: Flammarion, 1994), 32–33.

3. F. Poirié, *Emmanuel Levinas: Qui Êtes-vous?* (Paris: La Manufacture, 1987), 67.

4. Emmanuel Levinas, *Beyond the Verse: Talmudic Readings and Lectures*, trans. Gary D. Mole (New York: Continuum Press, 2007), xvi; *L'Au-dela du verset* (Paris: Les éditions de minuit, 1982), 10.

5. Poirié, *Emmanuel Levinas: Qui Êtes-vous?*, 68.

6. Myriam Anissimov, "Emmanuel Levinas se souvient," *Les Nouveaux Cahiers* 82 (Fall 1985): 32.

7. Poirié, *Emmanuel Levinas: Qui Êtes-vous?*, 69.

8. Poirié, *Emmanuel Levinas: Qui Êtes-vous?*, 69.

9. Lescourret, *Emmanuel Levinas*, 51.

10. Poirié, *Emmanuel Levinas: Qui Êtes-vous?*, 69. We will return to the question of why Levinas came to see philosophy as a "temptation."

11. Interested readers can find a more detailed discussion of the influence of Bergson, Levinas's Strasbourg teachers, Husserl, and especially Heidegger in my *Generation Existential: Heidegger's Philosophy in France, 1927–1961* (Ithaca, NY: Cornell University Press, 2005).

12. Levinas, *Éthique et Infini: Dialogues avec Phillipe Nemo* (Paris: Fayard, 1982), 16.

13. Lescourret, *Emmanuel Levinas*, 61–62.

14. Poirié, *Emmanuel Levinas: Qui Êtes-vous?*, 70. My additions in brackets.

15. Poirié, *Emmanuel Levinas: Qui Êtes-vous?*, 70

16. Emmanuel Levinas, *Éthique et Infini: Dialogues avec Philippe Nemo* (Paris: Librairie Arthème Fayard et Radio-France, 1982), 19; *Ethics and Infinity*, trans. Richard A. Cohen (Pittsburgh: Duquesne University Press, 1985), 28.

17. Levinas, *Éthique et Infini*, 19–20; *Ethics and Infinity*, 29.

18. Levinas, *Éthique et Infini*, 19; *Ethics and Infinity*, 29.

19. Levinas, *Éthique et Infini*, 20, 23; *Ethics and Infinity*, 29, 32–33.

20. Levinas, *Éthique et Infini*, 20, 29; *Ethics and Infinity*, 29, 38–39.

21. Poirié, *Emmanuel Levinas: Qui Êtes-vous?*, 75.

22. Emmanuel Levinas, *Theory of Intuition in Husserl's Phenomenology*, trans. André Orianne, 2nd ed. (Evanston, IL: Northwestern University Press, 1995), 150.

23. Whether or not Levinas's conclusion about the place of the "other" in Husserl, and ultimately Heidegger, was apt is a matter of scholarly debate.

24. Poirié, *Emmanuel Levinas.: Qui Êtes-vous?*, 79–80.

25. The naturalization file is in the Archives Nationales de France, class BB, file no. 24900X30.

26. We might also speculate that, as in the case of the return to the Jewish gymnasium in Kovno, Levinas's decision to take the post at the AIU was not based on choice but on a lack of choice. It was Léon Brunschvicg, neo-Kantian philosopher and a board member of the AIU, who told Levinas frankly, "With your accent I would never pass you on the oral part of the *aggrégation*." Thus placement in the Parisian academic world was not an option. See Kleinberg, *Generation Existential*, 42–45; Lescourret, *Emmanuel Levinas*, 90.

27. Hugo Ott, *Martin Heidegger: A Political Life* (London: HarperCollins, 1993), 177.

28. Emmanuel Levinas, "Reflections on the Philosophy of Hitlerism," trans. Seán Hand, *Critical Inquiry* 17, no. 1 (Autumn 1990): 63–71. This article was originally published as "*Quelques réflexions sur la philosophie de l'Hitlérisme*," in *Esprit*, no. 26, novembre 1934, 199–208. See also Samuel Moyn, "Judaism against Paganism: Emmanuel Levinas's Response to Heidegger and Nazism in the 1930s," *History and Memory* 10, no. 1 (Spring/Summer 1998): 25–58.

29. Emmanuel Levinas, "*De l'évasion*," *Recherches Philosophiques* 5 (1935/36): 373–92; translated by Bettina Bergo as *On Escape* (Stanford, CA: Stanford University Press, 2003). For an in-depth discussion of "On Escape" in relation to Levinas's philosophical trajectory and specifically in regard to Heidegger, see my *Generation Existential*, chapters 1 and 7. See also, Samuel Moyn, *Origins of the Other: Emmanuel Levinas between Revelation and Ethics* (Ithaca, NY: Cornell University Press, 2005), 103–8. For a critical assessment, see Simon Critchley, *The Problem with Levinas*, ed. Alexis Dianda (Oxford: Oxford University Press, 2015), "Lecture Two."

30. Levinas, "Reflections on the Philosophy of Hitlerism," 56.

31. The right-wing journal *Combat* has no relation to the daily newspaper

Combat that was clandestinely published by the Resistance throughout the war and that Camus directed after 1944.

32. See Jeffrey Mehlman, "Of Literature and Terror: Blanchot at *Combat*," *Modern Languages Notes* 95 (1980): 808–29; Dianne Rubinstein, *What's Left? The École Normale Supérieure and the Right* (Madison: University of Wisconsin Press, 1990), 113; Michael Holland, "Bibliographie I" and "Bibliographie II," in *Gramma* 3/4 and 5 (1976): 223–45 and 124–32; Phillipe Mesnard, "Maurice Blanchot, le sujet et l'engagement," *L'Infini* 48 (Winter 1994): 103–28. I take up some of these issues in chapter 6 of my *Generation Existential*.

33. Many of these articles were collected and published in a 1957 volume titled *En Découvrant l'Existence avec Husserl et Heidegger* (Paris: Vrin, 1957).

34. Raul Hilberg, *The Destruction of the European Jews* (Chicago: Quadrangle Books, 1961), 401. This policy did not apply to Jewish members of the Red Army or to former members of the Reich of Jewish origin who were serving in any army. These prisoners of war were either shot or sent to camps.

35. Salomon Malka, *Emmanuel Levinas: His Life and Legacy*, trans. Michael Kigel and Sonja M. Embree (Pittsburgh: Duquesne University Press, 2006), 69–71. Salomon Malka, *Emmanuel Levinas: La Vie et la trace* (Paris: JC Lattès, 2002).

36. Levinas was mobilized to serve in the French army but was captured in June 1940. See Lescourret, *Emmanuel Levinas*, 119–28; Kleinberg, *Generation Existential*, 246–48; Ethan Kleinberg, "The Myth of Emmanuel Levinas," in *After the Deluge: New Perspectives on the Intellectual and Cultural History of Postwar France*, ed. Julian Bourg (Lanham, MD: Lexington Books, Rowman and Littlefield, 2004) 212–13.

37. Recently published as Emmanuel Levinas, *Carnets de la captivité*, collected and annotated by Rodolphe Calin and Catherine Chalier (Paris: Bernard Grasset/IMEC, 2009). See Sarah Hammerschlag, "'A Splinter in the Flesh': Levinas and the Resignation of Jewish Suffering, 1928–1947," *International Journal of Philosophical Studies* 20, no. 3 (2012), and "Levinas's Prison Notebooks," in *The Oxford Handbook of Levinas*, ed. Michael L. Morgan (New York: Oxford University Press, 2019).

38. Levinas, *Carnets de la captivité*,75.

39. It is clear that Levinas completed the groundwork for what would become *De l'existence à l'existant* in these notebooks, but what is fascinating is the way that the category of "Judaism" is so readily apparent in the notebooks but obscured in the philosophical piece. Catherine Chalier and Robert Calin go so far as to suggest that the *être-juif* or *je suis juif* of the *Carnets de la captivité* are akin to the departure from the *je suis* articulated in *De l'existence à l'existant*; see the preface

in *Carnets de la captivité*, 22–23. For Levinas's postwar philosophical break with Heidegger, see Emmanuel Levinas, *De l'existence à l'existant* (Paris: Vrin, 1993), and Kleinberg, *Generation Existential*, 248–58.

40. Levinas, *Carnets de la captivité*, 134.

41. Levinas, *Éthique et Infini*, 38; *Ethics and Infinity*, 48.

42. Levinas, *Carnets de la captivité*, 186.

43. Levinas provides the Hebrew and the French, which reads "*la joie d'avoir la Thora*"; Levinas, *Carnets de la captivité*, 186.

44. Emmanuel Levinas, "Being-Jewish," trans. Mary Beth Mader, *Continental Philosophy Review* 40 (2007): 209; "*Être juif*," *Cahiers d'études levinassiennes*, 1 (2002): 104. This article originally published in *Confluences*, année 7, 1947, 253–64.

45. The notion of "election" is complex in Levinas because he uses it both in terms of the traditional Jewish association, God's choice of the Jewish people, and also in reference to the philosophical meaning of the way the other person's dependencies and vulnerabilities make a claim on the subject prior to any decision or act by the subject. There is a similar double valence to the concepts of "revelation" and "persecution."

46. Emmanuel Levinas, *Nine Talmudic Readings*, trans. Annette Aronowicz (Bloomington: Indiana University Press), 30; *Quatre Lectures Talmudiques* (Paris: Les éditions de minuit, 1968), 67.

47. Levinas, *Carnets de la captivité*, 188.

48. Kleinberg, "Myth of Emmanuel Levinas," 210–13, 219–21.

49. Emmanuel Levinas, "The Temptation of Temptation," in *Nine Talmudic Readings*, 36; "La tentation de la tentation," in *Quatre Lectures Talmudiques*, 79.

50. Emmanuel Levinas, "Temptation of Temptation," in *Nine Talmudic Readings*, 37; "La tentation de la tentation," in *Quatre Lectures Talmudiques*, 82.

51. Levinas, "Being-Jewish," 209; "*Être-Juif*," 103.

52. Levinas, "Being-Jewish," 209; "*Être-Juif*," 104.

53. Levinas, "Being-Jewish," 209; "*Être-Juif*," 104.

54. Levinas, "Temptation of Temptation," in *Nine Talmudic Readings*, 36; "La tentation de la tentation," in *Quatre Lectures Talmudiques*, 79.

55. Levinas, "Being-Jewish," 208; "*Être-Juif*," 103.

56. Levinas, *Carnets de la captivité*, 179–80.

57. Levinas, *Carnets de la captivité*, 210, 213. This is from the transcript of Levinas's 1945 radio broadcast "*L'expérience juive du prisonier.*"

58. Martin Heidegger, *Being and Time*, trans. John Macquarrie and Edward

Robinson (New York: Harper and Row, 1962), 286; *Sein und Zeit* (Tübingen: Max Niemayer Verlag, 1986), 242.

59. Heidegger, *Being and Time*, 294; *Sein und Zeit*, 250–51.

60. Levinas, *Carnets de la captivité*, 211. Transcript of Levinas's 1945 radio broadcast "*L'expérience juive du prisonnier.*"

61. Levinas, "Being-Jewish," 208; "*Être-Juif,*" 102–3; *Carnets de la captivité*, 173, 176.

62. Levinas, "Being-Jewish," 209; "*Être-Juif,*" 104–5.

63. In *De l'existence à l'existant*, Levinas makes the argument in philosophical terms by arguing that Heidegger's description of anxiety (angst) in the face of death is a misconception. Individual beings encounter anxiety, but after death they are returned to the realm of anonymous being which does not. Therefore, the cause of anxiety according to Levinas is not the finitude of death, which is the limit of our self, but instead the infinity of anonymous being that continues long after we have shed our mortal coil. Unlike death, being never stops but is always there in its anonymity. The question for Levinas is: "Anxiety before Being—the horror of Being—is this not more original than anxiety before death? (*De l'existence à l'existant*, 98–100, 20.) Thus for Levinas, what is frightening in death is not one's finitude but the realization that being continues infinitely after one dies—the realization that being has no need for any individual existent. But what is frightening at one level also proves to be the opening to the Other for Levinas via the category of Infinity. On this see Levinas, *Totality and Infinity*, trans. Alphonso Lingis (Pittsburgh: Duquesne University Press, 1980), 48–49.

64. Hilberg, *Destruction of the European Jews*, 196–208.

65. See Lescourret, *Emmanuel Levinas*, 110–46.

66. "Being-Jewish," 205; "*Être-Juif,*" 99. Sartre's work was originally published in 1946 as *Réflexions sur la question juive* and translated into English in 1948 with the title *Anti-Semite and Jew*.

67. Jonathan Judaken, *Jean-Paul Sartre and the Jewish Question* (Lincoln: University of Nebraska Press, 2006), 7.

68. On the faults, see Pierre Birnbaum, "Sorry Afterthoughts on *Anti-Semite and Jew*," trans. Carol Marks, *October*, no. 87 (Winter 1999); on addressing anti-Semitism and the Holocaust see Sarah Hammerschlag, *The Figural Jew: Politics and Identity in Postwar French Thought* (Chicago: University of Chicago Press, 2010), chap. 2; Judaken, *Jean-Paul Sartre and the Jewish Question*, 127.

69. For a succinct presentation, see Michel Rybalka, "Publication and Reception of *Anti-Semite and Jew*," *October*, no. 87 (Winter 1999).

70. The only remaining evidence of the actual lecture is a review by Françoise

Derins published in *La Nef* and subsequently translated for the special issue of *October* on Jean-Paul Sartre's *Anti-Semite and Jew*, no. 87 (Winter 1999), 24–26.

71. Sartre, "Reflections on the Jewish Question, A Lecture," trans. by Rosalind Krauss and Denis Hollier, *October*, no. 87 (Winter 1999). This issue also contains a translation of the introduction by Levinas. As a preface to the Sartre lecture, Pierre Birnbaum provides some thoughts on the written piece, our limited knowledge of its origin and/or completeness, and the conspicuous absence of mention of this lecture in most works on Sartre.

72. "Being-Jewish," 205; "*Être-Juif*"; "*Être-Juif*," in *Confluences*, année 7, 1947.

73. See Kleinberg, *Generation Existential*, 168–83.

74. Jean-Paul Sartre, *Anti-Semite and Jew*, trans. George J. Becker (New York: Schocken Books, 1976), 69.

75. Sartre, *Anti-Semite and Jew*, 90.

76. Jean-Paul Sartre, *L'être et le néant* (Paris: NRF Gallimard, 1943), 134. See Judaken, *Jean-Paul Sartre and the Jewish Question*, 135–37.

77. Peter E. Gordon, "Out from *Huis Clos*: Sartre, Levinas, and the Debate over Jewish Authenticity," *Journal of Romance Studies* 6, no. 1 and 2 (Spring 2006): 158–62.

78. See Kleinberg, *Generation Existential*, chap. 4, "Jean-Paul Sartre."

79. Emmanuel Levinas, "Existentialism and Anti-Semitism," trans. Denis Hollier and Rosalind Krauss, *October*, no. 87 (Winter 1999): 28.

80. "*Être-Juif*"; "Being-Jewish," 205; "*Être-Juif*," 99.

81. Levinas, "Being-Jewish," 206;"*Être-Juif*," 99–100.

82. Levinas, "Being-Jewish," 206; "*Être-Juif*," 100.

83. Levinas, "Being-Jewish," 206; "*Être-Juif*," 100.

84. Levinas, "Being-Jewish," 206; "*Être-Juif*," 101.

85. Levinas, "Being-Jewish," 206–7; "*Être-Juif*," 101.

86. Levinas, "Being-Jewish," 207; "*Être-Juif*," 101–2.

87. Levinas, "Being-Jewish," 208; "*Être-Juif*," 102.

88. Heidegger, *Being and Time*; *Sein und Zeit*.

CHAPTER 2

1. Aron Rodrigue, *Images of Sephardi and Eastern Jewries in Transition: The Teachers of the Alliance Israélite Universelle, 1860–1939* (Seattle: University of Washington Press, 1993), 7–21.

2. Rodrigue, *Images of Sephardi and Eastern Jewries in Transition*, 7.

3. "Appel à tous les Israélites," in Alliance Israélite Universelle, *Alliance Israélite Universelle* (Paris, 1860), 39.

4. "Appel à tous les Israélites," 11.

5. F. Poirié, *Emmanuel Levinas: Qui Êtes-vous?* (Paris: La Manufacture, 1987), 79–80.

6. Emmanuel Levinas, "L'Agenda de Léon Brunschvicg," in his *Difficile liberté* (Paris: Éditions Albin Michel, 1976), 69; "The Diary of Léon Brusnchvicg," in Emmanuel Levinas, *Difficult Freedom*, trans. Seán Hand (Baltimore: Johns Hopkins University Press, 1990), 43.

7. Levinas, "L'Agenda de Léon Brunschvicg," 68; "Diary of Léon Brusnchvicg," 43.

8. Levinas, "L'Agenda de Léon Brunschvicg," 71; "Diary of Léon Brusnchvicg," 45.

9. Levinas, "L'Agenda de Léon Brunschvicg," 67; "Diary of Léon Brusnchvicg," 42.

10. Levinas, "L'Agenda de Léon Brunschvicg," 63–64; "Diary of Léon Brusnchvicg," 39.

11. Levinas, "L'Agenda de Léon Brunschvicg," 70–71; "Diary of Léon Brusnchvicg," 44.

12. Emmanuel Levinas, "Être Occidental," in *Difficile liberté* (Paris: Éditions Albin Michel, 1976), 75; Levinas, "Being a Westerner," in *Difficult Freedom*, trans. Seán Hand (Baltimore: Johns Hopkins University Press, 1990), 48.

13. See Aron Rodrigue, *French Jews, Turkish Jews: The Alliance Israélite Universelle and the Politics of Jewish Schooling in Turkey, 1860–1925* (Bloomington: Indiana University Press, 1990). Also Jay R. Berkovitz, *The Shaping of Jewish Identity in Nineteenth Century France* (Detroit: Wayne State University Press, 1989).

14. Rodrigue, *Images of Sephardi and Eastern Jewries in Transition*, 9.

15. See Allan Nadler, *The Faith of the Mithnagdim* (Baltimore: Johns Hopkins University Press, 1997), esp. chap. 3.

16. "The Ark and the Mummy," in Emmanuel Levinas, *Difficult Freedom*, trans. Seán Hand (Baltimore: Johns Hopkins University Press, 1990), 54; "L'Arche et la Momie," in *Difficile liberté* (Paris: Éditions Albin Michel, 1976), 83.

17. Levinas, "L'Agenda de Léon Brunschvicg," 70; "Diary of Léon Brusnchvicg," 44.

18. Yair Sheleg, "Goodbye, Mr. Chouchani," *Haaretz*, September 26, 2003, www.haaretz.com/1.4707327.

19. See Salomon Malka's *Monsieur Chouchani: L'énigme d'un maître du XXe siècle* (Paris: JC Lattès, 2014).

20. Elie Wiesel, "The Wandering Jew," in *Legends of Our Time* (New York: Holt, Rinehart and Winston, 1968), 87–88.

21. Myriam Anissimov, "Emmanuel Levinas se souvient," *Les Nouveaux Cahiers* 82 (Fall 1985): 32. Salomon Malka, *Emmanuel Levinas: His Life and Legacy* (Pittsburgh: Duquesne University Press, 2006), 233.

22. Sheleg, "Goodbye, Mr. Chouchani."

23. François Poirié, *Emmanuel Levinas: Essais et entretiens* (Arles, France: Actes Sud, 1996), 152–53.

24. Poirié, *Emmanuel Levinas: Essais et entretiens*, 153.

25. Marie-Anne Lescourret, *Emmanuel Levinas* (Paris: Flammarion, 1994), 142. See also Malka, *Emmanuel Levinas: His Life and Legacy*, 241.

26. Poirié, *Emmanuel Levinas: Essais et entretiens*, 155. See also See Shmuel Wygoda, "Le maître et son disciplie: Chouchani et Levinas," *Cahiers D'Etudes Levinassiennes*, no. 1 (2002): 149–84. Also Jacob Meskin, "The Role of Lurianic Kabbalah in the Early Philosophy of Emmanuel Levinas," *Levinas Studies*, no. 2 (2007): 55–58.

27. Poirié, *Emmanuel Levinas: Essais et entretiens*, 155.

28. Poirié, *Emmanuel Levinas: Essais et entretiens*, 160.

29. Poirié, *Emmanuel Levinas: Essais et entretiens*, 156. See also Malka, *Emmanuel Levinas: His Life and Legacy*, 158.

30. Wiesel, "Wandering Jew," 88.

31. Malka, *Emmanuel Levinas: His Life and Legacy*, 84.

32. Jay Winter, "René Cassin and the Alliance Israélite Universelle," *Modern Judaism* 32, no. 1 (2012): 2–3.

33. Winter, "René Cassin and the Alliance Israélite Universelle," 4.

34. *Cahiers de l'AIU*, no. 198, May 1956, 11–12. Archives of the Alliance Israélite Universelle, Paris, Archives Modernes, Présidence 007C, Circular of April 11, 1956. See Lescourret, *Emmanuel Levinas*, 142. See also Malka, *Emmanuel Levinas: His Life and Legacy*, 150–51. Jacques Derrida, *The Work of Mourning*, ed. and trans. Pascale-Anne Brault and Michael Naas, trans. Pascale-Anne Brault (Chicago: University of Chicago Press, 2003), 199. Jay Winter and Antoine Prost, *René Cassin and Human Rights: From the Great War to the Universal Declaration* (Cambridge: Cambridge University Press, 2013), 311.

35. Cassin wrote that "only since the persecution of 1933 have I stood in solidarity among the persecuted." Archives of the Alliance Israélite Universelle, Paris, Archives Modernes, Présidence 001e, Cassin to Sam Lévy, directeur des Cahiers Sfaradis, Neuilly, April 12, 1948. In Jay Winter's words, "Cassin's personality is better captured in seeing him as a secular Jewish universalist, a man whose Jewishness

was not initially at the core of his personal identity; it was made so by racists and killers." "René Cassin and the Alliance Israélite Universelle," 9.

36. Archives of the Alliance Israélite Universelle, Paris, Archives Modernes, Présidence 005a, Commission des écoles, May 13, 1952.

37. Malka, *Emmanuel Levinas: His Life and Legacy*, 87.

38. Quoted in Malka, *Emmanuel Levinas: His Life and Legacy*, 91.

39. Levinas, "Reflections of Jewish Education," in Emmanuel Levinas, *Difficult Freedom*, trans. Seán Hand (Baltimore: Johns Hopkins University Press, 1990), 265; Levinas, "Réflexions sur l'éducation juive," in *Difficile liberté* (Paris: Éditions Albin Michel, 1976), 368.

40. Levinas, "Reflections of Jewish Education," 266; Levinas, "Réflexions sur l'éducation juive," 369.

41. Levinas, "Reflections of Jewish Education," 265; Levinas, "Réflexions sur l'éducation juive," 369.

42. Levinas, "Education and Prayer," in Emmanuel Levinas, *Difficult Freedom*, trans. Seán Hand (Baltimore: Johns Hopkins University Press, 1990), 271; Levinas, "Éducation et prière," in Levinas, "Réflexions sur l'éducation juive," in *Difficile liberté* (Paris: Éditions Albin Michel, 1976), 377. My emphasis.

43. Levinas, "Reflections of Jewish Education," 267; Levinas, "Réflexions sur l'éducation juive," 371.

44. Levinas, "Reflections of Jewish Education," 267; Levinas, "Réflexions sur l'éducation juive," 371.

45. Levinas, "Reflections of Jewish Education," 267–68. Levinas, "Réflexions sur l'éducation juive," 372.

46. Levinas, "Reflections of Jewish Education," 268; Levinas, "Réflexions sur l'éducation juive," 372.

47. "État d'Israel et Religion d'Israel," *Evidences*, no. 20 (September–October 1951), 6. Levinas, "The State of Israel and the Religion of Israel," in Emmanuel Levinas, *Difficult Freedom*, trans. Seán Hand (Baltimore: Johns Hopkins University Press, 1990), 220.

48. Levinas, "Reflections of Jewish Education," 268; Levinas, "Réflexions sur l'éducation juive," 372–73.

49. Levinas, "For a Jewish Humanism," in Emmanuel Levinas, *Difficult Freedom*, trans. Seán Hand (Baltimore: Johns Hopkins University Press, 1990), 273; Levinas, "Pour un humanism hébraïque," in Emmanuel Levinas, *Difficile liberté* (Paris: Éditions Albin Michel, 1976), 380–81.

50. Levinas, "For a Jewish Humanism," 275; Levinas, "Pour un humanism hébraïque," 382–83.

51. Levinas, "For a Jewish Humanism," 275; Levinas, "Pour un humanism hébraïque," 383.

52. "Comment le judaïsme est-il possible?," *L'Arche* 28 (1959): 34. "How Is Judaism Possible?," in Emmanuel Levinas, *Difficult Freedom*, trans. Seán Hand (Baltimore: Johns Hopkins University Press, 1990), 249; Levinas, "Pour un humanism hébraïque," 347.

53. "Comment le judaïsme est-il possible?," 34. "How Is Judaism Possible?," 248. My emphasis.

54. "Comment le judaïsme est-il possible?," 58. "How Is Judaism Possible?," 250–51.

55. "État d'Israel et Religion d'Israel," 6. "The State of Israel and the Religion of Israel," 220.

56. "Comment le judaïsme est-il possible?," 58. "How Is Judaism Possible?," 251.

57. "Comment le judaïsme est-il possible?," 58. "How Is Judaism Possible?," 252.

58. See Lescourret, *Emmanuel Levinas*, 137–40. Malka, *Emmanuel Levinas: His Life and Legacy*, 107–9; Catherine Chalier and Ami Bouganim, "Emmanuel Levinas: School Master and Pedagogue," in *Levinas and Education: At the Intersection of Faith and Reason*, ed. Denise Egéa-Kuhne (New York: Routledge, 2008); Chalier, "*Levinas Maitre,*" in *Levinas: Philosophe et Pédagogue*, (Paris: Éditions du Nadir de l'Alliance Israelite Universelle, 1998), 65–70.

59. Interview with Catherine Chalier on December 2, 2004.

60. Malka, *Emmanuel Levinas: His Life and Legacy*, 110. Catherine Chalier's recollection was that Levinas would lead with a passage from the Gemara, and that this was the only aspect of the day's lesson that he pre-planned.

61. Poirié, *Emmanuel Levinas: Essais et entretiens*, 158.

62. Poirié, *Emmanuel Levinas: Essais et entretiens*, 157–58.

63. Poirié, *Emmanuel Levinas: Essais et entretiens*, 158–59.

64. Chalier and Bouganim, "Emmanuel Levinas: School Master and Pedagogue," 13. *Lévinas Philosophe et Pédagogue* (Alliance Israélite Universelle 1998).

65. Prosper Elkouby quoted in Malka, *Emmanuel Levinas: His Life and Legacy*, 88.

66. Cohen is quoted in Malka, *Emmanuel Levinas: His Life and Legacy*, 99.

67. "État d'Israel et Religion d'Israel," 6. "The State of Israel and the Religion of Israel," 219.

68. Chalier and Bouganim, "Emmanuel Levinas: School Master and Pedagogue," 15. *Lévinas Philosophe et Pédagogue* (Alliance Israélite Universelle 1998).

69. Amin Bouganim, "Levinas Pedagogue and Philosopher," on p. 18 of Catherine Chalier and Ami Bouganim, "Emmanuel Levinas: School Master and Pedagogue," in *Levinas and Education: at the Intersection of Faith and Reason*, ed. Denise Egéa-Kuhne (New York: Routledge, 2008), 18. See also, Ami Bouganim, "*Lévinas Pédagogue*," in *Lévinas Philosophe et Pédagogue* (Paris: Éditions du Nadir de l'Alliance Israelite Universelle, 1998), 55–64.

CHAPTER 3

1. See André Neher, *Le dur Bonheur d'être juif* (Paris: Le Centurion, 1978), 164–72; Joseph Sunglowsky, "The Relationship of Edmond Fleg and André Neher," *European Judaism: A Journal for the New Europe* 35, no. 2 (Autumn 2002); Edward K. Kaplan, "André Neher: A Post-Shoah Prophetic Vocation," in *Post-Holocaust France and the Jew, 1945–1955*, ed. Seán Hand and Steve T. Katz (New York: New York University Press, 2015); Robert Aron, "Portrait: Léon Algazi, mon maître," *Le Nouveaux Cahiers*, no. 17 (Printemps 1968).

2. See David Banon, *L'École de pensée juive de Paris: Le judaïsme revisité sur les bords de Seine* (Strasbourg: Presses Universitaire de Strasbourg, 2017); Jonathan Judaken, "French-Jewish Intellectuals after 1968," in *Encyclopedia of Modern Jewish Culture*, vol. 1, ed. Glenda Abramson (New York: Routledge, 2005); Marie-Ann Lescourret, *Emmanuel Levinas* (Paris: Flammarion, 1994).

3. Lescourret, *Emmanuel Levinas*, 167.

4. Emmanuel Levinas, "L'assimilation aujourd'hui," in *Difficile liberté* (Paris: Éditions Albin Michel, 1976), 355; "Assimilation Today," in Levinas, *Difficult Freedom*, trans. Seán Hand (Baltimore: Johns Hopkins University Press, 1990), 255.

5. See Céline Trautmann-Waller, "Jacob Gordin ou le judaïsme d'un philosophe européen: Saint-Pétersbourg-Berlin-Paris," *Archives Juives* 46, no. 2 (January 2013).

6. Emmanuel Levinas, "Jacob Gordin," in Levinas, *Difficile liberté* (Paris: Éditions Albin Michel, 1976), 237; "Jacob Gordin" in Levinas, *Difficult Freedom*, trans. Seán Hand (Baltimore: Johns Hopkins University Press, 1990), 169.

7. François Poirié, *Emmanuel Levinas: Essais et entretiens* (Arles, France: Actes Sud, 1996), 158.

8. Steg is quoted in Salomon Malka, *Emmanuel Levinas: His Life and Legacy* (Pittsburgh: Duquesne University Press, 2006): 128–29.

9. Steg is quoted in Malka, *Emmanuel Levinas: His Life and Legacy*, 132. For an excellent account of the influence of Maimonides on Levinas, see Michael Fagenblat, *A Covenant of Creatures: Levinas's Philosophy of Judaism* (Stanford, CA: Stanford University Press, 2010), in particular chapter 3.

10. Steg is quoted in Malka, *Emmanuel Levinas: His Life and Legacy*, 128–29.

11. Emmanuel Levinas, "Towards the Other," in *Nine Talmudic Lectures*, trans. Annette Aronowicz (Bloomington: Indiana University Press, 1994), 13–14; Levinas, "Envers autrui," in *Quatre Lectures Talmudiques* (Paris: Les éditions de minuit, 1968), 31.

12. Jean Halperin quoted in Malka, *Emmanuel Levinas: His Life and Legacy*, 132.

13. Levinas, *Nine Talmudic Lectures*, trans. Annette Aronowicz (Bloomington: Indiana University Press, 1994), 4; Levinas, *Quatre Lectures Talmudiques* (Paris: Les éditions de minuit, 1968), 12. My emphasis.

14. Emmanuel Levinas, *Beyond the Verse: Talmudic Readings and Lectures*, trans. Gary D. Mole (New York: Continuum Press, 2007), xvi; Levinas, *L'au-delà du verset* (Paris: Les éditions de minuit, 1982), 10.

15. Jacob Neusner, *Understanding the Talmud: A Dialogic Approach* (Jersey City, NJ: Ktav Publishing House, 2004), 42–51.

16. Emmanuel Levinas, *Nine Talmudic Readings*, trans. Annette Aronowicz (Bloomington: Indiana University Press, 1990), 4; Levinas, *Quatre Lectures Talmudiques* (Paris: Les éditions de minuit, 1968), 12. My emphasis.

17. Richard A. Cohen, "Emmanuel Levinas: Judaism and the Primacy of the Ethical," in *The Cambridge Companion to Modern Jewish Philosophy*, ed. Michael L. Morgan and Peter Eli Gordon (New York: Cambridge University Press, 2007), 235.

18. Elizabeth Shanks Alexander, "The Orality of Rabbinic Writing," in *The Cambridge Companion to the Talmud and Rabbinic Literature*, ed. Charlotte Elisheva Fonrobert and Marti S. Jaffee (New York: Cambridge University Press, 2007), 40–41.

19. Levinas, "On The Jewish Reading of Scriptures," in *Beyond the Verse: Talmudic Readings and Lectures*, trans. Gary D. Mole (New York: Continuum Press, 2007), 109 and 202 n. 8; Levinas, "De la lecture juive des ecritures," in *L'au-delà du verset* (Paris: Les éditions de minuit, 1982), 135–36.

20. Levinas, *Nine Talmudic Readings*, 5–6; Levinas, *Quatre Lectures Talmudiques*, 15–16.

21. Alexander, "Orality of Rabbinic Writing," 42.

22. Levinas, "Spinoza's Background," in *Beyond the Verse: Talmudic Readings*

and Lectures, 166; Levinas, "L'arrière plan de Spinoza," in *L'au-delà du verset* (Paris: Les éditions de minuit, 1982), 203.

23. Alexander, "Orality of Rabbinic Writing," 44.

24. Quoted in Alexander, "Orality of Rabbinic Writing," 44.

25. Levinas, "Spinoza's Background," in *Beyond the Verse: Talmudic Readings and Lectures*, 166; Levinas, "L'arrière plan de Spinoza," in *L'au-delà du verset*, 203.

26. Levinas, *Nine Talmudic Readings*, 31; Levinas, "La tentation de la tentation," in *Quatre Lectures Talmudiques*, 69. Levinas examined this story from the Tractate *Shabbath*, 88I*a* and 88*b*, in his Talmudic reading, "The Temptation of Temptation," presented at a December 1964 colloquium on "The Temptations of Judaism."

27. Emmanuel Levinas, "The Temptation of Temptation," in *Nine Talmudic Readings*, trans. Annette Aronowicz (Bloomington: Indiana University Press, 1990), 46–47. Levinas, "La tentation de la tentation," in *Quatre Lectures Talmudiques* (Paris: Les éditions de minuit, 1968), 102.

28. Levinas, "Towards the Other," in *Nine Talmudic Lectures*, 21; Levinas, "Envers autrui," in *Quatre Lectures Talmudiques*, 47–48.

29. Levinas, "On the Jewish Reading of Scriptures," in *Beyond the Verse: Talmudic Readings and Lectures*, trans. Gary D. Mole (New York: Continuum Press, 2007), 109; Levinas, "De la lecture juive des écritures," in *L'au-delà du verset* (Paris: Les éditions de minuit, 1982), 136.

30. Levinas, "On Jewish Reading of Scriptures," in *Beyond the Verse: Talmudic Readings and Lectures*,112; Levinas, "De la lecture juive des écritures," in *L'au-delà du verset*), 140.

31. Levinas, "On Jewish Reading of Scriptures," in *Beyond the Verse: Talmudic Readings and Lectures*, 103; Levinas, "De la lecture juive des écritures," in *L'au-delà du verset*, 127.

32. Emmanuel Levinas, "Ethics and Spirit," in *Difficult Freedom*, trans. Seán Hand (Baltimore: Johns Hopkins University Press, 1990), 13; Levinas, "Éthique et esprit," in *Difficile liberté* (Paris: Éditions Albin Michel, 1976), 27.

33. Levinas, "Ethics and Spirit," in *Difficult Freedom*, 14; Levinas, "Éthiques et esprit," in *Difficile liberté*, 28.

34. Levinas, "Ethics and Spirit," in *Difficult Freedom*, 14; Levinas, "Éthiques et esprit," in *Difficile liberté*, 29.

35. Levinas, "Temptation of Temptation," in *Nine Talmudic Readings*, 32; Levinas, "La tentation de la tentation," in *Quatre Lectures Talmudiques*, 71. See

Kleinberg, "The Myth of Emmanuel Levinas," in *After the Deluge*, ed. Julian Bourg (Lanham, MD: Lexington Books, 2004), 210–13, 219–21.

36. Levinas, "Temptation of Temptation," in *Nine Talmudic Readings*, 12–29, esp. 25; Levinas, "La tentation de la tentation," in *Quatre Lectures Talmudiques*, 31–64, esp. 54–56. See Kleinberg, "Myth of Emmanuel Levinas," in Bourg, *After the Deluge*, 215–21.

37. See Michael Fagenblat, "Levinas and Heidegger: The Elemental Confrontation," in *The Oxford Handbook of Levinas*, ed. Michael L. Morgan (Oxford: Oxford University Press, 2019).

38. Levinas, "A Religion for Adults," in *Difficult Freedom*, trans. Seán Hand (Baltimore: Johns Hopkins University Press, 1990), 15; Levinas, "Une religion d'adultes," in *Difficile liberté* (Paris: Éditions Albin Michel, 1976), 29.

39. Levinas, "On the Jewish Reading of Scriptures," in *Beyond the Verse: Talmudic Readings and Lectures*, 102; Levinas, "De la lecture juive des écritures," in *L'au-delà du verset*, 126.

40. Levinas, "On the Jewish Reading of Scriptures," in *Beyond the Verse: Talmudic Readings and Lectures*, 102; Levinas, "De la lecture juive des écritures," in *L'au-delà du verset*, 126.

41. Levinas, "On the Jewish Reading of Scriptures," in *Beyond the Verse: Talmudic Readings and Lectures*, 103; Levinas, "De la lecture juive des écritures," in *L'au-delà du verset*, 127.

42. Levinas, "On the Jewish Reading of Scriptures," in *Beyond the Verse: Talmudic Readings and Lectures*, 110; Levinas, "De la lecture juive des écritures," in *L'au-delà du verset*, 137.

43. Levinas, "On the Jewish Reading of Scriptures," in *Beyond the Verse: Talmudic Readings and Lectures*, , 112; Levinas, "De la lecture juive des écritures," in *L'au-delà du verset*, 140.

44. Levinas, *Beyond the Verse: Talmudic Readings and Lectures*, 113; Levinas, "De la lecture juive des écritures," in *L'au-delà du verset* 141.

45. Levinas, *Beyond the Verse: Talmudic Readings and Lectures*, 113–14; Levinas, "De la lecture juive des écritures," in *L'au-delà du verset*,141.

46. Levinas, "A Religion for Adults," in *Difficult Freedom*, trans. Seán Hand (Baltimore: Johns Hopkins University Press, 1990), 16; Levinas, "Une religion d'adultes," in *Difficile liberté* (Paris: Éditions Albin Michel, 1976), 31.

47. Levinas, "On the Jewish Reading of Scriptures," in *Beyond the Verse:*

Talmudic Readings and Lectures, 114; Levinas, "De la lecture juive des écritures," in *L'au-delà du verset*, 142.

48. See Michael L. Morgan, "Levinas on God and the Trace of the Other," in *The Oxford Handbook of Levinas*.

49. Levinas, "A Religion for Adults," in *Difficult Freedom*, 15–16; Levinas, "Une religion d'adultes," in *Difficile liberté*, 30.

50. As Martin Kavka makes clear, Levinas has a willful and idiosyncratic interpretation of Hayyim of Volozhin. Martin Kavka, "For It Is God's Way to Sweeten Bitter with Bitter: Prayer in Levinas and R. Hayyim of Volozhin," *Levinas Studies*, ISSN 1544–7000 doi: Online First.

51. Levinas, "'In the Image of God,' according to Rabbi Hayyim Volozhiner," in *Beyond the Verse: Talmudic Readings and Lectures*, 149; Levinas, "'À l'image de dieu,' d'après rabbi Haïm Voloziner," in *L'au-delà du verset*, 183–84. My emphasis.

52. Jacob Meskin makes the case for a close connection between Levinas's reading of Hayyim of Volozhin and his philosophical work in "Toward a New Understanding of the Work of Emmanuel Levinas," *Modern Judaism* 20, no. 1 (February 2000), esp. 83–86. See also Catherine Chalier, *L'âme de la vie: Levinas, lecteur de R. Haïm de Volozhin* in *Cahiers de l'Herne: Emmanuel Levinas* (Paris: Editions de l'Herne, 1991), 442–60. One can track Levinas's references to Hayyim of Volozhin beginning with the 1963 essay "Pièces d'identité," in *Difficile liberté: Essais sur le judaïsme*, 74–78, esp. 75; "Means of Identification," in *Difficult Freedom: Essays on Judaism*, 50–53, esp. 50–51. 1974: "La volonté du ciel et le pouvoir des hommes," in *Nouvelles lectures talmudiques*, 9–42, esp. 10; "The Will of God and the Power of Humanity," in *New Talmudic Readings*, 47–77, esp. 49. 1976: "Les dommages causés par le feu," in *Du sacré au saint: Cinq nouvelles lectures talmudiques*, 149–80, esp. 167; "Damages Due to Fire," in *Nine Talmudic Readings*, 178–97, esp. 188. 1977: "Modèle de L'occident," in *L'au-delà du verset: Lectures et discours talmudiques*, 29–50, esp. 48; "Model of the West," in *Beyond the Verse: Talmudic Readings and Lectures*, 13–33, esp. 32. 1977: "'À l'image de Dieu,' d'après Rabbi Haïm Voloziner," in *L'au-delà du verset*, 182–200; "'In the Image of God,' according to Rabbi Hayyim Volozhiner," in *Beyond the Verse*, 151–67. 1979: "De la lecture juive des Écritures," in *L'au-delà du verset*, 125–42, esp. 135–36 n. 7; "On the Jewish Reading of Scriptures," in *Beyond the Verse*, 101–15, esp. 210 n. 8. 1984: *Transcendance et intelligibilité*, 41, 58; "Discussion Following 'Transcendence and Intelligibility,'" in *Is It Righteous to Be?: Interviews with Emmanuel Levinas*, 272, 281. 1984: "De la prière sans demande: Note sur une modalité de Judaïsme"; "Prayer

without Demand," in *The Levinas Reader*, 227–34. 1985: "Judaïsme et kénose," in *À l'heure des nations*, 133–51, esp. 138; "Judaism and Kenosis," in *In the Time of the Nations*, 114–32, esp. 120. In 1986 Levinas provided the preface to Benjamin Gross's French translation of *Nefesh ha Hayyim* as *L'âme de la vie* (Paris: Editions Verdier, 1986), vii–x; "Vladimir Jankélévitch," in *Hors sujet*, 123–33, esp. 131; "Vladimir Jankélévitch," in *Outside the Subject*, 84–89, esp. 88. 1987: "Dialogue sur la penser-à-l'autre," in *Entre nous: Essais sur le penser-à-l'autre*, 237–43, esp. 242; "Dialogue on Thinking-of-the-Other," in *Entre Nous: On Thinking-of-the-Other*, 201–6, esp. 206.

53. Levinas, "Spinoza's Background," in *Beyond the Verse: Talmudic Readings and Lectures*, 165; Levinas, "L'arrière-plan de Spinoza," in *L'au-delà du verset*, 202. My emphasis.

54. Levinas, "'In the Image of God,' according to Rabbi Hayyim Volozhiner," in *Beyond the Verse: Talmudic Readings and Lectures*, 150; Levinas, "'À l'image de dieu,' d'après rabbi Haïm Voloziner," in *L'au-delà du verset*, 84. My emphasis.

55. Levinas, "'In the Image of God,' according to Rabbi Hayyim Volozhiner," in *Beyond the Verse: Talmudic Readings and Lectures*, 151; Levinas, "'À l'image de dieu,' d'après rabbi Haïm Voloziner," in *L'au-delà du verset*, 185.

56. Levinas, "'In the Image of God,' according to Rabbi Hayyim Volozhiner," in *Beyond the Verse: Talmudic Readings and Lectures*, 151; Levinas, "'À l'image de dieu,' d'après rabbi Haïm Voloziner," in *L'au-delà du verset*, 185.

57. Levinas, " 'In the Image of God,' according to Rabbi Hayyim Volozhiner," in *Beyond the Verse: Talmudic Readings and Lectures*, trans. Gary D. Mole (New York: Continuum Press, 2007), 158; Levinas, " 'À l'image de dieu,' d'après rabbi Haïm Voloziner," in *L'au-delà du verset* (Paris: Les éditions de minuit, 1982), p. 194.

58. Levinas, "For a Jewish Humanism," in *Difficult Freedom*, trans. Seán Hand (Baltimore: Johns Hopkins University Press, 1990), 275; Levinas, "Pour un humanism hébraïque," in *Difficile liberté*, 382–83.

59. Levinas, "'In the Image of God,' according to Rabbi Hayyim Volozhiner," in *Beyond the Verse: Talmudic Readings and Lectures*, 159; Levinas, "'À l'image de dieu,' d'après rabbi Haïm Voloziner," in *L'au-delà du verset*, 195–96.

60. Levinas, "'In the Image of God,' according to Rabbi Hayyim Volozhiner," in *Beyond the Verse: Talmudic Readings and Lectures*, 161; Levinas, "'À l'image de dieu,' d'après rabbi Haïm Voloziner," in *L'au-delà du verset*, 198–99.

61. Levinas, "'In the Image of God,' according to Rabbi Hayyim Volozhiner," in *Beyond the Verse: Talmudic Readings and Lectures*, 163; Levinas, "'À l'image de dieu,' d'après rabbi Haïm Voloziner," in *L'au-delà du verset*, 200.

62. See Morgan, "Levinas on God and the Trace of the Other," in *The Oxford Handbook of Levinas*.

63. Levinas, *Nine Talmudic Readings*, 14; *Quatre lectures talmudiques*, 32.

CHAPTER 4

1. John Drabinski, *Levinas and the Postcolonial* (Edinburgh: University of Edinburgh Press, 2013), 6. In broad strokes, Drabinski attempts to "decolonize" Levinas's philosophy by first making explicit and then purging the problematic Eurocentric aspects of his thought with the goal of "universalizing" Levinas's ethical project. Even so, Drabinski remains concerned that the Jewish dimensions of Levinas's philosophy may very well be an intractable problem.

2. Andrew McGettigan, "The Philosopher's Fear of Alterity: Levinas, Europe, and Humanities 'without Sacred History,'" *Radical Philosophy* 140 (November/December 2006): 15.

3. McGettigan, "Philosopher's Fear of Alterity," 15.

4. Fred Moten, *Universal Machine* (Durham, NC: Duke University Press, 2018), 4.

5. Robert Gibbs takes up this issue in *Correlations* (Princeton, NJ: Princeton University Press, 1992), and it is worth consulting his work on this in relation to what follows. See esp. 157, 168, 170.

6. Emmanuel Levinas, "The Translation of the Scripture," in *In the Time of Nations*, trans. Michael B. Smith (New York: Continuum Press, 2007), 42; Levinas, "La traduction de l'écriture," in *A l'heure des nations* (Paris: Les éditions de minuit, 1988), 64–65.

7. Emmanuel Levinas, "The Translation of the Scripture," in *In the Time of Nations*, trans. Michael B. Smith (New York: Continuum Press, 2007), 36, 37; Levinas, "La traduction de l'écriture," in *A l'heure des nations*, 58–59.

8. Levinas, "'In the Image of God', according to Rabbi Hayyim Volozhiner," in *Beyond the Verse*, trans. Gary D. Mole (New York: Continuum Press, 1994), 149; "'À L'image de Dieu', d'après Haïm Volozhiner," in *L'au-delà du verset* (Paris: Les éditions de minuit, 1982), 183.

9. See Michael Fagenblat, "Levinas and Heidegger: The Elemental Confrontation," in *The Oxford Handbook of Levinas*, ed. Michael L. Morgan (New York: Oxford University Press, 2019).

10. Levinas, "Model of the West," in *Beyond the Verse: Talmudic Readings and Lectures*, trans. Gary D. Mole (New York: Continuum Press, 2007), 27–28;

Levinas, "*Modèle de l'Occident*," in *L'au-delà du verset* (Paris: Les éditions de minuit, 1982), 44.

11. Levinas, "Jewish Thought Today," in *Difficult Freedom*, trans. Seán Hand (Baltimore: Johns Hopkins University Press, 1990), 160–61; Levinas, "La pensée juive aujourd'hui," in *Difficile Liberté* (Paris: Albin Michel, 1976), 225.

12. Levinas, "A New Version of *Jesus Narrated by the Wandering Jew* by Edmond Fleg," in *Difficult Freedom*, 105; Levinas, "Une nouvelle version de 'Jésus raconté par le Juif errant,' d'Edmond Fleg," in *Difficile Liberté*, 151.

13. Levinas, "A Religion for Adults," in *Difficult Freedom*, 15; Levinas, "Une religion d'adultes," in *Difficile Liberté*, 29.

14. See chapter 3, p. XX.

15. Levinas, *Difficult Freedom*, 45 ("The Diary of Léon Brunschvicg"), 78 ("Messianic Texts"); Levinas, *Difficile Liberté*, 71 ("L'agenda de Léon Brunschvicg"), 114 ("Textes messianiques").

16. Levinas, "A Religion for Adults," in *Difficult Freedom*, 15–16; Levinas, "Une religion d'adultes," in *Difficile Liberté*, 30.

17. Levinas, "'In the Image of God,' according to Rabbi Hayyim Volozhiner," in *Beyond the Verse: Talmudic Readings and Lectures*, 158; Levinas, "'A l'image de Dieu,' d'après Rabbi Haïm Voloziner," in *L'au-delà du verset*, 194.

18. Levinas, "For a Jewish Humanism," in *Difficult Freedom*, trans. Seán Hand (Baltimore: Johns Hopkins University Press, 1990), 275; Levinas, "Pour un humanisme hébraïque," in *Difficile Liberté*, 382–83.

19. Levinas, "'A l'image de Dieu,' d'après Rabbi Haïm Voloziner," in *L'au-delà du verset*, 182–83; Levinas, "'In the Image of God,' according to Rabbi Hayyim Volozhiner," in *Beyond the Verse: Talmudic Readings and Lectures*, 151–52.

20. Levinas, "'In the Image of God,' according to Rabbi Hayyim Volozhiner," in *Beyond the Verse: Talmudic Readings and Lectures*, 149; Levinas, "'A l'image de Dieu,' d'après Rabbi Haïm Voloziner," in *L'au-delà du verset*, 183–84. My emphasis.

21. Drabinski, *Levinas and the Postcolonial*, xii

22. Levinas, "Revelation in the Jewish Tradition," in *Beyond the Verse* (New York: Continuum, 2007), 139; Levinas, "La revelation dans la tradition juive," in *L'au-delà du verset* (Paris: Les éditions de minuit, 1982), 172.

23. As discussed earlier, the concept of "election" is complicated because in addition to the historical or Jewish meaning that Levinas explores, he also provides a more technical philosophical meaning where election refers to the other's

preconceptual, original claim on the subject. The two senses are not the same but neither are they unrelated.

24. "Intention, Event, and the Other," in *Is It Righteous To Be?* ed. Jill Robbins (Stanford, CA: Stanford University Press, 2001), 149. The interview was conducted in German and originally published in *Humanismus des Anderen Menschen* (Hamburg: Felix Meiner Verlag, 1989), 132–50.

25. "Interview with François Poirié: in *Is It Righteous To Be?* ed. Jill Robbins (Stanford, CA: Stanford University Press, 2001), 79.

26. Levinas, "Jewish Thought Today," in *Difficult Freedom*, trans. Seán Hand (Baltimore: Johns Hopkins University Press, 1990), 165; Levinas, "La pensée juive aujourd'hui," in *Difficile Liberté* (Paris: Albin Michel, 1976), 231.

27. Fred Moten, *The Universal Machine* (Durham, NC: Duke University Press, 2018), 4.

28. Franz Rosenzweig, *The Star of Redemption*, trans. Babara Gali (Madison: University of Wisconsin Press, 2005), 43. Later, on p. 66, he states, "And yet: here as there, 'it was the Greeks' who brought the idea to its highest development possible in isolation. Again, they, and not the legendary peoples of the East."

29. Rosenzweig, *Star of Redemption*, 68.

30. Rosenzweig, *Star of Redemption*, 82.

31. Levinas, "Monothiesme et Langage," originated as a speech delivered to the French Students' Union at the Mutualité in 1959. Published in Levinas, *Difficile Liberté* (p. 249); *Difficult Freedom*, trans. Seán Hand (Baltimore: Johns Hopkins University Press, 1990), 178.

32. Levinas, "Monothiesme et Langage," published in Levinas, *Difficile Liberté* (p. 250); "Monotheism and Language," in *Difficult Freedom*, 178.

33. Levinas, "Monothiesme et Langage," published in Levinas, *Difficile Liberté* (p. 251); "Monotheism and Language," in *Difficult Freedom*, 179.

34. Rosenzweig, *Star of Redemption*, 127, 128. See Gil Anidjar, *The Jew, the Arab: A History of the Enemy* (Stanford, CA: Stanford University Press, 2003), "Appendix I: Rosenzweig's War"; Leora Batnitsky, *Idolatry and Representation: The Philosophy of Franz Rosenzweig Reconsidered* (Princeton, NJ: Princeton University Press, 2009); Peter Eli Gordon, *Rosenzweig and Heidegger: Between Judiasm and German Philosophy* (Berkeley: University of California Press, 2005); see also Drabinski, *Levinas and the Postcolonial*, and McGettigan, "Philosopher's Fear of Alterity."

35. Emmanuel Levinas, "Entre Deux Mondes (La voie de Franz

Rosenzweig)," in *Difficile Liberté*, 255; Levinas, "Between Two Worlds (The Way of Franz Rosenzweig)," in *Difficult Freedom*, 182.

36. Levinas, "Entre Deux Mondes (La voie de Franz Rosenzweig)," in *Difficile Liberté*, 261; Levinas, "Between Two Worlds (The Way of Franz Rosenzweig)," in *Difficult Freedom*, 187.

37. Levinas, "Entre Deux Mondes (La voie de Franz Rosenzweig)," in *Difficile Liberté*, 261–62; Levinas, "Between Two Worlds (The Way of Franz Rosenzweig)," in *Difficult Freedom*, 187.

38. Levinas, "Entre Deux Mondes (La voie de Franz Rosenzweig)," in *Difficile Liberté*, 268; Levinas, "Between Two Worlds (The Way of Franz Rosenzweig)," in *Difficult Freedom*, 192.

39. See Samuel Moyn, *Origins of the Other: Emmanuel Levinas between Revelation and Ethics* (Ithaca, NY: Cornell University Press, 2005), 12. See chap. 5, "Levinas's Discovery of the Other in the Making of French Existentialism."

40. Henry Corbin, "La théologie dialectique et l'histoire," *Recherches philosophiques* 3 (1933): 252.

41. Søren Kierkegaard, *Fear and Trembling*, trans. Alastair Hannay (New York: Penguin Putnam, 1985), 145–46.

42. Levinas, "Toward the Other," in *Nine Talmudic Readings*, trans. Annette Aronowicz (Bloomington: Indiana University Press, 1994), 21; Levinas, "Envers autrui," in *Quatre lectures talmudiques* (Paris: Les éditions de minuit, 1968), 48.

43. Levinas, "Entre Deux Mondes (La voie de Franz Rosenzweig)," in *Difficile Liberté*, 260; Levinas, "Between Two Worlds (The Way of Franz Rosenzweig)," in *Difficult Freedom*, 186.

44. Levinas, "Entre Deux Mondes (La voie de Franz Rosenzweig)," in *Difficile Liberté*, 269; Levinas, "Between Two Worlds (The Way of Franz Rosenzweig)," in *Difficult Freedom*, 193.

45. Emmanuel Levinas, "Franz Rosenzweig: A Modern Jewish Thinker," in *Outside the Subject*, trans. Michael B. Smith (Stanford, CA: Stanford University Press, 1994), 51–52; originally published as "*Franz Rosenzweig*: Une pensee juive moderne," *Revue de Theologie et de Philosophie 98* (1965): 208–21.

46. Levinas, "Entre Deux Mondes (La voie de Franz Rosenzweig)," in *Difficile Liberté*, 270; Levinas, "Between Two Worlds (The Way of Franz Rosenzweig)," in *Difficult Freedom*, 193.

47. Levinas, "Entre Deux Mondes (La voie de Franz Rosenzweig)," in

Difficile Liberté, 270, 277; Levinas, "Between Two Worlds (The Way of Franz Rosenzweig)," in *Difficult Freedom*, 194, 199.

48. Levinas, "Entre Deux Mondes (La voie de Franz Rosenzweig)," in *Difficile Liberté*, 281; Levinas, "Between Two Worlds (The Way of Franz Rosenzweig)," in *Difficult Freedom*, 201.

49. Levinas, "Entre Deux Mondes (Biographie spirituelle de Franz Rosenzweig," in *La Conscience Juive: Données et debates*, ed. Éliane Amado-Lévy-Valensi and Jean Halperin (Paris: Presses Universitaires de France, 1959), 148.

50. Fred Moten, *The Universal Machine* (Durham, NC: Duke University Press, 2018), 1, 10.

51. Moten, *Universal Machine*, 10.

52. Moten, *Universal Machine*, 11. My insertion.

53. Moten, *Universal Machine*, 23.

54. Levinas, "Model of the West," in *Beyond the Verse: Talmudic Readings and Lectures*, trans. Gary D. Mole (New York: Continuum Press, 2007), 31; Levinas, "*Modèle de l'Occident*," in *L'au-delà du verset* (Paris: Les éditions de minuit, 1982), 48.

55. Dipesh Chakrabarty, *Provincializing Europe* (Princeton, NJ: Princeton University Press, 2007), 8.

56. Emmanuel Levinas, "For a Place in the Bible," in *In the Time of Nations*, trans. Michael B. Smith (New York: Continuum, 2007), 3–4; Levinas, "Pour une place dans la Bible," in *A l'heure des nations* (Paris: Les éditions de minuit, 1988), 22.

57. Emmanuel Levinas, "Revelation in the Jewish Tradition," in *Beyond the Verse*, trans. Gary D. Mole (New York: Continuum, 2007), 138; Levinas, "La revelation dans la tradition juive," in *L'au-delà du verset* (Paris: Les éditions de minuit, 1982), 171.

58. Levinas, "Revelation in the Jewish Tradition," in *Beyond the Verse*, 134; Levinas, "La revelation dans la tradition juive," in *L'au-delà du verset*, 166–67.

59. Emmanuel Levinas, "The Translation of the Scripture," in *In the Time of Nations*, trans. Michel B. Smith (New York: Continuum Press, 2007), 40; Levinas, *À l'heure des nations* (Paris: Les éditions de minuit, 1988), 62.

60. Moten, *Universal Machine*, 4.

61. Moten, *Universal Machine*, 11. My insertion.

62. Levinas, "Revelation in the Jewish Tradition," in *Beyond the Verse*, 128; Levinas, "La revelation dans la tradition juive," in *L'au-delà du verset*, 159.

63. Levinas, "Revelation in Jewish Tradition," in *Beyond the Verse*, 135; Levinas, "La revelation dans la tradition juive," in *L'au-delà du verset*, 167.

64. Levinas, "For a Place in the Bible," in *In the Time of Nations*, 4; Levinas, "Pour une place dans la Bible," in *A l'heure des nations*, 22.

CONCLUSION

1. "But why don't we let ourselves go?" Fred Moten, *The Universal Machine* (Durham, NC: Duke University Press, 2018),xi.

2. On "being-Jewish," see chapter 1, pp. 36–52; also Sarah Hammerschlag, *The Figural Jew: Politics and Identity in Postwar French Thought* (Chicago: University of Chicago Press, 2010), chap. 2.

3. Emmanuel Levinas, "From Ethics to Exegesis," in *In the Time of the Nations*, trans. Michael B. Smith (New York: Continuum, 2007), 97; *A l'heure des Nations* (Paris: Les éditions de minuit, 1988), 128.

4. Emmanuel Levinas, "A Religion for Adults," in *Difficult Freedom: Essays on Judaism*, trans. Seán Hand (Baltimore: Johns Hopkins University Press, 1990), 21; Levinas, "Une religion d'adultes," in *Difficile Liberté* (Paris: Albin Michel, 1976), 39.

5. *D'Auschwitz à Israël: Vingt ans après la Libération*, ed. Isaac Schneerson (Paris: Centre de documentation juive contemporaine, 1968). Levinas's reference is to Blaise Pascale's *Pensées*, section XII, 759.

6. Levinas, "From the Rise of Nihilism to the Carnal Jew," in *Difficult Freedom: Essays on Judaism*, 221; Levinas, "De la montée du nihilism au juif charnel," in *Difficile Liberté* (Paris: Albin Michel, 1976), 309.

7. Levinas, "From the Rise of Nihilism to the Carnal Jew," in *Difficult Freedom*, 222; Levinas, "De la montée du nihilism au juif charnel," in *Difficile Liberté*, 311.

8. Judith Butler, *Parting Ways: Jewishness and the Critique of Zionism* (New York: Columbia University Press, 2012), 46. For an excellent account of Levinas on the issue of Israel, see Annabel Herzog, *Levinas's Politics: Justice, Mercy, Universality* (Philadelphia: University of Pennsylvania Press, 2020). As noted in the introduction, my chief difference with Herzog rests with her approach, which allows her to "square the circle" of some of Levinas's most problematic and promising tendencies. For a response to Butler's critique of Levinas that addresses the history of misascribing the term "faceless Palestinians" to him, see Oona Eisenstadt and Claire Elise Katz, "The Faceless Palestinian: A History of an Error," *Telos* 174 (Spring 2016): 9–32. Michael L. Morgan argues that Butler and Howard Caygill each use the confusion between what he calls the "ethical self" and the "political self" to claim there is a deep inconsistency in Levinas's thought. Critical accounts of Levinas include Tina Chanter, "Hands That Give and Hands That Take: The Politics

of the Other in Levinas," in *Levinas, Law, Politics*, ed. Marinos Diamantides (New York: Cavendish, 2007), 76; Kaveh Bassiri, "On Transformative Compassion," *Michigan Quarterly Review* blog, August 21, 2014, http://www.michiganquarterlyreview.com/2014/08/on-transformative-compassion/; John Drabinski, "The Possibility of an Ethical Politics: From Peace to Liturgy," *Philosophy and Social Criticism* 26, no. 4 (2000): 49–73; Catriona Hanley, "Levinas on Peace and War," *Athena Filosofijos Studijos* 2 (2006): 70–81; Anna Strahan, *Levinas, Subjectivity, Education: Towards an Ethics of Radical Responsibility* (New York: John Wiley and Sons, 2012), 1; David Campbell, "The Deterritorialization of Responsibility: Levinas, Derrida, and Ethics after the End of Philosophy," *Alternatives* 19, no. 4 (1994): 455–84.

9. See chapter 1, pp. 40–41, 51–52.

10. Levinas, "From the Rise of Nihilism to the Carnal Jew," in *Difficult Freedom: Essays on Judaism*, trans. Seán Hand (Baltimore: Johns Hopkins University Press, 1990), 223; Levinas, "De la montée du nihilism au juif charnel," in *Difficile Liberté* (Paris: Albin Michel, 1976), 311–12.

11. See Howard Caygill, *Levinas and the Political* (London: Routledge, 2002), esp. 164–72.

12. Levinas, "From the Rise of Nihilism to the Carnal Jew," in *Difficult Freedom*, 223; Levinas, "De la montée du nihilism au juif charnel," in *Difficile Liberté*, 312.

13. Levinas, "From the Rise of Nihilism to the Carnal Jew," in *Difficult Freedom*, 223–24; Levinas, "De la montée du nihilism au juif charnel," in *Difficile Liberté*, 312–13.

14. Levinas, "From the Rise of Nihilism to the Carnal Jew," in *Difficult Freedom*, 225; Levinas, "De la montée du nihilism au juif charnel," in *Difficile Liberté*, 314.

15. Levinas, "A Religion for Adults," in *Difficult Freedom*, 22; Levinas, "Une religion d'adultes," in *Difficile Liberté*, 40.

16. Levinas, "A Religion for Adults," in *Difficult Freedom*, 22; Levinas, "Une religion d'adultes," in *Difficile Liberté*, 39.

17. Levinas, "From the Rise of Nihilism to the Carnal Jew," in *Difficult Freedom*, 225; Levinas, "De la montée du nihilism au juif charnel," in *Difficile Liberté*, 315.

18. See chapter 1, p. 48; Levinas, "Toward the Other," in *Nine Talmudic Readings*, trans. Annette Aronowicz (Bloomington: Indiana University Press, 1994),

27–28; Levinas, "Envers Autrui," in *Quatre Lectures Talmudiques* (Paris: Les éditions de minuit, 1968), 61–62.

19. Judith Butler, *Parting Ways: Jewishness and the Critique of Zionism* (New York: Columbia University Press, 2012), 46.

20. See Levinas's interview with François Poirié in *Emmanuel Levinas: Essais et entretiens* (Arles, France: Actes Sud, 1996), 120.

21. Jacques Derrida, "Abraham, the Other," in *Judeities: Questions for Jacques Derrida*, ed. Bettina Bergo, Joseph Cohen and Raphael Zagury-Orly; trans. Bettina Bergo and Michael B. Smith (New York: Fordham University Press, 2007), 12. Derrida links his mistrust of the "*exemplarist* temptation" to that of "even more difficult and problematical language of *election*" (p. 16). While not coterminous the two go hand in glove.

22. Derrida, "Abraham, the Other," 23.

23. Emmanuel Levinas, "Being-Jewish," trans. Mary Beth Mader, *Continental Philosophy Review* 40 (2007): 209; "*Être juif,*" *Cahiers d'études levinassiennes*, 1 (2002): 104. This article originally published in *Confluences*, année 7, 1947.

24. Derrida, "Abraham, the Other," 23.

25. Levinas, "The Temptation of Temptation" in *Nine Talmudic Readings*, 41; Levinas, "La tentation de la tentation," in *Quatre Lectures Talmudiques*, 90. On Derrida and "messianicity," see "Abraham, the Other," 21; Jacques Derrida, *Archive Fever* (Chicago: University of Chicago Press, 1998), 72.

26. Judith Butler, *Parting Ways: Jewishness and the Critique of Zionism* (New York: Columbia University Press, 2012), 46.

27. Levinas, "On the Jewish Reading of Scriptures," in *Beyond the Verse: Talmudic Readings and Lectures*, trans. Gary D. Mole (New York: Continuum Press, 2007), 112; Levinas, "De la lecture juive des écritures," in *L'au delà du verset* (Paris: Les éditions de minuit, 1982), 140.

28. Levinas, "'In the Image of God,' according to Rabbi Hayyim Volozhiner," in *Beyond the Verse: Talmudic Readings and Lectures*, trans. Gary D. Mole (New York: Continuum Press, 2007), 159; Levinas, "'A l'image de dieu,' d'après Rabbi Haim Volozhiner," in *L'au delà du verset* (Paris: Les éditions de minuit, 1982), 195–96.

29. Levinas, "'In the Image of God,' according to Rabbi Hayyim Volozhiner," 161; Levinas, "'A l'image de dieu,' d'après Rabbi Haim Volozhiner," 198–99.

30. Levinas, "Spinoza's Background," in *Beyond the Verse: Talmudic Readings and Lectures*, trans. Gary D. Mole (New York: Continuum Press, 2007), 166;

Levinas, "L'arrière plan de Spinoza," in *L'au delà du verset* (Paris: Les éditions de minuit, 1982), 203.

31. Levinas, "On the Jewish Reading of Scriptures," in *Beyond the Verse*, 103; Levinas, "De la lecture juive des écritures," 127.

32. Levinas, "Contempt for the Torah as Idolatry," in *In the Time of Nations*, trans. Michael B. Smith (New York: Continuum Press, 2007), 55; "Mépris de la Thora comme idolâtrie," in *A l'heure des nations*, 79.

33. Levinas, "Revelation in the Jewish Tradition," in *Beyond the Verse* (New York: Continuum, 2007), 139; Levinas, "La révélation dans la tradition juive," in *L'au delà du verset* (Paris: Les éditions de minuit, 1982), 172.

34. Derrida, "Abraham, the Other," 34–35.

35. Derrida, "Abraham, the Other," 31.

36. Levinas, "Messianic Texts," in *Difficult Freedom*, 89; "Textes messianiques," in *Difficile Liberté*, 129.

Index

Abdima Bar Ḥama bar Hasa, 16, 37
Abraham: Abram and, 106–7, 108–10, 114; as the Other, 178; promise of universal humanity, 109–10, 112; sacrifice of Isaac, 41, 149
Abram: Abraham and, 106–7, 108–10, 114
Aeschylus: *The Eumenides,* 65, 66
Akiva, Rabbi, 105–6, 124, 125, 127, 152
Alexander, Elizabeth Shanks, 102
Algazi, Léon, 89, 90
Alliance Israélite Universelle (AIU): central committee of, 56, 67; decline of, 86, 87; international schools of, 59, 66–67, 82, 86–87; language of instruction, 59; Levinas and, 12, 29, 53–54, 187n26; mission of, 54, 55, 59, 61, 147; origin of, 29–30, 52, 54; reform of, 67; student enrollment, 87; during World War II, 67
Amar, André, 28
Amos, Book of, 101, 102–3
Amzalag, Emile, 69
anti-Semitism: in France, 32–33, 54; in Germany, 20, 31–32, 40; in Russian Empire, 17

"Anti-Semitism and Existentialism" (Levinas), 46
anxiety: conception of, 190n63
apikoros, 135, 136
Arab-Israel War (1947–48), 86
Aristotle, 21
Aronowicz, Annette, 129, 140
Askénazi, Léon (a.k.a. Manitou), 92, 99
assimilation of Jews, 49–50, 56–57, 58, 90–91, 121, 168–69, 170
atheism, 118, 119, 127–28, 137–38
Atlan, Henri, 92
Atlan, Liliane, 92

Babylonian Talmud, 102, 105
Baden decree, 31
Banon, David, 2, 183n2
Barrrès, Maurice, 30
Being: *vs.* beings, 28, 44; ego and, 42; idea of concrete, 28–29; ontological question of, 27, 33; of the "there is," 35–36
Being and Time (Heidegger), 26, 27, 51
"Being a Westerner" (Levinas), 58
being-Jewish: category of, 34–35, 36–37,

166; constitutive dissymmetry of, 173, 177–78, 179–80; *vs.* Dasein, 35, 36; emphasis on the past, 50–51; hierarchical understanding of, 52; meaning of, 48, 49, 52; ontology of, 38, 42, 43, 49–51, 62, 178; relation with the infinite, 175
"Being-Jewish" (Levinas), 37, 58
Berakhot (tractate), 89, 90, 94
Bergson, Henri, 21, 23–24
Beyond the Verse (Levinas), 125
bias of the modern, 161
Bible: humanism and, 138; Judaism and, 65–66, 73–74; openness of, 158; translation into Greek, 132–33
Birnbaum, Pierre, 191n71
Blanchot, Maurice, 32–33
Blondel, Charles, 21
Bouganim, Ami, 2, 85, 183n2
braid: metaphor of, 12
Brassillach, Robert, 33
Brunschvicg, Léon, 56–57, 58, 59, 61, 187n26
Butler, Judith, 167–68, 170, 172, 173, 174–75, 177, 207n8; *Parting Ways: Jewishness and the Critique of Zionism*, 167

Calin, Robert, 188n39
Carteron, Henri, 21
Cassin, René, 66, 67, 68, 86, 193nn34–35
Cassirer, Ernst, 22
Caygill, Howard, 207n8
Chakrabarty, Dipesh, 159
Chalier, Catherine, 2, 79, 81, 183n2, 188n39
Chanter, Tina, 207n8
Christianity: crisis of, 136; *vs.* Eastern cultures, 146; Judaism and, 147–48, 150–53; relation to time and history, 50, 153
Cohen, Gabriel, 82
Cohen, Hermann, 92

Cohen, Richard, 3, 4, 83, 102
Colloque des intellectuels juifs de langue française: conferences of, 89, 93–95; founders of, 89, 90; Levinas's Talmudic lectures at, 91, 94, 96–97, 127, 128
consciousness, 33
constitutive dissymmetry, 13, 173
"Contempt for the Torah as Idolatry" (Levinas), 177
contingency (*Geworfenheit*), 39
Corbin, Henry, 149
Corneille, Pierre, 81
cut off from the world to come, 139–40
cynicism, 77, 179

Damascus blood libel affair, 54
dancing, 155, 156, 157, 161. *See also* everything else is dancing
Dasein: *vs.* being-Jewish, 35, 36; concept of, 35, 39, 40–41; death and, 41; finitude of, 43; temporal totality of, 42
death, 16, 41
decolonization, 143, 144, 162, 163
"De l'Évasion" (Levinas), 33
De l'Existence à l'existant (Levinas), 35
Derrida, Jacques: "Abraham, the Other," 178; on category of being-Jewish, 173–74, 175, 178; on double gesture, 9; on exemplarist temptation, 209n21; *Glas*, 10; on the Other, 172–73, 178; "Tympan," 10
Descartes, René, 21
"Diary of Léon Brunschvicg, The" (Levinas), 56, 57–58
Difficult Freedom (Levinas), 128
disinterestedness, 138
divine inspiration, 116, 117
Divine will, 151
Dostoyevsky, Feodor, 19, 20, 21, 78; *The Brothers Karamazov*, 172
double gesture (*un double geste*), 9
Drabinski, John, 12, 141, 144, 159, 202n1; *Levinas and the Postcolonial*, 129

Dreyfus affair, 22–23, 57
Drieu la Rochelle, Pierre, 33
Durkheim, Émile, 21

Eastern Judaism, 120–21
École de Pensée Juive de Paris, 93, 95, 96
École Gilbert-Bloch d'Orsay: closure of, 96; comparison to ENIO, 92–93; educational goals of, 91–93; establishment of, 91; leading figures of, 91, 93; mission of, 92–93; ties to Jewish Scouts, 92
École Normale Israélite Orientale (ENIO): courses at, 78–80, 81–82; daily prayers, 69; educational mission of, 52, 66–67, 68, 85–86; establishment of, 66; international politics and, 86; Levinas's directorship of, 12, 29, 54, 63, 66, 67–69, 78, 85–86, 127; students of, 68–69, 86; transformation of, 87–88
École Normale Superieure, 67
"Education and Prayer" (Levinas), 70
ego, 34–35, 42
Einstein, Albert, 143, 163
Eleazar ben Azariah, Rabbi, 94, 108, 117
Election, 4, 9, 51; danger of deterioration into pride, 141–42, 177; language of, 209n21; meaning of, 164, 189n45, 203n23; possibility of death and, 40; revelation and, 39–40
Elijah ben Solomon Zalman, Gaon of Vilna, 15, 19, 60, 119, 125, 133, 134, 139
Eliphaz (Esau's son), 158, 159
Elkouby, Prosper, 82
end of philosophy, 130, 143–44, 163
Epstein, Rabbi, 82, 83, 94
eschatological sanction, 140
essentialism, 14, 150, 166, 167
ethics: of alterity, 166; anaesthetization of, 154; dis-interestment of, 138; as first philosophy, 166; idea of universal, 14; Jewish reason and, 158–59; politics and, 14, 22; religion and, 166–67; sources of, 6; universal, 13–14
European civilization: development of, 130, 144–45; end of domination of, 143–44
everyday life, 50–51
everything else is dancing, 142
exegesis, 122
exemplarism, 156, 163, 166, 167, 178, 209n21
Exodus: greatness of Israel in, 112; meaning of, 92, 95–96, 98, 165; memory of, 93, 96, 113, 161; as promise of liberty, 96–97
experience without experiencing, 20

faith, 38
Fasolt, Constantin, 4
February Revolution, 18
finite vs. infinite, 177
Finkelkraut, Alain, 2–3, 4
Fleg, Edmond, 89, 93
Fond Social Juif Unifié, Le, 75
"For a Jewish Humanism" (Levinas), 73
France: anti-Semitism in, 32–33; German occupation of, 56; Jewish community, 54, 89–90, 91, 133
"Franz Rosenzweig: Une pensee juive modern" (Levinas), 152
freedom, 33, 77–78, 91–92
freedom of choice, 16–17
French Revolution, 55, 56, 68
Friedlander, Judith, 4; *Vilna on the Seine*, 2
"From the Rise of Nihilism to the Carnal Jew" (Levinas), 167
fruit on a tree: metaphor of, 23–25

Gamliel, Rabban, 94
Gamzun, Robert (a.k.a. Castor), 91, 92, 93
Gaulle, Charles de, 67
Gemara, 60, 63, 99–100, 158
God: atheism and understanding of, 137–

38; humanism and idea of, 123–24, 138; intervention of, 76; memory and experience of, 91; power of, 123, 138; qualities of, 132; relations between human and, 176; saintliness of, 113
God on God's own side: *vs*. God on our side, 6–7, 9, 14, 111, 175–77; human assess to, 5–6; infinity of, 123, 175–76; transfer of meaning of Torah from, 124, 177
God on our side: ethical commitment, 6; *vs*. God on God's own side, 6–7, 9, 14, 111, 175–77; limitations of, 123; transfer of meaning of Torah to, 124, 177
Goethe, Johann Wolfgang von, 81
Gogol, Nikolai, 19
Gordin, Jacob, 91, 92, 96
Gordon, Peter, 47
Greek language: attributes of, 131, 132
Greek thought: ethics and, 136; monotheism and, 145; openness of, 158; universalism and rationalism of, 134–35, 141
Gregory, Brad, 4
Grossman, Vasily: *Life and Fate*, 90

Halakah (commandments and interdicts), 108, 109
Halbwachs, Maurice, 21
Hama bar Hanina, 23
Hasidic Judaism, 121, 134, 138–39, 157
Hayyim of Volozhin. *See* Volozhiner, Ḥayyim ben Isaac
Hebrew: in Jewish education, 70, 73, 76–77, 86; in relation to Greek, 140
Hegel, Georg Wilhelm Friedrich, 153, 155, 159, 170
Heidegger, Martin: on anxiety, 190n63; *Being and Time*, 26, 27, 51; criticism of, 31–32, 35, 36, 38, 52, 114; on death, 41; on everyday existence, 51; idea of Dasein, 35, 39, 41, 51–52; influence of, 2, 24, 26–28, 29, 166, 174; Jewish question and, 47; ontological phenomenology of, 28; political views of, 31, 46
Hering, Jean, 24–25
Herzog, Annabel, 185n21, 207n8
Hezekiah, 155, 161
historical teleology, 159
history, 33, 97–98; fatality of, 39; Judaism and, 153–54, 160–61; limits of secular, 4–5; memory and, 100; theory of, 185n22
Hitler, Adolf, 57
Hitlerism, 39–40, 90
Holocaust, 9, 14; God's intervention and, 124–25; Judaism and, 15, 65, 84–85, 104–5, 109–10; necessity of, 112–13; as Passion of Israel, 105–6; Western philosophy and, 44, 135
"How Is Judaism Possible?" (Levinas), 75
humanism: *vs*. atheism, 122, 138; Bible and, 138; finite nature of, 123, 124; Judaism and, 72, 73, 128, 135; origin of, 74–75
human universality, 108–10, 112, 114
humility, 179
Husserl, Edmund: concept of intentionality, 28; influence of, 2, 24, 25–26; Jewish origin of, 26; phenomenological project of, 26, 27; works of, 25

idolatry: as condition of inattention, 154; cutting off from the future, 140; logos and, 155, 157; prohibition against, 128; sources of, 144–45; Torah's relation to, 127–28, 129, 131, 133–34, 139, 150; worship of visible certainty, 140–41
il y a ("there is"): notion of, 35–36
"Il y a" (Levinas), 35
incompleteness, 133, 139
individual being, 44, 190n63
infallibility: notion of, 37–38

Information Juive (Levinas), 90
inhuman: notion of, 170, 172, 181
innovation: change of names as, 107; future and, 99, 181; memory and, 93, 181; sources of, 110; tradition and, 93, 94
Islam, 146, 147
Israel: continuation of, 104; equation to humanity, 170; greatness of, 111–12; hardships of, 89–90, 101, 103–4, 112–13; Jacob as, 111–12, 114, 165; meanings of, 168, 170, 180; particularism of, 171; place of, 15, 16; privileged position of, 75, 171; in relation to sacred texts, 170–71; in relation to the infinite, 175, 180–81; suffering of, 168
Israel, State of: creation of, 86, 167; evolution of, 168–69; universal responsibility of, 171, 172, 174; Zionist dream of, 167
Israel of Fact, 169–70

Jacob (Biblical patriarch): hardship of, 97–98; as Israel, 99, 111–12, 114, 165; story of, 76–77
Jewish education: decline of, 67–68; evolution of, 71–72; goals of, 83, 100, 113; Hebrew and, 70, 73, 76–77; importance of, 69, 77–78; Jewish mysticism and, 93; Levinas's model of, 84; meaning of, 69–70; Nazi rule and, 118; piety and, 77; scientific approach to, 77; in State of Israel, 86; task of, 75; in Western Europe, 70–71
Jewish identity: authentic understanding of, 127, 128, 141, 154–55, 158; displacement of the self in, 173; formation of, 91; Holocaust and, 165–66; Western culture and, 27
Jewishness: definition of, 68
Jewish Scouts, 92, 93
Jewish scriptures: in a post-Holocaust world, 109–10; reading technique of, 111–12, 117, 162
Jewish thought, 90, 91, 93, 133, 152, 153, 154, 178
"Jewish Thought Today" (Levinas), 135, 143
Jewish universalism, 166–67
Jewish way, 15–17
Jewish way of being, 15–16
Jews: Arab conflict, 86; authenticity of, 46–47, 51–52; Christians and, 146; cultural regeneration of, 59–60; danger of assimilation, 58, 121, 168–69, 170; definition of, 61; emancipation of, 54, 60; European *vs.* Eastern European, 158; as exemplary other, 141; hardships of, 89–90, 101, 103–4; inauthentic, 51–52; justification of survival of, 49; letting go of, 165, 166, 175, 182; migration of, 87; without mitzvot, 74–75, 181; Nazi persecution of, 167, 193n35; as the Other, 46–47; in post-Holocaust Europe, 58; prisoners of war, 188n34; privileged status of, 141, 156, 166, 167–68; relation to the world, 56; relation with the infinite, 175
joy: as promise of better world, 152; of singing, 152–53
Judaism: as accident of history, 153–54; authentic, 127, 154–55, 157; Bible and, 65–66, 73–74; Christianity and, 147–48, 150–53; competing strains of, 95–96; *vs.* Eastern cultures, 146; as eternal project, 153–54; Holocaust and, 53, 65, 90, 165–66; humanism and, 72, 73, 114, 128; without Jews, 27–28, 29; memory and, 113, 121; as mere abstraction, 28; mission of, 75, 76; modernity and, 45; myth and, 58–59; national pride and, 72; necessity of, 66, 72; oral tradition in, 97, 99, 102–3, 104–7; original meaning of, 40; origin of, 62–63, 76;

vs. other religions, 179; pietism and, 70–71; power of, 118; of reason *vs.* Judaism of prayer, 70, 71; relation to time and history, 149–50, 153, 160–61, 169–70; as religion for adults, 61, 112–13, 127, 137, 157; as revealed set of laws, 57–58; science and, 71, 72; skepticism in, 118–19; as spirituality, 75–76; values of, 72–73; Western philosophy and, 36–37, 115, 116–19, 120, 122, 136, 140
Judaken, Jonathan, 46
judges in Israel, 70, 71
justice, 138

Kafka, Franz, 178
Kahana, Rabbi, 71
Kant, Immanuel, 21, 128
Kaplan, Lawrence, 7–8
Kavka, Martin, 8, 200n50
Kierkegaard, Søren Aabye, 149, 150, 151
Kleinberg, Ethan, 9, 10, 11
knowledge, 21, 25, 38
Kook, Abraham Isaac Hacohen, 62
Kovno (Kaunas): German occupation of, 43; Jewish population of, 15–16; pogroms in, 43; Talmudic schools in, 15

law: oral *vs.* written, 147–48
Lermontov, Mikhail, 19, 20, 21
Levinas, Aminadav, 16
Levinas, Boris, 16
Levinas, Dvora, 16
Levinas, Emmanuel: academic career, 12, 21–22, 24–25, 29, 30–31, 53–56, 63, 66–69, 85–86, 93–94, 127, 147, 187n26; acknowledgment of his limits, 125, 126; allegiance to the State of Israel, 147; attitudes toward Europe, 130; authority of, 2–3, 12, 98, 125; awards, 68; celebration of the eightieth birthday, 1–2; commitment to Judaism, 29–30, 63–64; criticism of, 155–56, 207n8; early life, 1, 2, 12, 16–20; education and training of, 1–2, 3, 16–20, 101, 102, 112, 122, 144; evolution of ideas of, 61–62; family of, 16–17, 18, 19, 43; French naturalization of, 30, 56; ideals of French Revolution and, 55, 56; Lithuanian Talmudists, influence on, 134; military service, 33, 188n36; move to Paris, 29; philosophical studies, 20, 24–25, 27–28, 29, 52, 202n1; as prisoner of war, 33–34, 41–42; prison notebooks, 34–35, 36, 37, 40, 44, 188n39; public lectures and presentations, 93–94; racism of, 13, 156, 158, 174; Rashi course, 78–79, 82; reading technique, 111–12; reputation of, 2, 85; Russian literature, influence of, 19, 20–21; scholarship on, 6–7, 8, 129–30; Shushani and, 64–66; skepticism about religion, 4; Talmudic studies, 7–9, 19, 23, 35, 36, 53–54, 62, 66, 81, 98, 101–2, 125–26, 166; teaching activities, 2, 68–69, 75, 78, 79, 81–82, 154, 157; understanding of Judaism, 95, 157. *See also* Talmudic lectures; *individual works of Levinas*
Levinas, Yekhiel, 16
Lévi-Strauss, Claude, 143
Lévy, Benny, 3
Levy, Sylvain, 30
literary chauvinism, 30
Lithuania: German invasion of, 17–18, 43; reform of school system, 18
Lithuanian Talmudic tradition, 15–16, 62, 65, 72, 77, 124, 140, 167

Maimonides, 96, 115, 133, 136
Manasseh, the son of Hezekiah: story of, 155–58
Maurras, Charles, 30

McGettigan, Andrew, 12, 130, 141, 144, 159; "The Philosopher's Fear of Alterity," 129
meaning of life (*sens de la vie*), 19
memory: experience of God through, 91; freedom and, 92; future and, 180; of hardships, 90, 91, 99–100, 110–11; identity and, 114; innovation and, 93
Messianicity: idea of, 181
metaphysical "unease," 19, 26
Midrash, 92, 122, 133, 144
Mishnah, 54–55, 60, 66, 91, 99, 100, 147
Mitnageddic tradition, 60, 61, 119, 133, 138–39, 157
mitzvot: ethical significance of, 74, 75, 122–23, 138; performance of, 72, 74–75, 76
monotheism: affinity between religions of, 145–47; *vs.* atheism, 118, 127–28; as humanism, 73, 74; principles of Jewish, 137, 139
morality, 75, 76–78, 179–80
Morgan, Michael L., 207n8
morning prayer, 92–93
Morocco: Jewish population of, 86–87
Mortara affair, 54
Moses, 5, 102–3, 105–6, 151, 158
Moten, Fred, 12, 141, 144, 155–56, 158, 159, 174; *The Universal Machine*, 13, 130, 142, 165
Motherlant, Henri de, 33
Moyn, Samuel, 149
mysticism, 60, 93, 134

nationalism, 75, 169
National Socialism, 39
navel of the world, 64–65, 67
Neher, André, 89, 92, 94, 95
neo-Kantianism, 21
Nerson, Henri, 63–64, 83
Nietzsche, Friedrich, 151, 174
nihilism, 179
non-religious manifestations, 50

"On the Jewish Reading of Scriptures" (Levinas), 103–4, 110, 115
ontology, 27, 33
Other: ethical commitment to, 10, 18, 28; individual being and, 44; Jew as, 46–47; privileged place of, 172–73; *vs.* self, 13, 35
other Other, 35, 141, 157

Pascal, Blaise, 170
Passion of Israel, 105–6, 110, 112
past, 95, 96, 98, 99, 105
Peiffer, Gabrielle, 24, 25
Pentateuch, 132
phenomenology, 25, 26
philosophical writing: *vs.* Talmudic writings, 185n21
Plato, 21
Pradines, Maurice: on Dreyfus affair, 22–23; influence of, 21, 22–23
progress: logic of, 159, 162
Proust, Marcel, 78
Pushkin, Aleksandr, 19, 20, 21

Quatre lectures talmudiques (Nine Talmudic Readings), 104

Rabbinic literature, 102
racism, 75, 141
Rashi (Rabbi Shlomo Itzhaki), 78
rationality, 90–91
"Reflections on Jewish Education" (Levinas), 69, 72
"Reflections on the Philosophy of Hitlerism" (Levinas), 31
relationship with the future, 137
religion, 4–5, 166–67
"Religion for Adults, A" (Levinas), 112
Resh Lakish, 73–74, 102
Revelation: casual explanation of, 25; conditioned by the threat of death, 38; ethics and, 6; Levinas's claims about, 4, 9, 160; philosophical investigations

of, 19, 23; relational aspect of, 26; Torah as, 32, 144; written and oral, 5, 162, 163
Ricoeur, Paul, 2
Riveline, Claude, 96
Rodrigue, Aron, 59
Rosenberg, Shalom, 62
Rosenzweig, Franz: biography of, 94; criticism of, 148, 149, 151–52, 153–54; on development of civilizations, 144–45, 154; influence of, 146, 157; on Judaism and Christianity, 147–48; *The Star of Redemption*, 144

sacred texts: interpretations of, 4, 161, 162–64, 166–67; tradition of reading of, 99
sacrifice, 35, 171–72, 175, 179, 181
Sadducee and Raba: story of, 29–31, 108–9
Sanhedrin (juridical court of Jewish people): deliberation process in, 55–57; elitism of, 70–71, 78–79; as "a goblet," 68; Great and Lesser, 54, 58; Hellenic roots of, 54, 61–62, 63, 66–67, 72–73; hierarchical order of, 53–54, 58–59, 60, 78; *vs.* house of worship, 56; as navel of the world, 64–65, 67, 68, 169; novelty of, 56–57; openness of, 55–56, 61; public at, 58, 59; testimony before, 71–72; universal role of, 69–70
Sarai (and Sarah), 106–7, 108, 109, 110, 112, 114
Sartre, Jean-Paul: on authentic existence, 46; *Being and Nothingness*, 46, 47; critique of, 46, 47; on human condition, 47; influence of, 3; on Jewish question, 45–46, 47–48; lectures of, 45–46, 191n71; reflection on Jewish question, 44, 45–46, 47–48; on supreme commitment, 38–39
Scheler, Max, 22
Schwabe, Moses, 18–19, 26

Schweber, Moshe, 63
Science of Judaism (Wissenschaft des Judentums), 27
secularism: temptation of, 23, 27
self, *26*, 27, 34, 178
Septuagint, 132, 133, 151
servileness, 34
Shabbath (Tractate), 108–9
Shimon Gamliel, Rabbi, 132
Shushani (Chouchani), Monsieur, 1, 2, 12; authority of, 64–65, 80–81, 83, 101, 167; background and training of, 62–63; interpretative method of, 66, 80; *Pirke Avoth*, 80; teaching activity, 8, 64
snake: as representation of evil, 104, 105; in sacred texts, references to, 89, 100, 101, 102
solipsism, 20, 21
song, 152, 157, 161
Song of Songs, 64, 68, 70, 73
Stalinism, 90
"State of Israel and the Religion of Israel, The" (Levinas), 72
Steg, Ady, 1, 2, 94
Steinberg, Aron, 89
structuralism, 142–43
supreme commitment, 38
supreme freedom, 38–39
"Sur 'les Ideen' de M. Husserl" (Levinas), 28

Talmud: communication across time, 99; dynamic interpretation of, 105, 109–11, 115–16; elements of, 99–100, 162; ethical imperative, 137; as guideline for nation of Israel, 170–72; Judaism and, 62–63; language of, 100; *vs.* Old Testament, 163; as other form of Revelation, 163–64; Rashi's commentaries on, 78; structure and style of, 100; studies of, 61, 72, 77–78, 102, 143, 164; Torah and, 129; Western philosophy and, 62

Talmudic lectures: "As Old as the World," 12; audience, 96, 100–101, 133; "Between Two Worlds," 144, 147, 152; "Beyond Memory," 13, 165, 172; chronology of, xv–xviii; "Contempt for the Torah as Idolatry," 13; critique of, 4, 12, 13, 185n21; ethical message of, 13; "For a Place in the Bible," 160; goal of, 115, 137; intellectual history of, 10–11; language of, 100–101; "Model of the West," 135; "Monotheism and Language," 145; *Nine Talmudic Readings,* 129; oral and aural component of, 97, 99; preparation of the written text of, 97–98; presentation of, 9–10; "The Temptation of Temptation," 7, 12, 37, 114, 135, 174; "The Translation of the Scriptures," 131; "Towards the Other," 97, 114, 150

Talmudic studies: confessional approach to, 4; secular scholarship on, 3–4, 5

Talmudic writings: *vs.* philosophical writing, 185n21

temptation: remedy to, 32

temptation of secularism, 19–21

temptation of temptation, 18, 19–20, 22, 24, 26, 37, 38, 114, 174, 178

theory of history, 185n22

Theory of Intuition, The (Levinas), 28

three strands of the braid, 12, 16, 22, 54, 61, 71, 99, 112, 127, 155, 165

Timna, 158–59

Tolstoy, Leo, 19, 20, 21, 78

Torah: act of reading of, 105, 109–11, 130–31, 146, 149–50; as alternative to death, 17–18, 35; books of, 160–61; connection to the future, 147; denial of, 156; destiny of, 17, 130; divine nature of, 136, 137, 141–44; freedom of choice and, 16–17, 38; generative nature of, 106–7; as guideline for nation of Israel, 170–72; idolatry of, 127–28, 129, 131, 133–34, 139, 143, 149, 150, 157, 160; Jews' reception of, 25–26, 28–29, 32, 37, 176; learning of, 127, 150–51; as living Revelation, 144, 148; misreading and misunderstanding of, 134–37; Moses' reception of, 144; oral transmission of, 102–3, 104–7, 160–61; permanence of, 151–52; right and wrong way to engage with, 148; Talmud and, 129; testimony of, 71; transcendence of, 137; transfer of meaning of, 176–77; written *vs.* oral, 107–8

Totality and Infinity (Levinas), 123

Tractate Shabbat, 37

transcendence, 117–18, 130

translation of Hebrew into Greek: project of, 128, 131–33, 136–37, 139, 140–41, 158–60, 161, 164

truth, *16*, 169

Tsadikim (miraculous Rabbis), 139

Turgenev, Ivan, 19

universalism, 109–10, 127, 160, 181

University of Strasbourg, 20

Valéry, Paul, 81

Volozhiner, Ḥayyim ben Isaac: exegetic methods of, 19; influence of, 15, 119–20, 121, 123, 134, 139–40; Levinas's interpretation of, 5, 8, 104, 200n50; Mitnageddic tradition and, 60, 61; philosophy of, 122; *yeshivah* of, 120, 139–40

Wahl, Jean, 90, 133

Western philosophy: ethics and, 136, 137; Holocaust and, 135; Judaism and, 12, 115, 116–19, 122, 136, 140; limitations of, 114, 135, 140; temptation of, 65, 110, 114; viability of, 36, 44

Wiesel, Elie, 62, 64, 65

will of God, 37
will to extermination, 40
Winter, Jay, 193nn34–35
wolf, the lion, and the snake triad, 89, 100, 101
Wolzogen, Christoph von, 142
World Jewish Congress, 89

Yehoshua ben Korha, Rabbi, 127, 149, 150
yeshivah, 119, 139–40

Zakhor (commandment to remember), 91, 92
Zionism, 55, 167
Zola, Émile, 22, 30

Cultural Memory in the Present

Willemien Otten, *Thinking Nature and the Nature of Thinking: From Eriugena to Emerson*

Michael Rothberg, *The Implicated Subject: Beyond Victims and Perpetrators*

Hans Ruin, *Being with the Dead: Burial, Sacrifice, and the Origins of Historical Consciousness*

Eric Oberle, *Theodor Adorno and the Century of Negative Identity*

David Marriott, *Whither Fanon? Studies in the Blackness of Being*

Reinhart Koselleck, *Sediments of Time: On Possible Histories*, translated and edited by Sean Franzel and Stefan-Ludwig Hoffmann

Devin Singh, *Divine Currency: The Theological Power of Money in the West*

Stefanos Geroulanos, *Transparency in Postwar France: A Critical History of the Present*

Sari Nusseibeh, *The Story of Reason in Islam*

Olivia C. Harrison, *Transcolonial Maghreb: Imagining Palestine in the Era of Decolonialization*

Barbara Vinken, *Flaubert Postsecular: Modernity Crossed Out*

Aishwary Kumar, *Radical Equality: Ambedkar, Gandhi, and the Problem of Democracy*

Simona Forti, *New Demons: Rethinking Power and Evil Today*

Joseph Vogl, *The Specter of Capital*

Hans Joas, *Faith as an Option*

Michael Gubser, *The Far Reaches: Ethics, Phenomenology, and the Call for Social Renewal in Twentieth-Century Central Europe*

Françoise Davoine, *Mother Folly: A Tale*

Knox Peden, *Spinoza Contra Phenomenology: French Rationalism from Cavaillès to Deleuze*

Elizabeth A. Pritchard, *Locke's Political Theology: Public Religion and Sacred Rights*

Ankhi Mukherjee, *What Is a Classic? Postcolonial Rewriting and Invention of the Canon*

Jean-Pierre Dupuy, *The Mark of the Sacred*

Henri Atlan, *Fraud: The World of* Ona'ah

Niklas Luhmann, *Theory of Society, Volume 2*

Ilit Ferber, *Philosophy and Melancholy: Benjamin's Early Reflections on Theater and Language*

Alexandre Lefebvre, *Human Rights as a Way of Life: On Bergson's Political Philosophy*

Theodore W. Jennings, Jr., *Outlaw Justice: The Messianic Politics of Paul*

Alexander Etkind, *Warped Mourning: Stories of the Undead in the Land of the Unburied*

Denis Guénoun, *About Europe: Philosophical Hypotheses*

Maria Boletsi, *Barbarism and Its Discontents*

Sigrid Weigel, *Walter Benjamin: Images, the Creaturely, and the Holy*

Roberto Esposito, *Living Thought: The Origins and Actuality of Italian Philosophy*

Henri Atlan, *The Sparks of Randomness, Volume 2: The Atheism of Scripture*

Rüdiger Campe, *The Game of Probability: Literature and Calculation from Pascal to Kleist*

Niklas Luhmann, *A Systems Theory of Religion*

Jean-Luc Marion, *In the Self's Place: The Approach of Saint Augustine*

Rodolphe Gasché, *Georges Bataille: Phenomenology and Phantasmatology*

Niklas Luhmann, *Theory of Society, Volume 1*

Alessia Ricciardi, *After La Dolce Vita: A Cultural Prehistory of Berlusconi's Italy*

Daniel Innerarity, *The Future and Its Enemies: In Defense of Political Hope*

Patricia Pisters, *The Neuro-Image: A Deleuzian Film-Philosophy of Digital Screen Culture*

François-David Sebbah, *Testing the Limit: Derrida, Henry, Levinas, and the Phenomenological Tradition*

Erik Peterson, *Theological Tractates*, edited by Michael J. Hollerich

Feisal G. Mohamed, *Milton and the Post-Secular Present: Ethics, Politics, Terrorism*

Pierre Hadot, *The Present Alone Is Our Happiness, Second Edition: Conversations with Jeannie Carlier and Arnold I. Davidson*

Yasco Horsman, *Theaters of Justice: Judging, Staging, and Working Through in Arendt, Brecht, and Delbo*

Jacques Derrida, *Parages*, edited by John P. Leavey

The authorized representative in the EU for product safety and compliance is:
Mare Nostrum Group
B.V Doelen 72
4831 GR Breda
The Netherlands

www.ingramcontent.com/pod-product-compliance
Lightning Source LLC
Chambersburg PA
CBHW022007220426
43663CB00007B/995